THE AZTECS

THE AZTECS

BRIAN M. FAGAN

W. H. Freeman and Company
NEW YORK

Jorge Enciso (1880–1969) was a leading Mexican historian and collector, who did much to preserve pre-Columbian art. An influential artist, he drew the designs that appear as ornaments with each running head in this book from the hundreds of stone spindle whorls found in Mexican archaeological sites of all periods. Many of them come from Aztec sites, decorated with art motifs that were common throughout Mesoamerica for many centuries. Reproduced from Jorge Enciso, *Designs from Pre-Columbian Mexico,* New York: Dover Press, 1969.

Paperback Cover Art: An Aztec mask from the Museum of Anthropology in Florence. Courtesy, Scala/Art Resource.

Library of Congress Cataloging in Publication Data

Fagan, Brian M.
    The Aztecs.

    Bibliography: p.
    Includes index.
    1. Aztecs.   I. Title.
F1219.73.F33   1984   972'.01   83-16588
ISBN 0-7167-1584-8
ISBN 0-7167-1585-6 (pbk.)

Printed in the United States of America

9 8 7 6 5 4 3 2

To Lesley with love and gratitude for friendship

*"In mahan tixiuhtzintl, yn mahan tiqujltzintli:
otioalixcoac, otixotlac, oticuepon: in mahan noce
oticochia otioalicac."*

Fray Bernardino de Sahagun, *General History*, 10, p. 50

CONTENTS

CONTENTS

PREFACE

The Aztec civilization was first revealed to the English reading public, long before most of the research described in these pages was undertaken, by two famous works: the English edition of Francisco Clavijero's *History of Mexico* in 1787, and William Prescott's extraordinary *Conquest of Mexico,* published to popular acclaim in 1843. These works described a brilliant, militaristic empire that blossomed, within a few brief generations, to rule most of highland Mexico, only to fall in 1521 at the hands of a band of conquistadors in one of the most dramatic collapses of a civilization in history. The Aztecs have fascinated both scholar and general reader ever since. *The Aztecs* is an attempt to summarize what is known about this extraordinary civilization today.

Piecing together the anthropology and history of the Aztecs is more difficult than the most intricate of detective mysteries. The academic research comes from many disciplines, ranging from archaeology and anthropology to ethnohistory and colonial history. We are fortunate, however, that the quality of scholarship has been extremely high, ever since those memorable years in the mid-sixteenth century when a group of scholarly friars recorded the Aztecs' priceless oral histories from eye-witnesses who lived through the Conquest. The multidisciplinary account here, written by a nonspecialist, draws from many specialties to paint a picture not only of a civilization that rose from total obscurity within a few centuries, but of an innovative society that refined many cultural traditions developed centuries earlier.

In writing this book, I am deeply conscious of the debt I owe the many specialists whose work I use in these pages. Many of them have a lifetime's experience in Nahuatl and with the archives, codices, and sites that make up the Aztec story. Their dedicated researches have my deepest respect and admiration. It is with a sense of my own temerity that I have attempted to summarize them within the short compass of this volume.

A brief prologue covers Cortes' discovery of the Mexica and gives an account of research into Aztec history since the early sixteenth century. Part I discusses the rise of the Mexica; Part II, their economic life and governance. Part III deals with Aztec society and social organization, while Part IV examines their complex religious beliefs and philosophies. The story ends with the Spanish Conquest and its consequences. A brief Guide to Sources appears at the end of the book, following references for in-text quotations.

This book has seen many vicissitudes. It began as a projected volume in the *Scientific American Library,* then became a more ambitious work that required a complete redrafting in midstream. The process of research and writing has been a memorable learning experience. I am grateful to Mr. John Staples of W.H. Freeman, who boldly suggested that I write this book despite my lack of experience in the field. He overcame my objections with compelling counterarguments. His confidence and valuable advice have kept the project on track. My thanks, too, to the specialists who reviewed the many drafts of this book and criticized it unmercifully: Jan Gasco and Linda Pfeiffer of the University of California, Santa Barbara; Professors David Browman, T. Patrick Culbert, Charles Dibble, H.B. Nicholson, Jeremy Sabloff, Barbara Voorhies, and Gordon R. Willey. I learned a great deal from their comments and suggestions, but the errors and opinions in this volume are, of course, my responsibility. Lastly, a special debt of gratitude to Lesley Newhart, who worked on the photographs, and to Ricardo Lopez, who trained her for the assignment.

Brian M. Fagan

AUTHOR'S NOTE

The term "Aztec" is used throughout this book interchangeably with the word "Mexica." At the time of the Spanish Conquest, the Aztecs called themselves either Tenocha Mexica or Tlatelolca Mexica, depending on which part of the capital they lived in. "Mexica" could also be used alone, depending on the context. There were other groups in Texcoco, Azcapotzalco, Chalco, and elsewhere, who were also called Mexica, peoples probably descended from small bands that had split off from the main group of Mexica in the late thirteenth or early fourteenth centuries.

Nahuatl, the Aztec language, was a Mesoamerican *lingua franca,* used by ruling elites throughout much of the area, including both the Maya and Mixteca regions. Many rulers were probably descended from Nahuat-speaking military bands who were comparatively recent immigrants. The Nahuatl term *Azteca* or *Aztlaneca* is a word derived from Aztlan, the legendary place of their origin. But Huitzilopochtli, the Aztecs' patron diety, decreed that they were to be called Mexica, and, eager to obey, that is what they called themselves. The naturalist Alexander von Humbolt first popularized the term "Aztec" in his *Vues des Cordilleras* in 1810–1813, and William Prescott disseminated it widely in his *Conquest of Mexico.* The term has persisted ever since.

Archaeologists commonly refer to "Mesoamerica," a culture area that embraces Mexico and much of Central America. "Mexico" also has a specific use when referring to the modern nation of that name. For convenience, I have used the terms "Valley of Mexico" and "Basin of Mexico" interchangeably in this book.

The name Moctezuma has several spellings. In the interests of clarity, I have used Moctezuma rather than, say, Moteuhczoma here, because it is reasonably close in sound value to the original and is much easier to write.

I have omitted accents from Nahuatl and Spanish names in line with common practice in general books on the Aztecs. The specialist literature commonly uses accents, and the purist will find them there.

All distances and other measurements are given in inches, feet, and miles, with metric equivalents in parentheses.

NAHUATL PRONUNCIATION

Nahuatl, once the *lingua franca* of Mesoamerica, is an exotic language to European ears and a difficult one to learn. Although about a million people speak modern dialects of Nahuatl today, Classical Nahuatl is no longer spoken. Fortunately the Aztec language of four hundred years ago was transcribed by friars, but unfortunately they were linguistic amateurs. At the time, no one was competent to compile an analytical dictionary either.

The first (and perhaps the last) Nahuatl grammar was by the Franciscan Fray Andres de Olmos, his *Arte para aprendar le lengua Mexicana,* published in 1547. Two centuries later, the Jesuit Francisco Xavier Clavigero (1721–1787) compiled a manuscript booklet entitled *Reglas de la lengua mexicana* in which he summarized the grammar of the language as it was taught in the eighteenth century, using Spanish rules for Spanish sounds. It was a crude, but effective, means of training missionaries to converse with and preach to the Indians. Clavigero's system has since been adapted and improved to help English-speaking students acquire a knowledge of Classical Nahuatl in order to translate early manuscripts.

Since Classical Nahuatl was largely transliterated by Spanish missionaries, for the most part the language is pronounced as if it were Spanish. Nahuatl has five vowels (some authorities expand this to eight long and short ones). The vowel sounds approximate to *a-* (as in *bar*), *e-* (as in *let*), *i-* (as in *meet*), *o-* (as in *pole*), and *u-* (as in *rule*). Semi-vowels are *w-* (as *water*) and *y- (yet)*.

Here are some common phonetic values:

cu, as in *Culhuacan,* is pronounced *koo* (as in *cool*)

ch is pronounced *tch* (as in church)

c before *a* or *o* is pronounced as *k* (as in *cave*)

c before *e* or *i* is an *s* sound (as in *save*)

h is pronounced with a soft aspiration as it is in English
hu is sounded as *w* (as in *we*)
q is only found in the constructions *qua*, *que*, and *qui* where it is pronounced *ka*, *ke*, *ki*
tl, *ts*, and *tz* represent single sounds (as in spo*ts*) and should not be divided
u before *a*, *e*, *i*, and *o* is pronounced like the English *w*
x is always pronounced as *sh* (as in *sh*eet)
z before *e* and *i* is an *s* sound (as in mi*ss*)

Although pronunciation is normally like Spanish, Nahuatl speakers normally placed word stress on the next-to-last syllable. So Spanish-speaking writers add accents to Nahuatl words.

Here are some examples of Nahuatl words commonly used in the text:

Culhuacan	Kool-wah-kan
Huitzilopochtli	Wee-tseel-o/poch-tlee
Mexica	Me-shee-kah
Mexico	Me-shee-koh
Motecuhzuma (Moctezuma)	Mo-te-koo-suma
Quetzalcoatl	Ke-tsal-ko-atl
Tenochtitlan	Te/noch-tee-tlahn
Tlatelolco	Tla-te-lol-koh
Tolteca	Tol-te/ka
Tula	Too/lah

DISCOVERING AZTEC CIVILIZATION

All these things are concealed from us,
kept as a tightly guarded secret. The task
of discovering and making them known is
overwhelming. He who attempts [to do
so] will soon discover this, and of a
thousand other customs [he will be lucky
if he discovers] one half.

*Paving stones at the Templo
Mayor, Tenochtitlan, uncovered
in recent excavations. Photo,
Lesley Newhart.*

Fray Diego Duran, *History of the Indies of New Spain*, 1964, p. 55.

moteucalhujsque, njman
aocac maqujz. Auh in teu
njctico, njman ieic callacq̃
valmotzatzacutivetzque.
Auh in in muchiuh ietla
qualizpan: auh in jeiuhquj
njmā ieic teiximacho, te
çacaco: auh in jemuchintin
ōçacoque in moteucalhujsq̃
njmā ieic tatlatilo in tetel
puchcali.

Iuh cempoalli vmei Capitulo
vnian mjtoa in quenjn Moteu
çoma, yoan ce vei pilli tlatilul
co mjcque: auh min nacaio quj
vallaçque igujia oaioa qujia
oaioc incalli in vncan catca
Españoles.

Capitulo. 23. de como Mokeuco
ma y el gouernador del Tlatiluko
fueron echados muertos fuera de
la casa donde los españoles estaua
fortalecidos.

Despues delo arriba dicho, quatro dias
andados despues dela matança que
se hizo corel cu, hallaron los mexicanos
muertos a Motecuçoma, y al gouer
rador del Tlatlulco echados fuera
delas casas reales cerca del muro dō
de estaua vna piedra labrada como
gala pago que llamauā Teoayoc: y
despues que conocieron los que los

Auh ieiuh navilhujtl ne
teucalhujloc in qujmontla
çaco in Moteuçoma, yoan
Itzquauhtzin, omjcque, ate
co itvaisican. Teoaioc: ca
vncan catca injxiptla aioh,
tatl in tlaxiximtli, iuh qujn
aioll ipan mjxcuitia in
tatl. Auh ino ittoque, inoi

Prologue

"And when we saw all those towns and villages built in the water, and other great towns on dry land, and that straight and level causeway leading to Mexico, we were astounded. These great towns ... and buildings rising from the water, all made of stone, seemed like an enchanted vision.... Indeed some of our soldiers asked whether it was not all a dream.... It was all so wonderful that I do not know how to describe this first glimpse of things never heard of, seen or dreamed of before." So Conquistador Bernal Diaz de Castillo (1963, p. 214) described the Spanish Conquest of Mexico nearly half a century after that memorable day in November, 1519, when Hernando Cortes and his small band of adventurers gazed on the land of the Aztecs for the first time. Bernal Diaz was in his seventies when he wrote his account, but the passage of years never dimmed the vivid memories of that day. The conquistadors gaped in astonishment at an Indian metropolis larger than Seville and certainly better planned than many European capitals. Tenochtitlan, the hub of the Aztec world, seemed like a miracle in an unimaginable alien land, a miracle that promised untold wealth, enough gold for everyone. Diaz relished an old man's memories, then added: "Today all that I then saw is overthrown and destroyed ... nothing is left standing."

"Nothing is left standing...." Diaz wrote the literal truth. Today, the architectural, cultural, and material legacy of the Aztecs lies buried deep beneath modern Mexico City, only now being excavated under the city streets. The Aztecs themselves were decimated by the Conquest. Thousands died of exotic European diseases, others from harsh treatment and the rigors of forced labor. Fanatical friars burned priceless Indian codices and did everything they could to destroy all traces of

A page from Volume 12 of Sahagun's General History, *beginning, "In which it is told how Moctezuma and a great nobleman of Tlatilulco died and [the Spaniards] cast their bodies out before the gate...." Courtesy, University of Utah Press, Salt Lake City.*

3

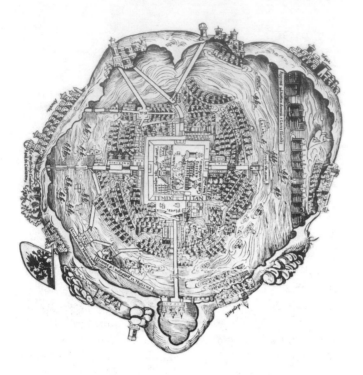

the ancient order. "Know ye that we are much busied with great and constant labour to convert the infidel . . . five hundred temples razed to the ground, and twenty thousand idols of the devils worshipped smashed and burned," wrote the zealous Bishop Zumarraga in 1531 (Ricard, 1966, p. 37). Within a few generations, most material traces of Aztec civilization had, to all intents and purposes, vanished.

Cortes and his conquistadors were confronted by a society so strange and alien to European eyes that it almost defied classification and understanding. Aztec civilization was immediately perceived as a culture of deep contradictions. On the one hand, the Indians lived in an orderly and highly organized society, ruled by a supreme monarch who seemed to the Spaniards to enjoy all of the panoply and splendor of a European king. They saw his nobles as equivalent to the Spanish *hidalgos,* leisured aristocrats and landowners. Some of the elite were skilled poets and sophisticated philosophers, others shrewd merchants or expert artisans. The

The city of Tenochtitlan as depicted in a German edition of Cortes's account of the Spanish Conquest, published in 1624. The drawing shows the ' main plaza, causeways, temples, and parks of the busy capital. UCSB Library. Courtesy, Regents of the University of California.

4

priests and the free peasants of Tenochtitlan seemed to be the Aztec equivalents of the clerics and the Castillian farmers in distant Spain. "The mode of life of [Tenochtitlan's] people was about the same as in Spain, with just as much harmony and order," wrote Cortes. "Considering that these people were barbarians, so cut off from the knowledge of God, and of other civilized people, it is wonderful what they have attained in every respect" (Cortes, 1928, p. 34). On the other hand, the Aztecs were passionate warriors, devoted to the rite of human sacrifice, and perhaps cannibalism as well. The Spaniards claimed that the Aztec priests sacrificed more than 20,000 victims to the gods each year—a highly unreliable estimate put together by Cortes's secretary Gomara. For their part, the Mexica were amazed to hear the Spaniards preach an alien creed that abhorred such ceremonies. Aztec society was so alien to Spanish eyes that contemporary observers tended to focus on the most exotic and horrifying aspects of Mexican life, notably human sacrifice and the cannibalism that they thought went with it. Because of this, the Aztecs have been dismissed as incorrigible cannibals to this day, when in fact their society was, in many respects, as sophisticated as that which replaced it. So total was the destruction of Aztec civilization at the hands of the conquistadors that more than four centuries of research in many disciplines have barely led us to even a provisional understanding of that society. Even the landscape in which the Aztecs flourished has been altered beyond recognition.

THE VALLEY OF MEXICO

"Towns and villages built in the water. . . ." Cortes and his men gazed on a landscape that bore little resemblance to that which surrounds Mexico City today. It is hard to believe that the Spaniards thought of the Valley as a miraculous paradise. The city itself—a sprawling, ever-expanding concrete jungle—houses more than 13,000,000 people. You can only see the surrounding

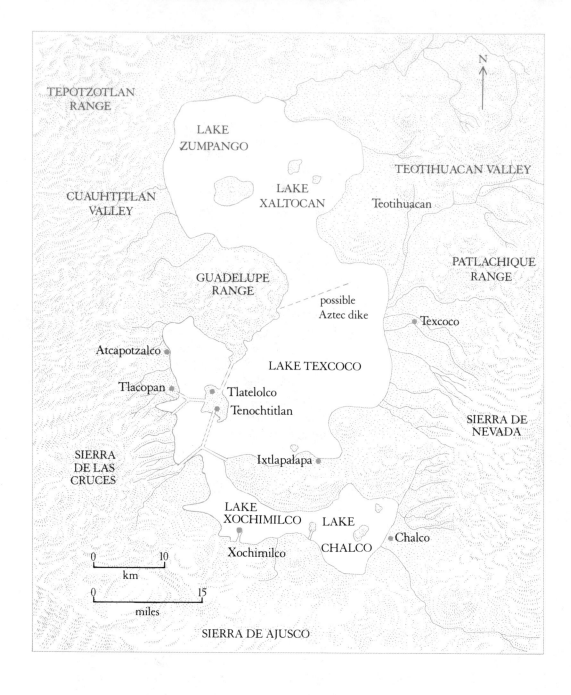

Map of the Basin of Mexico (left) showing major ecological zones and geographical features. After William Sanders, Jeffrey Parsons, and Robert Santley, The Basin of Mexico, *Map 1.*

Provinces and topographic features of modern Mexico (above).

mountain peaks on a rare clear day. The Spanish colonists drained the lakes that Diaz admired, and suburbs or farm lands now exist in their place. Dense smog mantles the superb view of the Valley of Mexico from the mountains.

The Valley of Mexico is an internal drainage basin of some 4,350 square miles (7000 sq km), about 75 miles (120 km) long by 43 miles (70 km) wide, at the top of the central highlands of Mexico. The valley floor lies at about 7,000 feet (2100 m) above sea level, surrounded by high mountains that give way in the north to less well-defined topography. Before the Spaniards dug drainage canals, water flowing off the mountain ranges fed a series of shallow, marshy lakes that covered more than 620 square miles (1000 sq km). Lake Xaltocan-Zumpango to the north was the highest, with fresher waters than low-lying Lake Texcoco in the center of the Valley. At a slightly lower elevation, Texcoco tended to collect salts deposited from its higher neighbors. Freshwater Lake Chalco-Xochimilco lay to the south, its shores and islands an important area for hydraulic agriculture in Aztec times.

7

These lakes were a unique resource in Mesoamerica, and the Aztecs exploited them intensively. They provided not only fish, but plentiful waterfowl, reeds for thatching and weaving, salt deposits, and abundant water for swamp (hydraulic) agriculture. In their unaltered state the lakeshore plains flooded occasionally, but they could be used for simple, relatively unproductive agriculture. The Aztecs and their immediate predecessors pressed the flat lands into service by draining some low-lying areas. They also partially drained the shallow waters of the lakes, creating thousands of agricultural plots. These *chinampas,* or swamp gardens, were organized in consolidated blocks, connected by myriad canals and drainage dikes that not only regulated water levels so that the water table remained within reach of the crop roots, but also provided easy communication between the fields and the bustling markets of Tenochtitlan and other centers. The Aztec capital lay within the confines of the lakes, connected with every part of the Valley of Mexico by canoe, causeway, and well-trodden mainland paths. Legend tells us that the site of Tenochtitlan was selected by the war god Huitzilopochtli himself in about 1325. The choice was a brilliant one. In less than two centuries this strategic place evolved from a tiny hamlet into the greatest city in Mexico.

Despite its shallow lakes, the Valley of Mexico is a high, semi-arid highland zone, with seasonal rainfall that is strongly localized and highly unpredictable. The rains fall from May through October, ranging from a low of about 18 inches (450 mm) a year in the north to some 40 inches (1000 mm) on the southern slopes. Away from the lake shores, the farmers had to rely entirely on the annual rains unless they could irrigate their fields. The sloping foothill zones above the plains could be cultivated, some of them by using floodwater or canal irrigation, but they enjoyed a short growing season and there was always a danger of losing maize plants to frost. Irrigation was vital wherever it was practicable, and the Aztecs cultivated every available patch of agricultural land on the floor and slopes of the Valley. The higher slopes of the mountains were, of course, unsuitable for agriculture, but they did provide a valuable source of forest products and game.

The Aztecs exploited a highland environment where different environmental layers, each with different economic potential, were "stacked" one above the other. In this sense, the Valley of Mexico was no different than other highland valleys, like Oaxaca. Its uniqueness lay in its highly productive lakes and its rich deposits of obsidian, a fine volcanic glass that was highly prized for ornaments, cutting tools, and sacrificial knives. The best deposits lay in the north, close to the ancient city of Teotihuacan, the great religious center where the Aztecs believed their world was created. The Aztec empire extended far beyond the Valley of Mexico—Tenochtitlan's merchants traded with the Maya lowlands and Veracruz and visited markets on the Pacific coast, reaching as far afield as Guatemala. But its hub was the Basin of Mexico and the diverse environment that fed the tens of thousands of people who flocked to Tenochtitlan. It was here that Aztec civilization was born and nurtured.

THE MISSIONARY HISTORIANS

This Mexican world was completely alien to European colonists and intellectuals alike. Columbus' voyages had unleashed a torrent of debate about the nature of the American Indians. The discovery of the Aztec civilization only added fuel to the controversy. Who were these Indians? Where had they come from? Were they descendents of the Ten Lost Tribes of Israel? Or fugitives from the Garden of Eden? As is so often the case with such debates, the amount of hard evidence was minimal, the speculation intense. Only a few scholars were curious enough to find out more about the Aztecs, and they did so for strictly practical reasons—to influence policy-making at the Spanish Court or to advance the Catholic missionary cause.

The first researches into Aztec culture were undertaken by missionaries who made it their business to

master all the intricacies of Aztec life, for, as one of them wrote, "the Indians will make a mockery of the Faith, and the minister will remain in the dark" (Duran, 1971, p. 55). Several missionary friars, mainly Franciscans, talked to Indian informants soon after the Conquest, among them Fray Toribio de Motolinia (c. 1495–1565). Their valuable efforts were among the many sources used by a brilliant scholar-Franciscan, Fray Bernardino de Sahagun (c. 1499–1590), whose research methods bear an uncanny resemblance to those used by students of oral history to this day. One of many friars attempting to describe Aztec history, his work provides an excellent example of the difficulties encountered by all of the earliest Aztec historians.

Fray Sahagun arrived in New Spain in 1529, less than a decade after the fall of Tenochtitlan. He soon learned Nahuatl, then busied himself studying Indian society in great detail. Sahagun really wanted to collect intellectual ammunition which would help prevent a return to idolatry, for he realized that the Indians' best protection against Spanish culture and Catholicism was their own closely knit society and age-old beliefs. He was also wanted to correct the widespread impression that the Aztecs had an inferior culture before the Conquest. The problem was to recover vital anthropological and historical information that had never been committed to paper. Fortunately, like a few of his colleagues, Sahagun realized that Aztec history was still walking around, but vanishing rapidly as many (but not all) of the older generation died without passing on their cherished traditions to their Spanish-speaking descendents. He had to tap this unique, firsthand source of information while there was still time.

Sahagun began by enlisting the assistance of prominent Aztec elders living at Tepepulco near Mexico City, some of them former merchants. He also chose four youths who had been educated in both the Aztec and Spanish cultures to act as his interpreters. "With these leaders and grammarians . . . I conversed many days, nearly two years," Sahagun tells us. He found

Bernardino de Sahagun. From a sixteenth-century portrait by an unknown artist. UCSB Library. Courtesy, Regents of the University of California.

that the Aztecs communicated with the aid of pictorial codices, most of which had been burned in an initial campaign against pagan ways soon after the Conquest. His informants produced hidden documents and went through them picture by picture, taking Sahagun back to the world of their ancestors, long before the Spaniards came. But these codices were not written scripts in the sense that we would use the term. They were not exact texts of spoken narratives. The pictorials contained only the bold outlines of religious concepts and social traditions. They served as *aides-memoire*, prompt books for the orators who were entrusted with the transmission of oral history and other knowledge to later generations.

Speaking well in public was fundamental to the education of an Aztec gentleman, just as weaving beautifully was to a lady. Speaking properly extended far beyond the normal proprieties of good manners. Trained orators learned the great discourses of the past, greeted diplomats with mellifluous words, and delivered congratulatory orations to priests and rulers. There were prayers to the gods, court speeches delivered on state occasions, exhortations from parents to their children, addresses given at weddings, even presentations by merchants, usually recited in standardized forms.

Fortunately, Sahagun realized the value of these *huehuetlatolli* (*huehue:* "old man"; *tlatolli:* "word" or "oration"). The Indians themselves noted that on such occasions, "it was then that the words of wisdom came forth." Sahagun understood that this was how the Aztecs perpetuated the fabric of their life and traditions, and he recorded dozens of these speeches in his notes. Not content with codices and orations alone, Sahagun also prepared a series of questionnaires that started asking for brief answers to single questions and then evolved into new sets of queries. About the Aztec gods, for instance, he formulated four questions about each diety: What were his titles and characteristics? What were his powers? What ceremonies were performed in his honor? What did he wear?

The dedicated friar spent years collecting and refining his data. Between 1547 and 1569 he compiled his master work, the priceless, bilingual *General History of the Things of New Spain,* a twelve-volume compendium of Aztec civilization. In its most complete form—the Florentine Codex, named after the Italian city which now houses it—it is a bilingual text, one column in Nahuatl, the second a paraphrase in Spanish. The first four volumes treat of the "gods worshipped by the natives," of religious rituals and sacrifices, and of many details of Aztec cosmology and divination. The central volumes describe astrology, omens, values, and theology "where there are Very Curious Things Concerning the Skills of Their Language." Books 8 to 10 describe the people themselves, their nobles, the history of their rulers, and "the merchants and artisans of Gold, Precious Stones, and Rich Feathers." Volume 11 is a treasure, a treatise on Aztec natural history and medicine. The twelfth book is perhaps the most interesting of all, for it describes the Conquest of Mexico through Aztec eyes. This last volume is so vivid that it can only be based on the personal experience of those who were there and survived. The tale is a sad one, but a story that displays remarkably little resentment toward Cortes and his adventurers.

Bernardino de Sahagun's historical masterpiece is of such seminal importance that an enormous scholarly literature has accumulated around the historical and anthropological riddles he left behind. But as a contemporary account, the *General History* stands almost alone. A small set of fifteenth- and sixteenth-century works add to his researches, among them various Indian writings and pictorials and the books of Fray Diego Duran (c. 1537–1588), a missionary who relied more heavily on written sources than Sahagun. He also used dozens of informants, among them an elderly conquistador turned friar who had taken part in the siege of Tenochtitlan decades before. Duran produced an ambitious three-part work: *The Books of the Gods and Rites* and *The Ancient Calendar,* detailed accounts of Aztec life and beliefs, and *The History of the Indies of*

New Spain, a magnificent work that covers several centuries of Aztec history. Thanks to Inquistadorial distrust, only a few indirectly quoted fragments of Duran's work appeared in print until the nineteenth century, as did only small portions of Sahagun's *General History.*

FROM SIGUENZA TO PRESCOTT

By the late seventeenth century, memories of the Aztec world had grown very dim. The Mexican authorities discouraged research and writing about the ancient civilizations and forbade publications in Nahuatl. Duran's and Sahagun's successors were mainly casual collectors and antiquarians more interested in the acquisition of manuscripts than in serious historical research. The first important collections of codices and documents were assembled by Mexican intellectuals, among them Carlos de Siguenza y Gongora (1645–1700), a priest, administrator, and university professor. Siguenza was a passionate collector who also carried out some archaeological investigations. An erudite scholar, he was one of the first to argue that the Mexico of his day was a unique blend of Indian and Spanish cultural traditions. Thus, he argued, it was necessary to recover the early history of the Indians from oblivion in order to achieve a greater understanding of the new nation that was Mexico. So fervently did Siguenza believe that "love of country" demanded that he delve deeply into Aztec customs that he labelled himself the "Presbytero mexicano" ("Mexican priest"). His sense of the historical continuity between Aztec times and colonial history has only been widely accepted in recent decades, and it is one of the cornerstones of Mexican nationalism. Most of his contemporaries were much less sophisticated, scholars like the Italian aristocrat Lorenzo Benaduci Boturini who assembled hundreds of manuscripts between 1736 and 1743. Unfortunately Boturini died before he could write his projected history of Mexico, and much of his collection was dispersed.

The late eighteenth and early nineteenth centuries saw little serious research into Aztec civilization. The celebrated German naturalist and traveller Alexander von Humboldt published some Aztec pictorials for the first time in his famous *Vues de Cordilleras* in 1810–1813. His book aroused considerable interest in Mexican history in Europe, as did the sumptuous publications of the eccentric Irish aristocrat, Lord Kingsborough. Convinced that the American Indians were the descendents of the Ten Lost Tribes of Israel, Kingsborough published nine richly illustrated folio volumes between 1830 and 1848, recording hundreds of Maya hieroglyphs and many more Aztec pictorials than Humboldt had included. The books drove Kingsborough to debtor's prison, but they stimulated all kinds of exciting research, including John Lloyd Stephens' and Frederick Catherwood's epic journeys to Guatemala and Yucatan in search of Maya ruins.

In 1843, just as New York was ringing with news of the spectacular Maya civilization, a book entitled *History of the Conquest of Mexico* appeared to ecstatic critical acclaim, a breathtaking work that wove the story of the Conquest into a whole tapestry depicting the background of the Aztec empire and its mercurial rise from obscurity in a few short generations. The author was William H. Prescott, a New Englander once destined for the law who had been accidentally blinded in one eye while at Harvard.

Instead of simply writing the history of the Conquest from the Spanish side, Prescott tried to throw light on the Aztec civilization by using unexploited sources in obscure archives on both sides of the Atlantic. Unemployed intellectuals sent him copies of unpublished documents from Madrid, Mexico City, and Paris that provided the rich source materials for *The Conquest*. A master of narrative, Prescott wove his diverse sources into a gripping story of astounding depth and vividness. Many people who read his accounts of Mexico and Tenochtitlan assumed—and would still assume—that Prescott had tramped over the battlefields himself and admired the scenery. In fact he never went further afield than Washington, D.C., while writing the book.

Prescott's *Conquest* was translated into Spanish almost immediately, and it became the basis for all later research into the Aztecs. In the fashion of the day, his history cast a somewhat romantic aura over the brutalities of the Conquest. He organized it as a study in dramatic contrasts, between Cortes, the wise instrument of progress, and the weak and superstitious Moctezuma, doomed by his own irresolution. Prescott stacked the cards against the Aztecs, depicting the Europeans as calm, heroic figures, the Indians as ill-disciplined, if brave, mobs of yelling warriors. He compared their stage of development to that of "our Saxon ancestors under Alfred." He made no attempt to understand the workings of either the Aztec mind or the society it created and sustained. For all the mediocre reasoning and contrived drama, the flowing pages of the *Conquest of Mexico* satisfied public curiosity about the Aztec people for more than a century. Only recently has a flood of new books about them appeared.

Mexico was a remote and little known country when Prescott published his *tour-de-force,* and so it remained for most of the nineteenth century. Only a handful of scholars followed in Prescott's footsteps, among them the French priest Brasseur de Bourbourg (1814–1873), who learned Nahuatl and travelled widely through Central America in the course of his pastoral duties. In 1857–1859 he published the *Histoire des nations civilisées du Mexique et de l'Amerique Centrale,* a vast monograph over 2,500 pages long that relied heavily on Indian sources. Brasseur was a tall, bespectacled scholar with the gift of writing clearly about incredible linguistic complexities. Unfortunately his interpretations were wild and woolly, based on weird distortions of the facts he collected so carefully. Like other scholars before him, he hypothesized that the Aztecs and earlier Mexican civilizations had come from the Lost Continent of Atlantis!

Brasseur was not entirely alone in his interest. As early as the 1880s, Mexican scholars began editing important but hitherto unpublished sources and producing syntheses of pre-Hispanic Mesoamerican ethno-history. But the trend has been towards specialization, simply because the linguistic and historical skills required by the subject matter militate toward the study of narrow problems rather than wide-ranging topics. The twentieth century has seen some remarkable researches, among them Miguel Leon-Portilla's brilliant studies of Aztec thought and literature, Alfonso Casos' inquiries into the Aztec calendar, and Eduardo Matos Moctezuma's meticulous reports of excavations uncovering the temple of the dieties Huitzilopochtli and Tlaloc in the heart of Mexico City. The most important work in the English language is surely Arthur Anderson and Charles Dibble's paleographic interpretation and translation of Sahagun's *General History,* which reads like an epic of Aztec history in its own right.

American, Spanish, and Mexican historians have taken over where Sahagun leaves off, studying Spain's shifting-sands policies towards New Spain and arguing passionately over the settlers' treatment of the Indians. Historian Charles Gibson has published a monumental study of the changes in Aztec society since the Conquest that is based on an exhaustive study of colonial archives and anthropological sources. But these works are just a beginning, the more spectacular achievements of a sometimes esoteric, but nevertheless fascinating academic specialty. Today, Aztec scholars are engaged in highly detailed research, in recording basic data, in assembling sources, and in speculating on what information is potentially available. As a result, we do know more about the Aztec civilization than we do about any other pre-Hispanic Mesoamerican society—but research is at such an early stage that this is not saying very much.

RECONSTRUCTING AZTEC HISTORY

Duran, Sahagun, and their contemporaries worked within an historical time-frame that began with the

Toltecs, if not earlier peoples, continued with the Aztecs' own legends of their arrival from a mythical land named Aztlan some centuries earlier, and ended with the bewildering events of the Conquest. They had some sense of pre-Aztec chronology, but this was at best fragmentary. Now, over four hundred years later, students of Aztec society see the empire in a much broader historical landscape that begins perhaps as long as 25,000 years ago, when mammoth hunters lived in the Valley of Mexico. They can call on archaeological excavations and surveys to trace the origins of Mexican civilization, rely on critical analyses of the *General History* for many details of the Aztec city of Tenochtitlan, and comb Spanish archives for details of colonial policy and administration.

Archaeology provides the long view, a chronicle of cultural change from the beginnings of plant cultivation before 6000 B.C., culminating in the rise of civilization in the Olmec lowlands with the great city of Teotihuacan some 1,800 years ago, and peaking with the emergence of the Mexica from obscurity in the fourteenth century. The archaeologist measures cultural change in centuries and millennia, dealing with the broad sweep of developing civilization, not with individual deeds or events. The few centuries of Aztec history are but a footnote to Mexican prehistory, so many surveys and excavations do little more than confirm the Spanish descriptions of the great temples of Tenochtitlan or data on artifacts and technology often ignored in codices and Spanish chronicles. Unfortunately, excavations at Tenochtitlan itself are seriously inhibited by the urban sprawl of Mexico City, which rose on the Aztec capital's foundations. Archaeologists have been able to do little more than get a glimpse of the old city when some urban development project exposes it by chance. Mexican archaeologists recovered thousands of artifacts and a small pyramid dedicated to Ehecatl-Quetzalcoatl, the God of Wind, during excavations for the Piño Suarez Metro station some years ago. Recent excavations downtown have uncovered much of the

Templo Mayor dedicated to the war god Huitzilo-pochtli and the rain god Tlaloc that once stood at the center of the Aztec capital.

Archaeology's most important contribution to Aztec studies has been the dispassion of its view of cultural development in the Valley of Mexico over many centuries. The Aztecs claimed that they conquered their empire through force of arms. True, but only partially true. Comprehensive archaeological surveys show that a dramatic population explosion accompanied the development of large-scale hydraulic agriculture in the high-land lakes as the Aztecs expanded their territorial conquests. Much higher crop yields enabled a large farming population to feed ever-growing numbers of nonfood producing priests, officials, soldiers, artisans, and commoners. The agricultural spiral expanded so rapidly that soon Tenochtitlan was importing food from all over the Basin of Mexico.

The Temple of Ehecatl-Quet-zalcoatl in the forecourt of the Piño Suarez Metro Station in Mexico City. Photo, Lesley Newhart.

Ethnohistory, the study of history using nonwritten sources, mainly oral traditions transmitted from generation to generation, is of great importance in understanding Aztec civilization. Fray Bernardino de Sahagun was one of the first, and perhaps the greatest, of the world's ethnohistorians, and his researches into Indian history collected soon after the Conquest provide some of the richest information about Aztec society.

Few fields of academic research require more specialized qualifications than Aztec ethnohistory. The linguistic skills alone would daunt many people: fluency in Nahuatl and in archaic and modern Spanish are an essential minimum. The prospective specialist needs the training of the documentary historian, an extensive background in anthropology and archaeology, a detailed knowledge not only of Mexican history but also of Spanish colonial policies, and a first-hand knowledge of archival sources that can take months, even years, to acquire.

Even a superficial glance at the ethnohistorical sources shows just how necessary these qualifications are. The primary sources were collected four centuries ago, and one must not only interpret the original material but analyze the way in which it was collected and put together. Simply understanding the pictures in the codices is also a problem. The pictographic-ideographic "writing system" used throughout the Aztec empire usually submits to interpretation in general terms. But many details of the genealogies, the dozens of place signs, and the rituals and divinations depicted in the pictorials are still imperfectly understood.

The early written sources present even more complexities. Every historian's work has to be examined to establish what is primary material, what is data quoted directly from informants, and what has been borrowed from others. Every text bristles with interpretative problems. How, for example, does one distinguish legend from historical events? Once analysis is complete and the primary data identified, one must evaluate reliability. Who wrote what, when, where, and why? For example, the account of the Conquest in Sahagun's *General History* is thought to have been told not by informants from the capital city, Tenochtitlan, but from the neighboring community of Tlatelolco. Her people play a prominent and partisan role in the story, and her soldiers' courage is praised during the siege: *yehica ca in tlatilulque cenca mochicauhque* ("the Tlatelolcans made themselves very strong"). Identifying the prejudices of the narrator is critical in evaluating the reliability of any document.

As the conquistadors found to their advantage, the various Indian states in the Valley of Mexico quarrelled incessantly with one another. All these quarrels took place within a framework of religious and cosmological beliefs that radically affected the ways in which Aztec histories were passed on from one generation to the next. All their traditional narratives are formalized accounts, a stylized image of the past, often designed for recitation on formal occasions and subject to constant change according to the theological and sociopolitical requirements of the moment. Each faction and each major ruler had a version of history to tell, tales of ancestors, of dynasties seeking, gaining, and holding on to power. The only way to construct a reasonably dispassionate, undistorted account of Aztec history is to analyze as many sources as possible. All too often, however, only a single codex is available, so the scholar must resort to value judgments that discount obvious hyperbole and unscramble telescoped chronologies and wrongly remembered names, to mention only a few problems. Even worse is the problem of dating. The Aztec calendar boasted several different year counts, all of which have to be reconciled before an accurate chronology for pre-European times can be agreed upon.

Historical documents cover the Conquest through Spanish eyes, but not until the mid-sixteenth century do ecclesiastical and government documents begin to provide any valuable insights into the drastic changes after the fall of the empire. Missionary records are a valuable primary source, and so are the letters and official documents of Spanish colonial administrators which contain useful information on native culture, land tenure, inheritance, and economic life. These include hundreds of technical memoranda, like the *Relaciones Geograficas,* inventories brought together between 1579 and 1585 by order of King Philip II of Spain. The demographer Sherborne F. Cook and historian Woodrow Borah made liberal use of the census data in the *Relaciones* when they prepared their famous study of the catastrophic declines in Indian populations after the Conquest. The same data has been invaluable for archaeologists studying changing prehistoric settlement patterns in the Basin of Mexico.

A number of Spanish-educated Indians and *mestizo* chroniclers also wrote annals of their communities in their own languages. These documents usually sought to establish their writers' genealogies as nobles who were entitled to privileges under the new regime. Seemingly an esoteric source, these annals do convey Indian attitudes and values far more effectively than any European could. In many cases, their genealogies and historical narratives derive directly from lost codices. Sometimes the chroniclers actually copied earlier pictures or wrote using annotated pictorial records.

Perhaps worst of all, all of these sources lie in widely scattered locations. Spanish colonial records are in Madrid, in the Archives of the Indies at Seville, in Mexico City, and at dozens of other ecclesiastical locations, and many, perhaps, still lie buried in uncataloged archives and private collections.

As Carlos de Siguenza pointed out in the seventeenth century, Aztec history did not end at the Conquest. It continues to this day and forms part of the tapestry of contemporary Mexican nationalism. Those who seek to understand the Aztec legacy should visit the National Palace in Mexico City, where the great artist Diego Rivera has commemorated the rise and fall of the Mexica in a series of epic murals. Rivera painted the past, present, and future of Mexico in a flowing march from the early millennia of simple tribal life,

through the heyday of the Aztecs and the rigors of the Conquest, to the bitter struggles and revolutions from which his nation was born. His greatest mural depicts Tenochtitlan floating in its highland lakes, the high temples of Huitzilopochtli and Tlaloc tinged with streams of human blood. The teeming market bustles in the foreground. Nobles in rich capes inspect the stalls, merchants barter, a dentist examines a boy's teeth, a prostitute displays her wares. The world is carefree, joyous—everyone shares in it. The serene, almost festive scenes give way to violence and oppression in the stairwell murals, where Rivera chronicles the trauma of the Conquest and the tumultuous colonial years. The Aztec world has gone for ever. Only the people remain, resigned to an inconspicuous, marginal role in the new society. But the legacy of their brilliant civilization is finally triumphant and forms part of the great indigenous tradition of modern Mexico. Rivera's

Diego Rivera mural in the National Palace, Mexico City. "The Great City of Tenochtitlan," painted in 1945. The mural shows the city with its temples and palaces. In the center is the great market of Tlatelolco, with various gods being offered for sale, a dentist examining a child's teeth, and a harlot plying her wiles. The regent Cihuacoatl dominates the entire scene. Diego Rivera drew on Bernal Diaz's description to paint this masterpiece.

panorama is idealistic, perhaps uncritical, but it makes its point. One cannot understand the modern nation of Mexico without comprehending the civilizations that preceded it.

I

THE RISE OF
THE AZTEC STATE

gun demonyo: todo esto dezian, que acon
tecia, porque estos dioses, de que aqui
se trata, se avian enojado contrael.
Despues de acabada la fiesta, otro dia
luego de mañana, el que avia hecho,
la fiesta: juntauan asus parientes,
y asus amigos, y alos de su barrio, cō
todos los de su casa: y acabauan de
comer, y beuer, todo lo que avia so
brado de la fiesta. A esto llamavan,
apeoalo, que quiere dezir: añadidura
alo que estaua comjdo, y beujdo: nin
guna cosa quedaua de comer, nj de be
uer, para otro dia. Dezian que los
gotosos, haziendo esta fiesta, sanaua
de la gota: ode qualis quiera, de las
enfermedades, que arriba se dixero
y los que avian escapado, de algun
peligro de agua: con hazer esta fies
ta, cumplian con su voto. Acabada
toda la fiesta: los papeles, y adere
cos, conque avian adornado, estas y
magines: y todas las vasijas, que
ayan sido menester, para el combite:
tomauanlo todo, y lleuauanlo, a vn
sumjdero, que esta enla laguna de
mexico: que se llama pantitlan, y
alli lo arronjauan todo.

ichiua ntla paloaia, yn tlach tia
yia inmanel can tepiton ocon
palo: iuh nytoaia tenne cuylivia
tepantiliuia, avie momamana
avie xoquyvi yntze: yoan intza
matzicoliuja, yma quicue
cuetza, icxi quicue cuetza, ma
copichauj, icxicopichauj, icxi
cuecuechca, yhixatotoco, ten
papatlaca, tenvivioca, icch
quyneca: mjtoa, oquitlavelique
inzoxouhque tepeme. Auh
ynotlathuje, njman ie ic apeoa
lo: ynapeoa can iehoan, ymi
c aniolque, in vel icalloc, inean
tlaca, comeoa, in vel icujtlax
colloc, yn vel jmecaioc: motene
oa apeoalo, iquac cempoliuja
tlatlamj, in quex qujch mocdoa
ia mitl, intla qualli: yoan inoc
quex qujch omocauh xatocamye in
vetli, maiuctli, intla chisaluctli, in
iztacuctli, in ochuctli. Auh ynte
pi qujsnj, intepieqnj: intla coaci
vi, y njuh omyto tlacpac, ic patz:
yoan ynaquyn atlan miqujzqaja

CHAPTER 1   Tolteca and Chichimeca

*These thus mentioned called themselves
Chichimeca Mochanecatoca, that is to say
Tolteca. It is these who caused the Toltecs to
disperse when they went away, when
Topiltzin Quetzalcoatl entered the water,
when he went to settle in the place of the
red color, the place of burning.*

Fray Bernardino de Sahagun, *General History,* 10, p. 175.

*Page 24: Quetzalcoatl. From
original drawing by Alonso
Caso. Courtesy, Fondo de
Cultura Economica Mexico
City.*

*Left: A page from Volume 1
of Sahagun's* General History,
*beginning, "which telleth of
those called Tepicteton (Little
Molded Ones) who belonged
among the Tlalocs. . . ."
Courtesy, University of Utah
Press, Salt Lake City.*

"In order to discuss the real and truthful account of the
origin and beginnings of these Indian nations, so mysterious and remote to us, and to discover the real truth
about them, some divine revelation or spirit of God
would be needed," wrote Fray Diego Duran in despair
after years of trying to unravel Aztec history (1964, p.
2). Modern scholars are sometimes tempted to agree
with him. After more than four centuries of historical
and archaeological research, we know tantalizingly little
about the very earliest development of Aztec civilization. We do know, however, that the flames of Mexican civilization were kindled over three thousand years
before the conquistadors gazed on Tenochtitlan. The
Aztecs inherited a complex legacy of religious beliefs
and philosophies from their predecessors. Their trade
routes and markets were an expansion of commercial
activities that had flourished for centuries, surviving
shifts in political power, the rise and fall of gods and
religious cults, even entire civilizations. They merely
refined and changed what had been established cen-

27

turies before. Therefore we must begin our survey of Aztec civilization by examining some of its antecedents.

The earliest complex societies of Mesoamerica appear to have developed among the Olmec peoples of lowland Veracruz and with the Maya farmers of the steamy rain forests of the Yucatan before 1500 B.C. These peoples traded for obsidian and other essential commodities with highland villages in the far interior, sending such exotic luxuries as conch shells, tropical feathers, and ritual paraphernalia to communities far from the Gulf of Mexico. The lowlands exported far more than just exotica, however. They passed on pervasive symbolic ideas and compelling religious beliefs surrounding earth, water, and fertility that were to survive and flourish for centuries.

Three thousand years ago, highland Mexico was home to hundreds of village communities, many of them owing loose allegiance to nearby larger settlements, also in the Basin, that boasted of modest public buildings and temples. It was the priests in these towns that donned the imported regalia, who gashed their bodies with sting-ray spines from the coast in rituals of penance that were to survive into Aztec times. In time, the center of political power and state development may have shifted from Olmec country and southern Mesoamerica to Monte Alban in the Valley of Oaxaca and to the Valley of Mexico. Around A.D. 100, the great, pre-Aztec city of Teotihuacan, 30 miles east of modern Mexico City, was coming into prominence, a metropolis that was to dominate the highlands and the Basin of Mexico for more than eight centuries.

TEOTIHUACAN (c. 200 B.C. to A.D. 750)

Teotihuacan bestrides the history of pre-Aztec Mexican civilization like a colossus. In its heyday during the early part of first millennium A.D., the city housed between 125,000 and 150,000 nobles, priests, artisans, and farmers, and covered more than 8 square miles (20 sq km). We do not know the linguistic or tribal affilia-

Central America.

tions of its inhabitants, but the city was teeming with crowded neighborhoods, apartment buildings, and imposing public monuments. Its great market attracted merchants and merchandise from all over Mesoamerica. Thousands of people attended the elaborate rituals and ceremonies conducted in its imposing plazas. The city was a cosmopolitan metropolis, at once a commercial center, an imperial capital, and a place of pilgrimage. More than half a millennium after its final collapse, the Aztecs still revered its silent shrines and abandoned pyramids. Teotihuacan was one base of the Aztec spiritual world.

Teotihuacan was an important inspiration for Aztec civilization in more practical ways, too. The master plan for Teotihuacan was established very early in the second century A.D. when the great Street of the Dead was laid out. The wide roadway was lined by temples, pyramids, and palaces. The vast pyramids of the Sun and Moon rose alongside the street, massive artificial

Teotihuacan from the Temple of the Moon. The city dates from about 200 B.C. to A.D. 750. Photo, Lesley Newhart.

mountains of rubble, adobe, and earth encased with stone. The city's public architecture was calculated to maintain an illusion of height and mass. From whatever angle one approached Teotihuacan, one's eye was led to a point of interest, guided by the arrangement of the planes and masses. The architects managed to conquer the diminishing effect of distance. Their monuments overwhelmed the visitor. Like the great Maya ceremonial centers of the lowlands, Teotihuacan served as a blueprint for the imposing temples and pyramids that would later dominate the Aztec capital, Tenochtitlan. The ceremonial precincts of both cities were carefully designed to dominate the viewer with the sheer weight of divine power.

By the fifteenth century, the central plaza of Tenochtitlan had become the center of the Aztec world. The unknown builders of Teotihuacan set the precedent for this, making their Street of the Dead the hub of their world. Both Tenochtitlan and Teotihuacan were divided into four residential quadrants, the quarters of each city meeting at the most sacred place in the metropolis. Both stood at the center of a carefully organized hinterland which supplied most of their food. Merchants from hundreds of miles around converged on both cities, where every conceivable kind of merchandise was sold and distributed in the great markets.

Teotihuacan inherited religious beliefs that had probably been nurtured for over a thousand years in the lowlands. Modified forms of the same beliefs became a vital part of Aztec theology. The city's dominant god Tlaloc, the rain diety, may have originated among the jaguar fertility cults of the Olmeca of Vera Cruz. The name Tlaloc derives from *tlalli,* "earth," for the god was associated with fertility and the regeneration of crops. Tlaloc's goggled and fanged countenance appears not only on Teotihuacan's public buildings, but on figurines found at archaeological sites throughout Mexico. The rain god was still worshipped by the Aztecs, as was another diety that appears at Teotihuacan, the Feathered Serpent. No one knows when the cult of the Feathered Serpent Quetzalcoatl first began. The name Quetzalcoatl is derived from *quetzalli,* "green feather," and *coatl,* "serpent." The Feathered Serpent cult may have derived from the jaguar cult of Olmec and other early peoples, for the jaguar represents the fertility of

Effigies of the Rain God Tlaloc and of the Feathered Serpent Quetzalcoatl on the Temple of Quetzalcoatl at Teotihuacan. Photo, Lesley Newhart.

31

the earth, while the serpent represents that from the water. But at this time the Feathered Serpent had far less importance than Tlaloc. Only in later centuries, in Toltec times, did Quetzalcoatl rise to extraordinary prominence and his cult spread throughout central Mesoamerica, persisting up to the Spanish Conquest.

The cultural and spiritual legacy of Teotihuacan to the Aztecs was both pervasive and subtle. Many of the obvious characteristics of Aztec civilization—long-distance trade, great markets, swamp agriculture, and spectacular religious architecture designed as a setting for elaborate public ceremonies—developed in earlier times. It was at Teotihuacan that many of the Aztecs' most cherished religious beliefs originated. Such was the city's spiritual power that it held an intensely sacred place in Aztec thought. It was also associated with the legendary origins of the Aztec world, that of the Fifth Sun.

THE LEGEND OF THE FIFTH SUN

Teotihuacan declined during the seventh and eighth centuries A.D. for reasons that are still little understood. Some authorities believe that the city's agricultural base collapsed as a result of overpopulation, others point to an increased militarism represented in the city's art, as if armed conflict weakened the metropolis. Whatever the reason, by A.D. 800 Teotihuacan was little more than a series of scattered villages. Its leaders had moved elsewhere and Mexican civilization had gravitated to other areas. But, according to Aztec legend, momentous religious events had occurred just before the city's demise.

Sometime in the 1470s, the Aztec ruler Axayacatl dedicated a new sacrificial stone in the temple of the war god Huitzilopochtli at Tenochtitlan, the famous Stone of the Sun that symbolized the Aztec cosmos. The twenty-four ton stone was lost for more than two centuries after the Spanish Conquest until it was dug up by accident in 1790. Now housed in the Aztec gallery of the National Museum of Anthropology, it has

The Aztec Stone of the Sun. Courtesy, The Bettmann Archive.

become a national symbol. The Stone of the Sun depicts the perpetual struggle between the forces of good and evil that caused the creation and destruction of no less than four worlds, or suns. The circular carving is dedicated to Tonatiuh, the Sun God, whose face lies in the center. Surrounding his countenance are four square panelled reliefs depicting the dates when the four earlier worlds ended. No source agrees with the other on the chronology of the first four suns, but a figure of 2028 mythical years for earlier eras appears in at least two codices.

33

All was darkness after the destruction of the Fourth Sun. Fray Bernardino de Sahagun records one version of what happened next:

It is told that when yet all was in darkness, when yet no sun had shone and no dawn had broken—it is said —the gods gathered themselves together and took counsel among themselves there in Teotihuacan. They spoke; they said among themselves:

"Come hither. O gods! Who will carry the burden? Who will take it upon himself to be the sun, to bring the dawn?"

And upon this, one of them who was there spoke: Tecuziztecatl presented himself. He said: "O Gods, I will be the one."

And again the gods spoke: "And who else?"

Whereupon they looked around at one another. They pondered the matter. They said to one another: "How may this be? How may we decide?"

No one dared; no one else came forward. Everyone was afraid; they all drew back. There was present how- ever a god named Nanauatzin, the little Syphilitic God. As he stood listening, the gods called to him and said: "Thou shalt be the one." He eagerly accepted the deci- sion, saying: "It is well O gods; you have been good to me" (Sahagun, 7, p. 4).

The two gods chosen to represent the Sun and Moon did penance for four days and nights, just as Aztec rulers did in later centuries, performing their ceremonies on the Pyramids of the Sun and Moon. Then they were dressed in the correct ritual regalia and immolated themselves in a great fire while the other gods watched. Nanauatzin jumped boldly into the fire, but his companion procrastinated. The Syphilitic God suddenly emerged from the flames. "With a rabbit he came to wound in the face this Tecuziztecatl; with it he darkened his face; he killed its brilliance. Thus doth it appear today" (Sahagun, 7, p. 7). Tecuziztecatl be- came the Moon, the imprint of the rabbit, the dark shadows on its surface. But the Sun and Moon were

Pyramid of the Sun at Teotihuacan. Photo, Lesley Newhart.

still stationary. So the wind god Ehecatl "arose and exerted himself fiercely and violently as he blew. At once he could move him [the Sun] who thereupon went his way. And when he had already followed his course, only the moon remained there. At the time when the sun came to enter the place where he set, then once more the moon moved" (Sahagun, 7, p. 8).

Thus was the Fifth Sun born, but a deep sense of fatalism surrounded the Aztec legend of creation. The Stone of the Sun does not commemorate the birth of the Fifth Sun, but its eventual destruction by catastrophic earthquakes. The central design of the stone is the day-sign—each day in their calendar had a specific number and symbol—of the day known to the Aztecs as "4 Movement." The Fifth Sun was finite, a world destined to end. In the meantime, however, the Aztecs believed that they could ensure the continuity of life by nourishing the sun with the magic elixir of human hearts. It was for this reason that human sacrifice was such an integral part of Aztec religious belief and ritual.

But even with diligent sacrifices, the best that mortals could do was to postpone the day of reckoning for a while.

TAMOANCHAN, "THE PLACE OF DESCENT"

The myth of the Fifth Sun has been pieced together from many sources, not only from the Stone of the Sun, but from Sahagun's research and several other codices. The Fifth Sun was the last of the five worlds that made up the complicated origin myths of the Aztecs described in Chapter 9. Like all origin myths, the legend of the Suns attempts to establish and explain a relationship between the natural and supernatural worlds. Its historical interest lies in its associations with the great city of Teotihuacan. The Aztecs were well aware that theirs was not the first civilization in the highlands. Many of their venerated religious beliefs and philosophies and some of their social and economic institutions, they knew, had originated centuries before. Their oral traditions contain constant, repetitive references to the decline of Teotihuacan when her gods departed. They also refer to a mysterious place of fullness and abundance, a location associated with mist, water, jaguars, and plenty, a place named Tamoanchan.

No two experts seem to agree on what Tamoanchan means. Sahagun said that the word meant "we seek our home," but his Nahuatl rendering may be incorrect. Perhaps Tamoanchan is in fact *temo-ichan,* "the place of descent," a version that is grammatically acceptable but historically undocumented. All sorts of places have been associated with Tamoanchan, among them a fabled region named Tlalocan in the coastal lowlands to the east, where the sun rose. Historian Nigel Davies argues that possibly two Tamoanchans existed, the first a mythical place associated with the distant Gulf Coast, the second a more specific location, perhaps the general area where the city of Teotihuacan came into being. As time passed, Davies believes, Teotihuacan itself became the revered symbol of a magnificent civilization that

had vanished forever, the cradle of the gods, Tamoanchan itself, the place where the Fifth Sun was born.

Archaeologists date the eventual collapse of Teotihuacan to the seventh and eighth centuries A.D. This
appears to have been a period of political and economic
confusion. Perhaps the city was weakened by partial
ecological collapse, or conquered by invaders, perhaps
from the north. The evidence is highly uncertain. Both
the archaeological record and Sahagun's carefully collected oral traditions paint a highly confused picture of
the centuries that followed. Sahagun tells of constant
comings and goings of tribes, of the departure of most
of Teotihuacan's *tlamatinime*, "wise men," to the east.
They carried the image of their gods on their backs,
following, they said, their Lord and Master Tloque Nahuaque, the primeval creator. They took their codices
and their expert artisans with them. The common people remained behind under the charge of four wise men
who expressed confidence in the future of the world
despite the departure of their god and the sacred writings. So they devised a new Book of Days, and a year
count, the *xiuhamatl:* "And thus was time recorded
during all the time the Tolteca, Tepaneca, the Mexica,
and all the Chichimeca reign endured" (Sahagun, 7, p.
10). It may be that the legend of the Fifth Sun com-
memorates this critical moment, for the wise men created a new world that was sanctified by the gods. The
people made offerings at Teotihuacan; leaders were
elected who "all were worshipped as gods when they
died; some became the sun, some the moon." The
Fifth Sun legend looks back and in retrospect gives
gods the credit for a new political order, one that
emerged from the ruins of Teotihuacan.

As Teotihuacan fell apart, so different peoples
moved away from the disintegrating metropolis, perhaps in search of new agricultural land. The codices
mention various peoples, some of them original inhabitants of the city, others perhaps newcomers, nomadic
peoples from the desert north, moving into hitherto
tightly controlled lands. Among the migrants were the
Tolteca, "the ones who took the very lead." Other

groups split off, including the Mexica, who went on to Chicomoztoc, a place "of seven caves" that figures prominently in later Aztec history.

All these references to population movements and Tamoanchan exist in oral tradition, little more than pure myth, but they do highlight the legacy of Teotihuacan, with its powerful religious beliefs and highly effective political and economic institutions, to the Aztecs centuries later. It is with some relief that we can now move onto firmer historical ground with the emergence of the Tolteca as a dominant force in the Basin.

THE TOLTEC LEGACY (A.D. 900 to 1150)

The Tolteca were among those who were the heirs of Teotihuacan and the revered ancestors of the Aztecs. The Mexica thought of them as the rulers of a Golden Age, an era of such magnificence that civilization reached its most brilliant apogee. So they tried to emulate their predecessors' perceived splendor. "The Tolteca were wise. Their works were all good, all perfect, all marvellous; their houses beautiful, tiled in mosaics, smoothed, stuccoes, very marvellous.... The Tolteca were skilled; it is said they were feather workers ... in truth they invented all the wonderful, precious, marvellous things which they made" (Sahagun, 10, pp. 165–66). They were expert herbalists, jewelers, the originators of calendars and year counts—righteous, wise people in every way, it was claimed. The oral histories depict the Tolteca as tall people who excelled in all the arts and sciences. Hunger and unhappiness were unknown. Toltec farmers even grew colored cotton and huge ears of maize.

Eventually the Toltec rulers became mythical heroes. The ultimate birthright for an Aztec noble was to claim descent from one of the Toltec heroes. Said to be fabulous artists and artisans, they built a wonderous capital at Tula to the north of the Valley of Mexico. Sahagun's informants regaled him with tales of the magnificent temple of Quetzalcoatl and its four precincts, one of gold facing east, another of turquoise facing towards the sunset, and white and red shell-decorated shrines facing south and north. This temple, wrote Sahagun, stood as the ultimate symbol of a people of learning and genius, the inspiration for all that was best in Aztec life. The Tolteca loom larger than life in Aztec legend.

What is the historical reality? In 1941, Mexican historian Jimenez Moreno used place names near the modern city of Tula in Hidalgo province to identify the archaeological site of Tula with the legendary Toltec capital, Tollan Xicoctitlan, "the place nearby to Xicococ," a famous hill near Tula. *Tollan* itself means "the place of rushes," and the word came to signify a great congregation of people who were crowded together as thick as rushes. The archaeological site of Tula is far less spectacular than the vastness of Teotihuacan, but recent researchers have shown that the settlement was a spread-out urban center that covered 7 square miles (11 sq km). Perhaps as many as 120,000 people lived in the city itself or within the radius of a few miles.

The site of Tula was already a small farming settlement around A.D. 650. But the Tolteca who adopted it as their capital built a ceremonial precinct on a high promontory around A.D. 900. The pyramid that dominated the north side of the precinct bore a temple dedicated to the Feathered Serpent god Quetzalcoatl, in his role as the God of the Morning Star. Its workmanship is crude compared with that of the pyramids of Teotihuacan. Great warrior figures with flat heads supported the roof of Quetzalcoatl's temple. The shrine stood on a pyramid faced with panels of walking jaguars and eagles consuming human hearts. The north side of the pyramid boasts a serpent wall, or *coatepantli,* an artifice that was to surround Aztec temples in later centuries. The wall demarcated the pyramid from the outside of the precinct. The friezes on the serpent wall include gruesome scenes of a snake swallowing a human being except for the head. The head is not devoured, the dismembered limbs lie among the serpent's coils. Everything honors Quetzalcoatl, the Feathered Serpent, the great Creator, the God of the

Temple of Quetzalcoatl at Tula. Photo, Lesley Newhart.

Great warrior figures from Tula. Photo, Lesley Newhart.

Tula: a serpent devouring a dismembered human being. Detail from a temple frieze at Tula. Photo, Lesley Newhart.

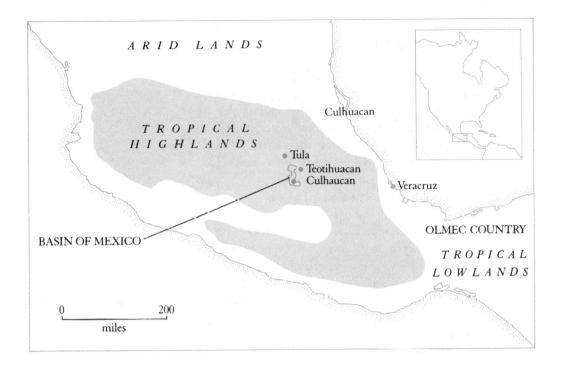

Teotihuacan and Tula.

Wind and the Morning Star. Now Quetzalcoatl, not Tlaloc, is the dominant god. The religious legacy of Teotihuacan has evolved into a far more militaristic theology based on human sacrifice.

The Tula excavations reveal a battle-scarred, militaristic Toltec civilization, one in which oppression was a way of life and human sacrifice second nature, a far cry from the Golden Age of Aztec legend. The Toltecas' vaunted empire was certainly much smaller than that of Teotihuacan. Although their trading contacts extended far into the lowlands, their actual domains embraced only the northern part of the Valley of Mexico and portions of Hidalgo province. The militaristic rulers of Tula engaged not only in conquest, but in extensive irrigation works, settling people in garrisoned regions where they could collect tribute in produce and labor. Thus they established precedents of tribute gathering and imperial governance that would serve the Aztecs well.

Not even in physical appearance did the Tolteca live

up to the heroic, master race of legend. The skeletons recovered at Tula show that the Tolteca were indeed slightly taller than their neighbors, but with big noses, poor teeth, and projecting faces—hardly the super-people of early legend. The contrast between myth and reality is so dramatic that some authorities believe that the "fabulous Tolteca" were in fact the Teotihuacanos whose vast capital had indeed been the center of an imposing and magnificent civilization centuries earlier.

THE LEGEND OF QUETZALCOATL

Why, then, did the Aztecs endow the Tolteca with such an extraordinary aura of high achievement and sanctity? As we shall see, their imperial ambitions had firm roots in a mythical and heroic past, a past dominated by the perpetual battle between the forces of annihilation and those of survival.

The most important diety at Teotihuacan had been the rain god Tlaloc. But the Feathered (or Plumed) Serpent had always had power. Both gods were associated with earth and water, two elements symbolically linked in Indian belief from the earliest days of highland civilization, and that belief endured long after the Conquest. The Tolteca gave Quetzalcoatl preeminence. His effigies dominate Tula's ceremonial precincts. According to Henry Nicholson, the concept of Quetzalcoatl had two aspects. He was the Wind, as part of the Tlaloc complex so popular at Teotihuacan. But he was also God of the Heavens. Quetzalcoatl actually played a triple role, for he was thought of by the Tolteca as the Creator as well. So the Quetzalcoatl worshipped by the people of Tula fused many theological elements into one all-powerful god who dominated all other deities in the Tolteca pantheon.

According to Fray Sahagun, the wise men who departed from Teotihuacan (or Tamoanchan) carried the image of their gods with them. They may also have been searching for a new god or hero figure. Nigel Davies believes a new cult of Quetzalcoatl had emerged in the lowlands, perhaps in coastal Tabasco, before bursting onto the highlands during the confused centuries that followed the decline of Teotihuacan. Quetzalcoatl was instantly popular and emerged as a powerful political force at such places as Xochicalco, southwest of the Basin of Mexico, and, later, at Tula. One high priest adopted the name Topiltzin, or Quetzalcoatl. He became the primeval hero of Aztec legend: Ce Acatl-Topiltzin, the founder of Tollan-Xicoctitlan, or Tula.

One commonly accepted version of the legend has Ce Acatl-Topziltzin becoming ruler of the Tula in about A.D. 968. There he assumes the title of high priest of the Feathered Serpent and becomes a fanatical religious reformer. Topziltzin Quetzalcoatl was an austere leader who soon ran afoul of the powerful warrior class personified by the bloodthirsty war god Tezcatlipoca. After vicious internal strife, the Tezcatlipoca faction prevailed. Legend has it that his sorcerers got Topziltzin Quetzalcoatl so drunk and befuddled that he slept with his sister. These sins ended Tollan's golden age. The disgraced Topziltzin Quetzalcoatl fled from Tula, and his victorious rivals, the warriors, continued to reign for nearly a century before the city fell.

Another interpretation plays out the drama as a struggle for supremacy between two factions at Tula, the one religious, the other secular. In the end both Topziltzin Quetzalcoatl and his rival fled, and Tula was abandoned.

The two legends are chronologically incompatible, one claiming that Topziltzin Quetzalcoatl left soon after the founding of the city, the other that he left as it perished. H.B. Nicholson has looked closely at the sources of both versions of the legend and pointed out that the interpretation problems are so complex that neither version can be more than a speculative folk tale. But whether the character in this story was an actual person, an imaginary figure out of fable, or simply the embodiment of a religious concept, the spiritual legacy of this story to the Aztecs was enormous. Many believed that it was the god Quetzalcoatl himself, not the syphilitic Nanauatzin, who gave his life by jumping into the fire to create the Fifth Sun, the world that would one day be destroyed by giant earthquakes.

Several legends of Topiltzin Quetzalcoatl's departure from Tula were widespread in the Aztec empire. Sahagun writes how he departed to meet his destiny in Tlillan Tlapallan, the mythical lowlands where the sun rose. He "looked toward Tula, and then wept; as one sobbing he wept.... And when he had done these things, he went to reach the sea-coast. Then he fashioned a raft of serpents. When he had arranged the raft, there he placed himself, as if it were his boat. Then he set off across the sea" (Sahagun, 3, p. 12). Some versions had the god setting fire to himself and becoming the Morning Star, others that he set sail vowing to return in the year 1 Reed to regain his homeland. Historical and symbolic fiction they may have been, but these were the legends to which Moctezuma and his advisers turned for explanation when they heard rumors of strange visitors to Mexico from over the sea in 1519, by grotesque historical coincidence, the year 1 Reed.

THE CHICHIMECA

The Toltec empire did not flourish for long. Perhaps drier weather caused repeated droughts after 1100, forcing farmers living in settled lands on the northern frontiers of the empire to move southwards into the more fertile territory near Tula. In any case, Tula was burned and destroyed in the mid-twelfth century, perhaps at the hands of outsiders from the north, the Chichimeca. These peoples also figure prominently in Aztec legends; indeed, the Tolteca were sometimes described as Chichimeca, "the first who settled here in the land." The arrival of these marginal, semi-acculturated barbarians compounded the ecological problems facing the settled populations of the Basin. The next two centuries saw intense political and military conflict between the farmers of the Basin and the nomadic

Diego Rivera's depiction of Quetzalcoatl setting sail on his raft. National Palace, Mexico City. Photo, Lesley Newhart.

Chichimeca who were moving onto lakeside lands. The Toltec empire evaporated. Archaeological surveys reveal that the center of population moved from around Tula to the southern areas of the Basin. Several noble Toltec lineages did survive, the most prestigious at Culhuacan in the south, where people were beginning to settle by the lake shore and experiment with swamp cultivation. The daughters of Culhuacan's rulers were much sought in marriage, for the city was the bastion of Toltec culture and all that meant in terms of prestige and legitimacy to the many contenders for leadership of the Valley.

The Chichimeca included a large number of nomadic groups. The Teochichimeca were regarded as the true Chichimeca, nomadic hunter-gatherers, depicted in sixteenth-century codices dressed in skins and using bows and arrows. "These were the ones who lived far away; they lived in the forests, the grassy plains, the deserts, among the crags. These had their homes nowhere. They only went about travelling, wandering. . . . Where night came upon them, there they sought a cave, a craggy place; there they slept" (Sahagun, 10, pp. 171–172).

Then there were the Tamime, "shooters of arrows," an offshoot of the Teochichimeca, who, Sahagun tells us, made their homes in caves and gorges, and sometimes lived in small grass huts. They were hunters, but they also cultivated maize, and wore tattered capes. The Tamime had mingled enough with the farmers to acquire some advanced culture. "These were vassals of some ruler, some nobleman, to whom belonged the land, the city where they dwelt. Their tribute payments became that which they caught . . ." (Sahagun, 10, p. 171). They were expert herbalists and healers. Perhaps the first Aztecs were Tamime, semicivilized wanderers who drifted into the Valley of Mexico.

Later Aztec propagandists made much of their Chichimeca ancestry, of the "rags to riches" legitimacy that became almost a status symbol. Their heroes, the Tolteca, were also Chichimeca, the "first to settle here in the land." So they copied them, picturing themselves as strong and virile folk who had been used to a rough life and to the hardships of campaigning. This tribal ancestry was perhaps as important a part of the "official" view the Aztecs held of themselves as the long tradition of civilization epitomized by the civilizations at Teotihuacan and Tula.

In all probability, the Chichimeca migrations into the Valley took generations and involved many groups and leaders. The oral traditions for these two centuries are so confusing that they are almost useless, little more than garbled speculations. There seems to be some agreement, however, that sometime in the mid-thirteenth century an invading Chichimeca leader named Xolotl settled first at Tenayuca and later at Texcoco on the east shore of the Lake Texcoco. By the time Xolotl settled his new capital, the choice agricultural lands of the Valley were occupied, although no one group dominated the highlands. Cholula, outside the confines of

Sites mentioned in this chapter.

the Valley, was another important center. So were the Toltec bastion at Culhuacan and the city of Xochimilco. But the most significant players of all were the Mexica (Aztecs), still an obscure tribal people when Xolotl settled at Texcoco. It was not until the year 1325 that these folk founded a tiny hamlet close by, at Tenochtitlan in the swamps of Lake Texcoco. Less than two centuries later, these same people were the masters of all of Mexico.

vn poco, despues de la media noche
y llegaua hasta la mañana la luz
della la encubria. De manera
que salliendo el sol, no parecia mas
segun algunos, viose vn año ente
ro, y segun otros, quatro años arreo.
Quando aparecia de noche esta
cometa, todos los yndios, dauan
grandissimos alaridos, y se espan
tauan esperando, que algun
gran mal auja de venjr.

Otro mal aguero acontecio aqui
en mexico, que el cu, de vitzilobuch
tli, se encendio, sin auer razon yn
guna humana para ello, parece
que milagrosamente, se encendio:
y salian las llamas de dentro los
maderos, hazia fuera, y de presto
se quemo: dieron bozes los satrapas,
para que traxessen agua, para
matarlo, y quanto mas agua echa
uan, tanto mas ardia, del todo se
quemo.

tlac tlacujuitl, vel illi tlapa tlaltitech
ac viac viuci itloca vnipa tlap
copa motlitoquetzaya, oiuh onquiz
ioaltica tomila iniecoa tlachiuhtia
ca, ipan tlatlapa Qujnichoatl
qujoalpoloaia tetonatiuh, injc tic
oal qujquiza: vel cexiujtl motimo
quetzaya (çan machictlonxome
calli jmpeuh) auh injcoac necoc
tlacaoaloaia, netenujttecoaa, netço
ujloia, tlacemmachoia.

Injc vntetl tetzaujtl muchiuh
njpan mexico, çanmonomauj in
tlatlac caotlan, aiac ma qujtleco
uj çanmonoma tletauj, injtl dia
blo vitzilobuchtli, mjtoaia
itoaiocan Tlacateca innoz ietlatla
mela quechalli itlic oalqujça, intle
mjtacatl, mtlenenepilli, mtleca
çelluatl, cenca çan iaichat compalo
mixqujch calquaujtl. Niman ict
tlacaoaia qujtoa Mexiae, ma
oallatotoca, tlaceujloz, amapilol
auh mjcoac aatequjaia, inquj
ceujznecaja, amic ilhujce mopitza
aocmouel ceuh uellallac.

CHAPTER 2

The Rise of the Mexica

By what right do we deserve such good fortune? Who made us worthy of such grace? We have at least fulfilled our desires; we have found what we sought, our capital. Let thanks be given to the Lord of All Created Things, our god Huitzilopochtli.

Fray Diego Duran, *History of the Indies of New Spain*, 1964, p. 31.

A page from Volume 8 of Sahagun's *General History, beginning, "In which it is told how signs and omens appeared and were seen when the Spaniards had not yet come to this land . . . ." Courtesy, University of Utah Press, Salt Lake City.*

"Huitzilopochtli commands us to look for this place. When we discover it we shall be fortunate, for there we shall find our rest, our comfort, and our grandeur. There our name will be praised and our Aztec nation made great . . . . We will rule over these people, their land, their sons and daughters. They will serve us and be our subjects and tributaries" (Duran, 1964, p. 30). Thus does Diego Duran begin his account of the founding of Tenochtitlan, during the Aztecs' extraordinary rise to supremacy. The major events of their history are comparatively well-documented in the writings of the sixteenth-century friars, although many details are still debated.

These sixteenth-century sources have been subjected to critical analysis since the eighteenth century. At first the experts believed that the codices and chronicles stated literal, historical truth, even though they also depicted myth. Orozco y Berra and other nineteenth-century Mexican scholars went to the opposite extreme and treated the entire story as pure myth. They thought of Aztlan, the Mexica homeland, for example, merely as metaphor for the island capital of Tenochtitlan. The investigator has to untangle layer upon layer of symbolic stories and actual events that were interwoven over the centuries into repetitive, colorful orations. Modern scholars look for a balance between legend and historical fact, for, like the Homeric epics and other well-known sagas, the Aztec codices do ring of certain convincing historical truths. The synthesis here uses the critical studies of dozens of English-speaking and Mexican scholars since the 1840s in attempt to identify areas of controversy and general agreement.

THE MIGRATION LEGENDS
(A.D. 1111 to 1319)

Although their own historians could not locate it, the Mexica themselves were in no doubt that their homeland was an island in a lake named Aztlan, a place where their ancestors lived by fishing from boats. Modern historians cannot agree on the exact location of Aztlan, although most argue that it lies to the northwest of the Basin of Mexico, not too far from Tenochtitlan. Perhaps it is a mistake to search for the precise location of Aztlan, except to locate it in general terms to the northwest. Like Tamoanchan and other legendary places, Aztlan is more important as a concept, even though it may have been a specific place. In all probability the original Mexica were Tamime, semicivilized, settled people who were also Chichimeca. The Tamime had lived, at least for some time, within the boundaries of the original Toltec state, even if originally they had come from elsewhere. The concept of a homeland surrounded by water may have persisted simply because Tenochtitlan, the great capital, was itself an island surrounded by lakes, and the idea of having originated in such a place also made good political propaganda.

In the year 1609 Don Fernando de Alvarado Tezozomoc, an Indian noble and a grandson of Moctezuma Xocoyotzin, the Aztec ruler at the time of the Conquest, set down what he called "the story of the elders," an account of early Aztec history. In fact, it is a slightly modified version of the account given by Diego Duran and others. His *Cronica Mexicayotl* begins with the legends of Aztlan and describes the legendary departure of the Mexica from the mythical assembly point that is a cornerstone of so many origin legends of the peoples who descended on the Valley of Mexico in the mid-twelfth century: "The rock is called Chicomoztoc, which has holes on seven sides; and from there came forth the Mexicans, carrying their women, when they came out of Chicomoztoc by pairs; that was a fearsome place, for there abounded the countless wild beasts established in the area . . . and it is full of thorns, of sweet agave, and of pastures; and being thus very far-off, no one still knew later where it was" (Tezozomoc, 1949, pp. 7–8).

Mexican historian Jimenez Moreno worked out the major dates in Aztec history by calculating the number of "New Fire" ceremonies during their wanderings. New fire rites marked the end of each fifty-two-year calendar cycle, and there were five during the migration, the last at Tenochtitlan in 1351. Using this chronology, the Mexica probably set off on their migrations in about A.D. 1111.

The legends tell how a heterogeneous group of at least seven clans of Mexica travelled under the guidance of several priests, who were also political leaders. The Codex Boturini shows one of the priests carrying the idol of their patron god Huitzilopochtli. But an obscure divine in the Mexican pantheon at the time, Huitzilopochtli was far less significant, even to the Mexica, than were Quetzalcoatl and other major gods. His patronage assumed much greater importance in later centuries, when Aztec propagandists compiled an "official" version of their early history. Only then did they build up Huitzilopochtli as a major cult figure, the all-powerful god of war. But even at this early time, the people built a temple to Huitzilopochtli wherever they stopped, and there they performed human sacrifices.

Numerous hardships along the way were borne stoically, for the priests of Huitzilopochtli promised the god would make them "lords and kings of all that is in the world," receivers of tribute, rich in gold, emeralds, and feathers. As they tarried along the way, the early

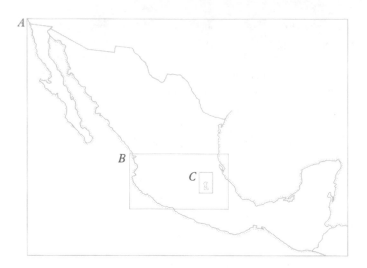

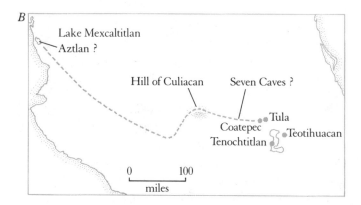

Mexica built temples, even ball courts. Human sacrifices were already commonplace, an act of devotion to the god and also, perhaps, a way of controlling factionalism. The wanderers' lives were already regulated by a religious and secular calendar that culminated in fifty-two year cycles. The Mexica had developed a complex religious life, but they were still relatively unsophisticated wanderers, very much less civilized than many of their more settled neighbors. Caught up in the confusion that followed the decline of the Tolteca, the wanderers lost themselves, so an Aztec footnote to a codex tells us, "in the mountains, the woods, and the place of

Possible migration routes of the early Mexica from Aztlan to Tenochtitlan. (A) Locator map. (B) Generalized route. (C) Valley of Mexico and its peoples around the thirteenth and early fourteenth centuries. These are highly provisional maps based on Nigel Davies, The Aztecs, pp. 9 and 10.

52

C

- - - - - route of
the Mexica

Tula

Atitlaquia

Apaxco

CHICHIMECA AND OTOMIS

Zumpango

Xaltocan

Teotihuacan

Tenayuca

Texcoco

Azcapotzalco

Tepeyacac

Tacuba

Tlatelolco
Tenochtitlan

Coatlichan

Tilapan

ACULHUAS

Chapultepec

Culhuacan

TEPANECA

Chalco

Xochimilco

0   15
miles

CHULHUAS
AND OTHERS

crags. They are said to have visited the ruins of Tula, to have wandered widely in the northern reaches of the Basin of Mexico, and to have attacked their neighbors on many occasions. They took prisoners on these forays, whom they sacrificed to Huitzilopochtli. The early Mexica wanderings often read somewhat like the meanderings of the Israelite hosts under Moses—hardly surprising, given the strong Catholic influence on many sixteenth-century informants. Near Tula, at a place called Coatepec, "the Hill of the Serpent," the Mexica celebrated the first New Fire in about 1163, the begin-

ning of a new fifty-two year cycle in the ritual calendar.
Their wanderings finished, five cycles later they were
established in their final capital.

Coatepec was where, later Aztec chronicles tell us,
the war god Huitzilopochtli assumed supreme spiritual
leadership. He had emerged fully grown from his
mother Coatlicue's womb some time before, brandish-
ing Xiuhcoatl, the Serpent of Fire that was to become
the weapon of the god. His devout mother already had
four hundred sons and a single daughter. Although she
had then sworn herself to chastity, one day she picked
up a feather floating in the air while sweeping a temple. Soon she was pregnant with Huitzilopochtli,

*The Seven Caves of Chicomoz-
toc. Feather-decked Toltec
warriors are asking the
wanderers for help in battle.
From the* Historia Tolteca-
Chichimeca.

54

whose brothers and sisters were far from overjoyed at the prospect of a new rival. They marched against Huitzilopochtli, who smote and killed his sister with his Serpent of Fire and routed her brothers in confusion. This symbolic tale may reflect internal dissension among the different clans of the Mexica that erupted in open rebellion against the authority of the priests of Huitzilopochtli. The latter fought their rivals and established the clan of the god as the dominant power in Mexica society. And it was Huitzilopochtli who would guide the Mexica destiny until the Conquest.

This symbolic event at Coatepec was of cardinal importance to the Mexica and later propagandists made much of it. The new god's name means "the hummingbird of the left (handed)." The hummingbird was closely linked both with human sacrifice and with rain, since it appears in the rainy season, so the bird was associated with the form of death believed to feed the sun and with fertility as well. Huitzilopochtli was no longer just an obscure earth deity, he was now the Lord of the Daylight Sky, the Rising Sun, and his symbol, the hummingbird, also came to represent the fallen warriors who accompanied the sun on his daily journey. Among his other attributes, the Mexica came to believe in Huitzilopochtli as the God of War, not as a pacific earth god of fertility, but a burning symbol of militarism, ambition, and imperious dynamism. Unlike the omnipresent Quetzalcoatl, Lord of Creation, Huitzilopochtli was the official mouthpiece who incited his cho-

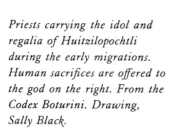

Priests carrying the idol and regalia of Huitzilopochtli during the early migrations. Human sacrifices are offered to the god on the right. From the Codex Boturini. Drawing, Sally Black.

sen people to greatness, not by his favor, but by the force of their own hearts and their arms which would "lift the Mexican nation to the clouds." These same hearts and arms were also to provide the vital, nourishing blood that sustained the god and the Aztec world.

After 1168 the Mexica came into increasing contact with the sedentary communities around Lake Texcoco in the Basin of Mexico. These were civilized petty states, centered on small cities with impressive monumental architecture. Each polity traded with its neighbors and maintained far-reaching exchange networks with areas outside the Valley. Their leaders presided over stratified societies of priests, skilled artisans, merchants, and thousands of free citizens who cultivated the fertile swamp lands of the lake shore. The various states vied with each other, attempting to enlarge their domains through conquest and a complex network of political alliances and well-timed marriages. Bravery in war, shrewdness in trading, political acumen, and careful exercise of brute force: these were the keys to power and personal success in the Valley. The Mexica found themselves unwelcome visitors in this sophisticated world, for their new neighbors despised their unsophisticated barbarity. Tough, single-minded people, they learned to hold their own in this environment of Byzantine political intrigue and double-dealing. They wandered from place to place, eventually arriving at Tenayuca, once the capital of Chichimeca ruler Xolotl.

Two peoples were now dominating the affairs of the Basin, the Acolhua, living around Texcoco on the eastern shores of the lake, and the Tepaneca, who lived to the west of the lagoon in the ancient settlement of Azcapotzalco, now a suburb of Mexico City. The two groups faced each other across the lakes, at a time when dozens of petty kingdoms bickered with one another in a constant state of barely suppressed rivalry. They shared a common culture, deeply rooted in Toltec civilization, a sacred calendar of 260 days, and a theology that revered a pantheon of deities including both Tlaloc and Quetzalcoatl. One reason for the constant quarrelling was a shortage of agricultural land, for nearly all the prime farming acreage had been taken up. So the Mexica were even more unwelcome guests in the Valley. Harried by their neighbors, they moved in 1299 from Tenayuca to Chapultepec, "the Hill of the Locust," which is close to downtown Mexico City today. There they enjoyed a commanding view of Lake Texcoco but were hemmed in by hostile neighbors on all sides.

FROM CHAPULTEPEC TO TENOCHTITLAN (1299 to 1325)

By this time the Mexica were probably a consortium of as many as twenty clans headed by authoritative military leaders and ambitious priests. On the face of it, their situation was precarious, for they owned little land and their numbers were increasing rapidly. But they were pushy, aggressive people. Soon their activities began to worry their neighbors, who threatened to attack them and wipe them out before it was too late. Huitzilopochtli exhorted the people never to relax and settle down comfortably, so the clans chose a single leader named Huitzilihuitl, "Humming Bird Feather," to lead their army. But it was to no avail. After repeated battles, the Mexica were forced to abandon Chapultepec in about 1319. Some of them fled to nearby Culhuacan, others dispersed to other centers. The Codex Boturini depicts the events at Chapultepec. The hill has a locust perched on top of it, while pieces of wood symbolize the lighting of a new fire at the beginning of a new calendar cycle. The Mexica are seen weeping brokenheartedly while Huitzilhuitl and his daughter are dragged away by their hair as sacrificial prisoners of war.

The Mexica who straggled into Culhuacan in about 1319 were down but not out. The Culhua were somewhat at a loss as to what to do with these unwelcome guests, but they permitted them to settle at Tizapan, 6 miles (9.6 Km) west of their city, in a desolate environment where, thought the wise men, "they will perish ... eaten by the serpents, since many dwell in that place." Far from perishing, the Aztecs thrived. Not only did they eat the snakes, but they combined hunting and farming with trading and flourished in a modest way, much to the consternation of the Culhua. Soon the Mexica were entering the city freely and intermarrying with their neighbors. Within a few generations, they had acquired the polish and sophistication of a much older and more civilized people. Their nobles now claimed descent from hallowed Toltec lineages.

Hard pressed by the armies of nearby Xochimilco, Culhuacan now asked the Mexica for military assistance. Not only did they rout the enemy, they began to threaten their hosts. Matters came to a head when Huitzilopochtli advised the departing Mexica to find a female sacrificial victim whose death would provoke the Culhua to war. So the Mexica asked for the hand of one of Culhuacan's rulers, a beautiful girl whom they promptly killed and flayed. Her father arrived to attend her wedding, only to be confronted by a priest dancing in her flayed skin. Fighting broke out at once, and the Mexica retreated into the swamps of the lagoon, finally reaching the safety of a reed-covered island near the center of what is now Mexico City. There they rested. Huitzilopochtli appeared before one of the priests, ordering him to search for a cactus where a great eagle perched. This, said the god, was a place he had named Tenochtitlan, the "Place of the Fruit of the Prickly Pear Cactus."

Next day, the people found the cactus with the eagle perched upon it. The priests recognized the symbolism of the place, for the eagle was the symbol of the sun, of Huitzilopochtli himself. The cactus fruit were red, and in the shape of the human hearts that the god devoured. This was a place among reeds, too, another Tollan, a "place of rushes," like the revered Tula of the Tolteca. The Mexica were overjoyed, for they knew this was their final destination, the place where their city was to be built. Immediately they piled up a sod platform where they erected a reed temple to Huitzilopochtli. The temple was founded in the year Two

The founding of Tenochtitlan, with the eagle perched on the cactus, surrounded by ten Mexica leaders. The interior border symbolizes the lake, the bisecting lines, the four quarters of the future city. Below, Aztec warriors conquer Culhuacan and Tenayuca in the city's first military triumphs. The glyphs of the exterior border represent the fifty-two years of a calendar cycle. The fire ceremony that marked the beginning of a new cycle is depicted at bottom right. From the Codex Mendoza. Courtesy, Bodleian Library, Oxford. MS. Arch. Selden A.1. folio 2.

House, probably around A.D. 1325, although some authorities place the date twenty years later.

The site was an ideal choice for a capital, not only because of abundant food supplies and easy water communications, but because of its strategic advantages. The Mexica never had to abandon their city, although they were dangerously dependent on their powerful neighbors for vital supplies such as timber, building stone, and potable water. The capital was also vulnerable to unpredictable floods. Tenochtitlan was on the boundaries of Acolhua and Tepaneca land, to say nothing of the Mexicas' old adversaries from Culhuacan. At first, the settlement was little more than a hamlet. A century and a half later, Tenochtitlan was a great imperial capital.

THE MEXICA RISE TO POWER
(1325 to 1430)

The foremost Mexica ruler of the time was Tenoch, who continued to rule until a quarter-century or so after the founding of the capital. He maintained a low profile, wisely trimming his political sails to those of his neighbors, especially Culhuacan. The latter's armies had been driven away from Tenochtitlan with showers of spears, and an uneasy peace persisted while the insult of the flaying was forgotten. In about 1372, the Mexica nobles made a policy decision of the utmost importance. Although they wanted to remain completely independent, and despite earlier events, they decided to ally themselves with a royal dynasty of Culhuacan. In fact, the city was a logical choice, for the Mexica enjoyed ever closer ties with its people, and it had been revered as a hallowed heir of Toltec civilization for generations. A man from Culhua named Acamapichtli ("handful of reeds") was selected as the Aztec ruler, and he came to live in Tenochtitlan. He was an ideal political choice, a leader with close connections with the Acolhua, his mother a princess of Culhuacan. The Aztecs thus allied themselves with several powerful factions in the Valley. Soon nearby Tlatelolco, the swamp-based trading city close to Tenochtitlan, acquired a dynasty from the Tepanecas. So the obscure settlements deep in the lake began to acquire useful ties throughout the Valley of Mexico.

Acamapichtli assumed the reins of power in Tenochtitlan at a time when the Tepaneca, under Tezozomoc of Azcapotzalco on the northwest shore of the lake, were expanding their domains not only by conquest but by skillful diplomacy as well. Tezozomoc reigned for over half a century, during which time he developed the art of diplomacy and empire building to new and sophisticated heights. His aim was to seize supreme power over the Basin. With the aid of his Mexica allies, he conquered Tenayuca and Culhuacan, leaving only the Acolhua of Texcoco standing in his way. Within a few decades the Tepaneca dominated almost all the Basin of Mexico. Their influence extended as far as the Valley of Toluca and the cotton-rich Valley of Morelos to the south. Tezozomoc replaced local rulers with his own relatives and created an empire that was fundamentally a tribute-gathering organization of great ruthlessness and sophistication. Later empire builders, and especially the Aztecs, would follow his innovative model.

At first the Mexica found life uncomfortable under Tezozomoc's harsh regime. His tribute levies were ever more insatiable. But when Tezozomoc realized just what valuable military allies the Mexica were, their status changed. Soon they became valued associates as much as vassals. Their tribute assessments were lightened, and prominent nobles were connected by well-timed marriages to the Tepaneca nobility. The successful campaigns of the Mexica not only aided Tezozomoc, they added to their own scanty agricultural lands and opened up valuable trading connections with the lowlands where prestigious tropical bird feathers and precious stones were found.

By the time Tezozomoc died in 1426, Tenochtitlan and Tlateloco boasted impressive ceremonial buildings and fine stone dwellings for the nobility. Mexica society evolved rapidly into well-defined classes of nobles, artisans, and commoners, a social structure that was to be refined again and again in later years. As the population rose, the Mexica experimented successfully with irrigation techniques, perfecting hydraulic agriculture and creating thousands of acres of swamp gardens for intensive cultivation. From the very beginning, the Mexica rulers realized that control of good agricultural land, not long distance trade, war, or religious prestige, must be their primary power base. Their long term political objectives were simple: to acquire land, land, and still more land.

Tezozomoc spent his last years trying to overcome his Acolhua rival Ixtlilxochitl of Texcoco. Eventually

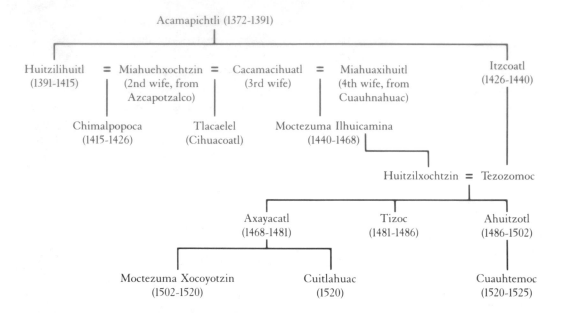

Acamapichtli (1372-1391)

Huitzilihuitl (1391-1415) = Miahuehxochtzin (2nd wife, from Azcapotzalco) = Cacamacihuatl (3rd wife) = Miahuaxihuitl (4th wife, from Cuauhnahuac)   Itzcoatl (1426-1440)

Chimalpopoca (1415-1426)   Tlacaelel (Cihuacoatl)   Moctezuma Ilhuicamina (1440-1468)

Huitzilxochtzin = Tezozomoc

Axayacatl (1468-1481)   Tizoc (1481-1486)   Ahuitzotl (1486-1502)

Moctezuma Xocoyotzin (1502-1520)   Cuitlahuac (1520)   Cuauhtemoc (1520-1525)

the Tepaneca prevailed, stripped Texcoco of tribute, then gave it to the Mexica. At one stroke the land-hungry Aztecs became tribute collectors for the first time, a real force in the balance of power in the Basin of Mexico. They were in an ideal position to step into the shoes of the Tepaneca for their dominance did not survive long after Tezozomoc's death, indeed was already crumbling in the closing years of his reign. In the same year he died a leader named Itzcoatl, "Serpent of Obsidian," assumed the Mexica throne. Urged on by the official orators, Itzcoatl reversed foreign policy sharply. No longer were the Mexica to be subservient, they were to be warlike and aggressive. The people were rightly afraid of the Tepaneca and begged their leaders to subordinate themselves. But two outstanding nobles, Moctezuma Ilhuicamina and Tlacaelel, a high official who later acquired the title *Cihuacoatl,* "Woman Snake," advocated war. They argued that Tenochtitlan and Texcoco formed a highly effective partnership for waging war. This alliance was to evolve into the famous Triple Alliance of these two cities and the lesser center of Tlacopan.

Genealogical table of the Aztec rulers. Data from Frances Berdan, The Aztecs, *p. 8.*

The Triple Alliance was a close political arrangement among three polities, a core at the center of an empire that relied on a patchwork of alliances and tribute relationships to control a much larger area of territory. The Alliance worked well, but Tenochtitlan soon became the dominant member. In 1428 the three allies besieged and eventually captured the Tepaneca capital of Azcapotzalco after fierce fighting and a more than four-month siege. The Mexica later boasted that they overthrew the Tepaneca singlehanded. In fact, they received help not only from Texcoco, but from other communities that had been cruelly oppressed by their hated masters. These allies soon found they had made a mistake. In overthrowing the Tepaneca, they had merely exchanged one harsh overlord for another even worse. The Mexica had achieved supremacy not by sudden conquest or a dramatic feat of arms, but because they had spent generations consistently strengthening their position in an ever-shifting political landscape. Their leaders were weaned on war, with ruthless armies at their backs made up of people who believed themselves the chosen of Huitzilopochtli himself. When a city was conquered, its gods were toppled and images of Huitzilopochtli erected in their place. Thus, the new cult spread widely wherever the Mexica conquered.

Tlacalel, the first "Woman Snake," the ruler's vizier, appears to have been the principal architect of Aztec imperial ambitions. He even prevailed on Itzcoatl to burn all earlier tribal records on the grounds that they would undermine established authority. Official versions of Aztec history compiled by official propagandists replaced tribal histories. These promoted the cause of Huitzilopochtli, raising him to supreme heights in the divine pantheon. The war god became the great presence, the arbiter and justification for military conquest and punishment. A later chronicler was to write cynically of Tlacaelel that "he was the one who was always busy demonstrating that the devilish Huitzilopochtli was the god of the Mexicans" (Chimalpahin Quauhtlehuanitzin, 1889, p.5).

THE GREAT CONQUERORS (1430 to 1502)

For the remainder of his reign, Itzcoatl consolidated the position of Tenochtitlan in the Basin. He achieved dominance over many other centers, among them Coyoacan and Xochimilco, in campaigns during which armies were transported in canoes. At the same time the Mexica nobility reorganized the conquered lands, leaving most of the land under the jurisdiction of local lords, and thereby ensuring their loyalty to the new order.

Itzcoatl was duly succeeded by his nephew Moctezuma Ilhuicamina ("the Angry Lord, the Archer of the Skies") in 1440. Moctezuma was forty-two, a statesman and warrior of great reputation. He turned his conquering eyes outside the Basin, marching against Chalco in a war that continued sporadically for twenty years. The campaigns faltered when a plague of locusts hit the Basin in 1446, followed three years later by catastrophic floods that innundated Tenochtitlan. So serious was the danger that Moctezuma himself helped construct a great embankment of earth and stone slabs over 9 miles (14 km) long. Then a series of bad harvests brought famine to the Basin. At first everyone lived off stored reserves and food imported from the Gulf Coast. After four years of famine thousands had died. Desperate parents bartered their children for maize. Thousands more sold themselves into slavery to coastal cities in exchange for food. Aztec officialdom, concerned as it was in the main with tribute gathering, was ill-equipped to distribute food supplies. In the end Moctezuma was forced to tell the people that they were on their own. His empire was in administrative tatters.

The famine ended in the abundant harvests of 1455 that coincided with the close of a fifty-two year cycle, a cycle that had seen the wrath of the gods visited on the Mexica. For generations, the priests had appeased the gods with fresh blood. What more fruitful way to ensure the future than by increasing the tempo of human sacrifice? Moctezuma Ilhuicamina proclaimed that war was to be considered the principal occupation of the

Moctezuma Ilhuicamina's conquests. The burning temples signify victories. The border is decorated with glyphs giving the years of his reign. "... Moctezuma was a very grave lord, good tempered, of sound judgement, virtuous, and a hater of evil ...." From the Codex Mendoza. Courtesy, Bodleian Library, Oxford. MS. Arch. Selden A.1. folio 7.

Mexica, thus ensuring a constant supply of prisoners to supply the insatiable maws of the gods. The immediate consequence was almost continuous warfare, for Moctezuma now sacrificed not single victims, but hundreds of people to Huitzilopochtli each year.

First his armies marched southeastward in 1458, against the Mixteca of Coixtlahuaca. They routed the Mixteca regiments, burned their city temple, and strangled their ruler before appointing an Aztec tribute collector over the new district of the empire. The Mixteca were required to pay carefully specified quantities of tribute every eighty days. A specially appointed official in Tenochtitlan saw to it that the consignments were received on time. This campaign set a pattern of conquest and tribute-gathering that became the hallmark of all later Aztec conquest.

The great famine left an indelible mark on Moctezuma Ilhuicamina. Determined to assure reliable food supplies through conquest and tribute assessments, he now embarked on campaigns directed at the fertile, well-watered lowlands, as usual demanding only nominal tribute from key leaders. When this was refused he moved against the Totonaca of the Veracruz area. It took several bloody campaigns, but subduing these wealthy domains gave the Mexica ready access to the food, jewels, and bright feathers upon which so much of the panoply of state depended. Throughout these campaigns, Moctezuma was more interested in tribute than in adding territory to his empire, for he realized that the regular collection of taxes served quite eloquently to express the dominance of the Mexica over their neighbors. But tribute was far more than a political instrument: it was an economic device as well, stimulating production of the goods specified and desired by the conquerors.

With each successful conquest Moctezuma gained territory, subject people, and goods or services. He made tribute a primary goal of conquest when his armies marched against the prosperous lands of the Huaxteca to the northeast, a people whose markets competed with those of Tenochtitlan. Using the murder of several merchants as a pretext, Moctezuma's soldiers ambushed a Huaxteca army and took hundreds of captives who were sacrificed to the Flayed God, Xipe Totec. Moctezuma was careful to invite many foreign leaders to watch the prisoners go to meet the gods, and the priests wore the victims' skins in triumph throughout the festival of the Flaying of Men in Tenochtitlan.

Moctezuma's last campaign in 1466 was a punitive raid against Tepeaca, a consortium of cities lying astride key military and trade routes to the south and southeast. The vizier Tlacaelel ordered the conquered rulers not only to bring tribute, but to "pay special care

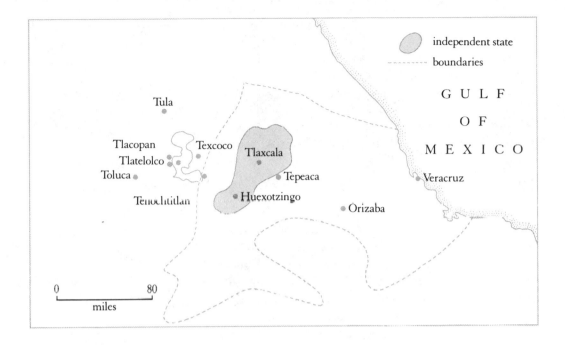

Tula

Tlacopan
Tlatelolco
Toluca
Tenochtitlan

Texcoco

Tlaxcala

Tepeaca

Huexotzingo

Orizaba

GULF
OF
MEXICO

Veracruz

independent state
boundaries

0   80
    miles

*Approximate boundaries of the
Aztec empire at the end of
Moctezuma Ilhuicamina's
reign. Data from Nigel
Davies,* The Aztecs, *p. 160.*

to protect the merchants who go to trade in Xocon-ochco and Guatemala and in all the land, because it is these who enrich and ennoble the earth . . ." (Duran, 1964, p. 102). Closely tied to trade and commerce, Aztec imperialism was based on the assumption that the state was a commercial organization, an entity that flourished to meet the spiritual and material needs of Huitzilopochtli.

By this time the Aztec empire was big business, a complex organization that required the services of thousands of petty officials simply to keep track of the tribute payments and commercial transactions that passed through Tenochtitlan and its satellite cities. Moctezuma Ilhuicamina himself created a complex system of government with carefully defined rules that governed not only tribute, but clothing, rank, and personal conduct. He based the rules of society on two criteria: birth and bravery in battle. Everything consolidated the power of the king and his nobles, with Moctezuma himself assuming all the remoteness and dignity of a mighty potentate, adorned in the finest jewels and cotton raiment, with bright feathers in his headdress. The great *tlatoani* (ruler) only appeared before the people on rare occasions. He took care to regulate the behavior and dress code of everyone else, even the mightiest noble in the land. Moctezuma's administrative reforms extended to a harsh law code that regulated everything from adultery to drunkenness, as well as more serious offenses. Even thieves could be executed or forced to serve as slaves to those they had robbed.

The state allowed conquered local rulers considerable latitude—provided they paid their annual assessments. The tax collectors were the hated symbols of Aztec control. Seldom carrying arms, they went about their business secure in the knowledge that nonpayment of tribute would result in swift and savage reprisals—and hundreds of sacrifices back in Tenochtitlan. The entire fabric of the empire depended not only on a carefully orchestrated terror policy, but on a network of alliances with neighbors and with distant states. Moctezuma and his successors presided over a loosely knit domain that collected tribute from the labors of several million people. This tribute supported not only the splendors of the court, but the costs of public administration and of the elaborate ceremonies and lavish presents distributed to foreign dignitaries.

Moctezuma Ilhuicamina himself embarked on ambitious public works at Tenochtitlan. He was determined to turn his capital into a city without peer. His major undertaking was a temple for Huitzilopochtli, one of a series of vast buildings that formed the nucleus of the sacred precinct at Tenochtitlan. The great pyramid was not finally completed until 1487, nineteen years after Moctezuma's death. Even during his reign it boasted more than one hundred steps leading to the shrine of the great god at the summit. Thousands of slaves and conscripts labored on the public buildings even during the great famines, carrying stone and timber across the lagoon on canoes to build a huge edifice that reached towards Huitzilopochtli's sky.

Moctezuma Ilhuicamina died in 1468. He had the satisfaction of defeating his first enemy, Chalco, at last, and he laid out magnificent gardens, complete with an elaborate irrigation system, near Huaxtepec in Morelos. There he planted flowers, herbs, and all manner of exotic plants from the coastal lowlands. The garden, dedicated with intricate rites to Xochipilli, the God of Flowers, was still flourishing at the time of the Conquest. Moctezuma's successors inherited not only his gardens, but an empire that was founded on conquest and dependent on a mounting crescendo of human sacrifice, a rising tide of bloodshed that was to become a macabre obsession.

The next two Aztec leaders had less success than their mighty predecessor. Axayacatl reigned for twelve years and died in 1481 after winning an internecine quarrel with Tenochtitlan's twin city of Tlatelolco. He killed the rival leaders and installed a military governor, making it a commercial satellite of Tenochtitlan. This was a political and economic development of the greatest importance, for it gave Tenochtitlan control over Tlatelolco's powerful merchant community and her flourishing markets. He also campaigned unsuccessfully against the Tarascans, who lived in what is now the modern state of Michoacan. This left the Mexica with a major rival on their western flanks.

Axayacatl's elder brother Tizoc was elected to succeed Axayacatl but ruled for only five years, during which the Aztec armies campaigned inconclusively against Metztitlan, an independent territory to the north. Tizoc's performance as ruler may have dissatisfied his nobles, for there is some reason to believe he was assassinated. Next the Mexican leaders elected a great general to succeed him, Ahuitzotl, the second of the great Aztec conquerors. He immediately embarked on a series of punitive campaigns to the northwest of Tenochtitlan. These victories provided the sacrificial victims for Ahuitzotl's coronation, to which he invited hundreds of neighboring leaders. Many, however, refused to come, despite bribes proffered in the form of lavish gifts. Ahuitzotl distributed the equivalent of a year's tribute to his guests, including 33,000 handfuls of exotic feathers, an extraordinary largess which measures the importance the Mexica placed on prestigious display.

Ahuitzotl was soon in the field again, suppressing rebellion among the Huaxteca. He collected thousands of prisoners who featured in the final dedication of Huitzilopochtli's great temple in 1487. Visiting chiefs were ordered to bring additional sacrificial victims on their own account and were again showered with fine gifts. For five days Ahuitzotl and his priests sacrificed long lines of victims until the temple steps ran with blood. The exact number is in dispute, but some sources claim that as many as 87,000 people met their death. The actual number must have been considerably less: it would have taken prodigious efforts to offer up even 8,000. But the sacrifice was obsessive. The festival was "an awesome spectacle: the streets, squares, market places and houses were so bursting with people that it looked like an ant hill. And all of this was done with the purpose of lifting up the majesty and greatness of Mexico," wrote Diego Duran (1964, p. 196).

Ahuitzotl soon lusted after new conquests. He made an determined thrust to the shores of the Pacific between 1491 and 1495, subjecting a vast stretch of territory extending 150 miles (500 km) northwest of Acapulco, an area that became a major cotton producer. He also extended Mexica influence into the Valley of Oaxaca, which provided abundant gold, cochineal, and mantles for his coffers, and conquered the Zapoteca of Tehuantepec. In 1499 he even subdued the distant state of Soconusco, a major cacao producer on the borders of modern Mexico and Guatemala, over 600 miles (965 km) from Tenochtitlan. Three years later Ahuitzotl died, perhaps as a result of his exertions during an unexpected flood that threatened to engulf Tenochtitlan when an ambitious fresh water canal dug to harness the springs of Coyoacan for the capital burst its bounds.

THE OBSESSIVE EMPIRE (1502 to 1521)

By this time Tenochtitlan was a vast and imposing city, rivalling in size the largest European metropolises, the seventy-eight imposing structures of its ceremonial precinct surrounded by a fortified wall. Tenochtitlan and its gods fed on conquest, more conquest, and still more conquest. The Aztec rulers became obsessed with prestige, appeasement of the insatiable gods, and military prowess. The Mexica were locked into a vicious circle that forced them to expand and conquer simply to obtain more victims and tribute. Now that their closest neighbors were part of the empire, they were forced to campaign farther and farther afield. Even their own soldiers complained. Ahuitzotl had had to resort to bribery and shared loot to keep the warriors happy and the tempo of conquest unabated. He left his successor an empire at the apogee of its brilliance, but an empire very vulnerable to rebellion and with a government that was probably incapable of adapting to new, more centralized systems that would ensure the long-term stability of the kingdom. Unfortunately, religious pressures for further conquest were so strong that probably no one leader could hope to put the ravenous Huitzilopochtli on a more temperate diet.

In 1502 the Aztec nobles chose thirty-four-year-old Moctezuma Xocoyotzin, a nephew of Ahuitzotl, as their new ruler. He had a reputation as a valiant warrior and as a grave and wise counsellor, attributes important at a time when many nobles felt the empire was overextended. Moctezuma was a proud and haughty man, capable of great humility and yet harsh cruelty, a man of deep religious conviction. He concentrated on consolidating territory won by his predecessors, relying not on lightning campaigns, but on efforts at longer-term subjugation that brought Oaxaca closer to the fold and led to constant fighting with the powerful city of Tlaxcala and her neighbors in the Puebla-Tlaxcala valley, cities that were to play a vital role in

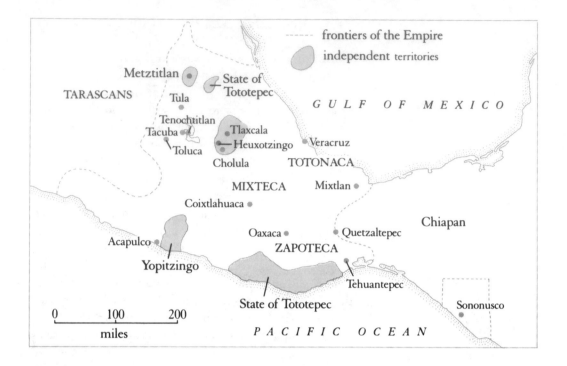

Aztec empire at the time of the Spanish Conquest in 1519. Data from Nigel Davies, The Aztecs, *p. 220.*

the Spanish Conquest. Tlaxcala had long enjoyed good trade relations with the lowlands to the east and was determined to maintain independence from Tenochtitlan, even when the Mexica began an economic blockade of the valley that cut vital salt supplies down to almost nothing. Between 1504 and 1519 Moctezuma's armies marched against the Tlaxcalans again and again without conclusive result. This military standoff cost him dearly. The Spaniards found in Tlaxcala an ally who was only too anxious to join forces against a hated neighbor.

The campaigns against Tlaxcala were at their height when Moctezuma Xocoyotzin began to receive ominous signs that new and momentous events were afoot. When a coastal Indian reported seeing a mountain moving on the sea, he was imprisoned for his story-telling. The next time Moctezuma heard rumors that strangers from the east had landed on the coast, he remembered the legend of Quetzalcoatl, the Plumed Serpent god who had promised to return and reclaim his kingdom. It is hardly surprising that he assumed the strangers were gods—all his other enemies were of the Mexican world. So the doomed leader grected Hernando Cortes and his adventurers, presenting them with regalia appropriate for a returning deity. Within two years of this encounter, his empire was in ruins.

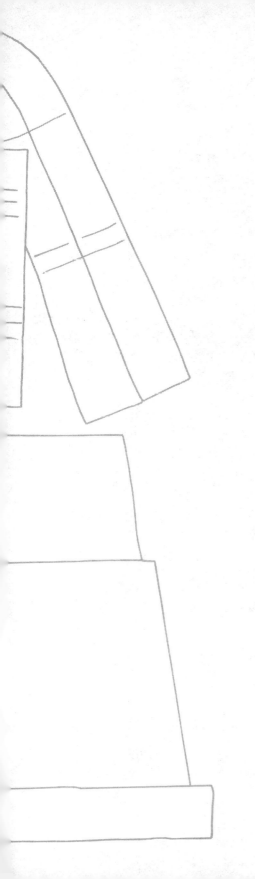

II

THE IMPERIAL STATE

neuh, cioatlauehtloc, cioa cuecuel,
cue cue tolcioatl, ichpuchpil, ich
puchtontli, quin uehicaton, uel
ica cioatl, ichpuchtli, ichpuch=
pol, ilama, ilamapol, ilanton, a
uililama, anenqui apan, apan
nemini, atzintlaltechpachiui, v
tli, quitotocatinemi, vtli quimama
tililiti ✠ tianqui ✠ quiui ✠
tectinemi, tianquiztli, quicuite
tinemi, vtli quicuecuecuelpacheti
nemi, moiacatinemi, temamátine
mi, acan chariltta, cacan uetzi,
cacan cuchi, cacan tlatui, caque
uetzin tooalli, maçuilhuitl.

¶ Picienamacac: quinamaca
pieatl, xicoitetl, tlalietl. quima
xaqualoa, inaca quitta picietl,
quiqua, Auh ce quintin iztauhiatl
inquipicie pca, inpicietl tetech
quiz, teiuinti, tetlatemouili, te
ciauiz pópoloa.

Iniccempoalli onchicome
capitulo: intechpa tlatoa
incuitlaxculli, ioan inix

¶ El que vende picíete muc
le primero las hojas del mezcla
dolas con vna poca de cal, y an
si mezclado, estregalo muy
bien entre las manos. halgunos
hazen lo de el axenxo de la tie
rra. y puesto en la boca haze
desuanecer la cabeça, s embriaga
cha. haze tambien digerir lo co
mjdo, y haze prouecho para qui
tar el cansancio.

Capitulo veinte y sie
te de todos los mjembros
exteriores, e interio

CHAPTER 3

The Subsistence Base

Thus can be seen today the great quantity
of hills and slopes that were once worked,
and they [the inspectors] had charge, by
province, of providing maize and all
necessary things to Mexico . . . .

Francisco del Paso y Troncoso, *Epistolario de Nueva Espana,* 4, pp. 169–170

"The good farmer is strong, diligent, and careful; rises early so as not to lose his holding, and works to increase it; he eats and sleeps little; he works hard at his trade . . . ." Fray Bernardino de Sahagun (10, p. 41) was in no doubt about the importance of agriculture to the Mexica. He devoted page after page of the *General History* to farmers and farming.

The good peasant was a productive member of Aztec society, a giver and provider: agriculture and the exploitation of wild vegetable foods were the primary means of providing subsistence in the Basin of Mexico, where meat supplies were scarce. Farming was so important to the Mexica after the disastrous famines of the early 1450s that Moctezuma Ilhuicamina and his successors used official inspectors to ensure that every acre of arable land was planted, by force if necessary. Even with these harsh measures the standard of living was probably lower than today. The average farmer produced only the smallest of food surplusses in a diverse environment, even with every acre of land used to its practical limit. These served as the tribute and the produce that flowed into the vast markets of Tenochtitlan. The Mexica had to use highly effective farming methods to

Page 74: Huitzilopochtli. From original drawing by Alonso Caso. Courtesy, Fondo de Cultura Economica, Mexico City.

Left: A page from Volume 10 of Sahagun's General History, *"tells of the atole sellers and the sellers of prepared chocolate." Courtesy, University of Utah, Salt Lake City.*

ensure a basic subsistence for everyone: maize cultivation could be a chancy venture; leaving little margin for error.

AGRICULTURE

Cultivation in the Basin of Mexico for at least 3,500 years has drastically modified the original natural vegetation. Soil erosion after loss of plant cover denuded the land and overcultivation has reduced its fertility. But then, even more than now, the Valley of Mexico provided an exceptionally diverse environment for agriculturalists. The aboriginal vegetation in the southern parts of the Basin may have been broadleaf forest, giving way to scrub woodland in areas up to 8,600 feet (2600 m). Coniferous forest predominated between 8,600 and 15,000 feet (4500 m), providing an abundant source of timber for building. Alpine meadows and snow fields at the highest elevations provided yet another environment.

The native vegetation was easy to clear, and fertile Basin soils were easily cultivated with simple hoes and digging sticks. The productivity of the soil varied with its depth, being less fertile in the north than in the south. Since the prehistoric farmer often used sloping ground, he had a constant erosion-control problem with the loamy, loose-textured soils of the Basin. Fertility was maintained by simple restoration techniques: using animal and vegetable fertilizers, rotating crops, and leaving exhausted fields to lie fallow for a number of years.

Rain and frost set serious limits for Basin agriculture. The rainfall and temperature of the southern parts of the Basin are more favorable for maize agriculture, the staple Aztec crop. The drier northern tracts suffer from irregular rainfall, early frosts, and frequent droughts, making maize a relatively high-risk crop. If the farmer waits for the rains to start and they are late, then planting is late, and fall frosts can damage the germinating seed. The new plants also require plenty of moisture while the all-important ears are forming. At elevations above 9,000 feet (2700 m) 15 percent of the Basin surface has a long frost season. In addition, the sloping terrain rendered at least 45 percent of the Basin's surface area liable to serious erosion. The immediate lakeshore plain and the lower slopes of the foothills were relatively frost free and provided good maize land when not otherwise used, but here the early farmers ran into drainage problems. Only in later centuries was the high water table lowered by canals.

Agriculture took many forms in the Basin of Mexico. Our knowledge of Aztec practices is based on sixteenth-century accounts as well as research into modern peasant farming where it is practiced without benefit of twentieth-century machines and chemicals.

CROPS AND IMPLEMENTS

The basic subsistence crop was maize. The Indians ate it in tortillas and in a gruel known as *atolli*, served in many variations: "maize gruel with honey, with chili and honey, with yellow chili," lists Sahagun. Then there was "white, thick gruel with a scattering of maize grains," to say nothing of "maize gruel with fish-amaranth seeds and honey." The Aztecs enjoyed a rich variety of tamale recipes, too: "white tamales with beans forming a sea shell on top," or "tamales made of maize flowers with ground amaranth seed and cherries added" (Sahagun, 8, pp. 37–39).

Today, at least 65 percent of the Basin soils are planted with corn, even in areas where the crop is at best marginal. The two kinds of maize normally grown today were also in use in prehistoric times: a lower yielding, faster maturing corn that produced ears in three to four months, normally planted late in fields where irrigation is impracticable; and a slower growing variety, planted in irrigated fields, that matures in six months with a much higher yield. The latter was more commonly used. By the time of the Spanish Conquest, the Mexica controlled maize-growing territory in such a variety of ecological zones that they could get corn in nearly every month of the year. Despite these imports sometimes "there was much hunger, when dried maize was costly," in the lean months before the harvest.

The festivals of the mid-summer month Uey Te-chuilhuitl honored the young maize plant. The ruler would provide an abundance of tamales over a week-long festival, then green corn tortillas to commemorate the newly ripening maize. Corn occupied a highly honored place in Aztec society, and had its own goddess, Chicomecoatl, "Seven Serpent." "She is truly our flesh, our livelihood," cried the people as they dedicated the seed for a new growing season. Sahagun lists a complicated agricultural vocabulary for maize cultivation, defining different characteristics of corn cobs, such as *xiuhtoctli,* "tender maize stalk," or, at the other end of the spectrum, *cimpala,* "rotten ear of maize." Maize was so closely identified with people that an honored person might be described as one who had "reached the season of the green maize ear" (Sahagun, 6, p. 235).

Maize may have been the staple, but a variety of other crops were important components in the Aztec diet. Beans were a vital source of protein, either planted alongside maize or grown on thinner hillside slopes where corn was a high-risk crop. The *Relaciones Geograficas* of 1580 and other Spanish sources record large acreages of amaranth, along with maize, the two major sources of caloric energy for the Aztecs. Amaranth seeds were made into a gruel known as *pinole* and sometimes mixed with ground maize in tamales. The farmers also grew a grain called *chia (Salvia),* several varieties of fruit trees, including prickly pears that yielded the popular fruit *nochtli,* and gourds for containers. Several varieties of squash yielded seeds and fruit that were eaten raw or cooked, as were flowers that provided valuable flavorings. Tomatoes flourished in the chinampa, while chili peppers were a universal accompaniment to meals. So important was chili that some fasts were defined as full meals taken without chilis.

Every inch of soil was used. the acreages with thinnest soil in low rainfall areas to cultivate cacti like nopal

Maguey farmers. From the Florentine Codex. Courtesy, University of Utah Press, Salt Lake City. Drawing, Sally Black.

or maguey *(agave),* a crop often used as a field boundary and fermented to make the intoxicating beverage known as *ochtli,* or *pulque.* The maguey plant also yielded some medicinal preparations, fibers for cape manufacture, and the thorns used as needles in sewing and in rites of penance. Maguey had its own four-hundred-breasted goddess, Mayahuel. She and her children, the Four Hundred Rabbits, inhabited the world of drink and drunkenness. The consumption of alcohol was strictly controlled and, theoretically, confined to people over fifty—some sources say seventy—years of age. But in practice alcohol was widely consumed, often as a medicine for ailments such as gout. Maguey leaf pulp and salt were used to dress open wounds.

Cacao (chocolate) and cotton were farmed in the tropical lowlands and other outlying parts of the Aztec

81

empire. Cacao beans were a universal currency, and chocolate was the favorite drink of the nobility and a major item of tribute from lowland areas. The intricately decorated capes and regalia of the nobility were woven from cotton, and only the ruler himself could wear the finest grades of cotton raiment.

The fifteenth-century Basin farmers had to have a complete technical knowledge of their basically simple agricultural systems to support the pre-Conquest Valley population of about 1,000,000 people. At least half of these lived in urban centers, up to 20 percent of them based in the greater Tenochtitlan area. At least 400,000 people lived in a 231-square-mile (370 sq km) zone of foothills, alluvial plains, and lake bed between the Sierra de Guadalupe southward to the foothills of the Ajusco foothills. This Aztec heartland included not only Tenochtitlan, but at least nine provincial centers and a large number of smaller settlements, the largest and densest population concentration in the entire history of pre-Hispanic America. The only way to feed everyone was by efficient, government-controlled agriculture. Moctezuma Ilhuicamina and his successors maintained a small army of inspectors who oversaw every acre of land, making sure that it was planted and that surplus foodstuffs were sent to the capital. "In this manner the city was the best provisioned in the world," we are told.

Fifteenth-century Aztec farmers had not only chinampa plots, they may have had many other soils now completely degraded by erosion. They used every patch of available soil, even abandoned village sites rich in organic nutrients, and brought silt and water to their land wherever possible.

Using but the simplest of cultivation techniques, the Aztecs fertilized the soil carefully. They knew that intercropping and interplanting of maize and beans maintained fertility (in fact such practices do retain organic material and replenish the nitrogen level). Having no animals to feed on the stalks, the farmers probably removed only the maize ears and bean pods at harvest time, digging the rest of the plant back under

the soil. They left gardens fallow after two or three years and allowed them to rest for at least that length of time before recultivating them.

Along with this fallowing, known as *tlacolol,* they used a variety of natural fertilizers, rotten leaves, for example. In 1519 Bernal Diaz saw the Indians selling canoe loads of human excrement in the great markets of Tenochtitlan. He claimed this was "for the manufacture of salt and the curing of skins, which they say cannot be done without it" (Diaz, 1963, p. 233). Special huts were erected by city streets and alleys for people to relieve themselves. This urban sanitation system may have yielded human fertilizer for the fields.

Whether planting, weeding, or harvesting, the conscientious farmer worked hard to break up the soil properly, to maintain its fertility, and to wrest maximum yield from his fields.

The codices depict farmers preparing the soil with a wooden, shovel-like artifact known as a *uictli.* Laborious and time-consuming in use as these implements must have been, they turned over the soil just as effectively as a plow, if more slowly. (A plow takes about a quarter of the time to do the same work.) Pointed wooden sticks were used to dig holes for the seed, simple knives were used to prune and harvest. The actual technology of tillage was simple in the extreme, but the measures taken to protect, enrich, and irrigate were comparatively sophisticated.

A diligent farmer using a digging stick to cultivate maize. From the Florentine Codex. Courtesy, University of Utah Press, Salt Lake City. Drawing, Sally Black.

DRY AGRICULTURE

The different methods of cultivation in the Basin required very different labor inputs. Crop yields varied sharply from location to location. Cultivation depending on rainfall alone probably flourished all over the Basin in the deep, arable soils of the plains and on gentle foothill slopes where irrigation was impracticable. Reasonable maize crops can be grown in good rainfall years. But the Mexica used dry agriculture wherever they could, building huge terrace systems to protect steeper hill slopes against soil erosion. Carefully designed terrace systems covered most of the central and northern basin slopes in the fifteenth century. These systems worked magnificently as long as the people maintained them properly. In Aztec times the farmers built their houses close to their terrace systems, living among their fields and maintaining them in a high state of repair. Once the Spanish colonists started rounding up the farmers into concentrated settlements, the intensive maintenance and the system fell into disuse.

IRRIGATION AGRICULTURE

One obvious solution to the frost and rainfall problems was, and still is, irrigation, watering the land by artificial means before the rains begin. The simplest systems, hillside schemes which need water runoff from rainier, higher elevations, flourished in the central and northern Basin where the soils had an unusually high water-retention rate. Sahagun tells us the farmers began watering between January and March, planting the maize in April or early May, after which the growing crops depended on normal rainfall. The planting dates varied from location to location, depending on rainfall and temperature. The farmers organized their irrigation systems so that mountain runoff watered their lands at progressively higher altitudes as the threat of annual frost receded. This is difficult farming, further complicated because Basin rainfall is so localized that drought can affect one area, while another fertile region only a few miles away has abundant crops.

Along with these simple irrigation techniques they often used stone-walled terraces, or equivalent constructions built of indurated subsoil or other convenient, durable materials. The terraces helped to retain moisture and to prevent soil erosion and were sometimes watered by floodwater channels or permanent irrigation canals. Villagers on the plains built ditches linked to natural waterways that drained off surplus water during the rainy season. The same channels, perhaps only a few serving a single village, or an elaborate complex linking several communities, also brought irrigation waters in to the crops.

Floodwater irrigation systems can still be seen in the Teotihuacan valley and elsewhere. Floodwater systems depend on storing local rainfall on the slopes, then releasing it by opening wooden floodgates. The farmers do everything they can to retain moisture in the soil by breaking up clods of the loose, crumbly soil, and by planting maguey to control erosion. They maintain a highly intensive, very productive agricultural system, provided the entire operation is carefully managed. The success of irrigation systems like this depends not only on cooperation among individual farmers, but also among families and often several villages or towns.

Angel Palerm has combed documentary sources and found convincing evidence that pre-Hispanic irrigation systems utilized all major water resources fully and in much the same way that they are used today. Communities like Teotihuacan which were fortunate enough to locate near perennial springs could develop large-scale irrigation systems. Teotihuacan's spring-based systems are described in the *Relaciones Geograficas* of 1579 as extending all the way from the springs at San Juan Teotihuacan to the lake shore—and this after catastrophic depopulation. "The city of Acolman is located in a plain; at the foot of a high ridge; it is cleared land; does not have any permanent water sources; a river called the San Juan passes by the town; it is divided into three canals of water, from which they irrigate a large piece of land, almost a league long and half a league wide; it is fertile in pasture and crop land," states the *Relacion de Tecciztlan* (quoted in Sanders, Parsons, and Santley, 1979, p. 261).

The Basin lakes were where the Mexica developed their most impressive drainage projects and irrigation works, especially within the confines of Lakes Chalco and Xochimilco. Both lakes were covered with artificial, island-like gardens, the famous *chinampas*. Chinampa agriculture was absolutely vital to the Aztecs, a form of drainage cultivation that made use of swamps and heavy soils with water tables so high that they retained moisture for much of the year. Once such areas can be drained and the water table lowered, both agriculture and irrigation are possible, provided that the farmers are prepared to put in the intensive labor necessary to organize and build the artificial plots. Anthropologist Pedro Armillas has surveyed the chinampa areas and shown that the lake bottoms were shaped like very shallow saucers, so shallow that the water depth probably never exceeded 3 to 7 feet (1.0–2.25 m). By laying out a vast network of drainage ditches that reduced the water table to the point where the higher points in the former lake bottom could be cultivated, the Indians created their chinampas. Armillas also shows that these drainage projects first centered around offshore islands and mainland peninsulas, then rapidly spread over the lake. The main drainage canals also served as arteries of travel and communication. The whole system was so regularly laid out that it could only have been planned and executed under strong, centralized administrative control.

The chinampas themselves consisted of alternate layers of lake-floor mud and vegetation, protected by "fences" of huejote trees to retain the silt. The dark, organic soils of these fields were, and still are, highly productive. A continuous succession of crops were produced, a corner of the plot serving as a nursery for seedlings as the previous crop matured. The chinampas were watered with buckets or by splashing water on to them from canoes. The farmers simply loaded the har-

A modern-day chinampa at Xochimilco, near Mexico City. Photo, Lesley Newhart.

vest into their canoes and took the produce straight to the markets at Tenochtitlan and other centers.

Recent surveys have revealed that the chinampa system had existed at least as early as 100 B.C., but it expanded to its full extent during the fifteenth century as the Mexica were reaching the apogee of their power. Extensive chinampas once flourished east of Lake Texcoco, along much of the Cuautitlan River, north of Lake Xaltocan, and east to Lake Chalco. No one would consider reclaiming these heavy, badly drained or swampy soils until the requirements of a very dense population forced the cultivators to open up new fields. Once they decided to undertake the necessary communal work, the rewards were considerable: the swampy soils were highly fertile, and the high water table protected the crops against frost. The irrigation waters brought in silt that fertilized the fields each year, making intensive harvesting possible. A chinampero cultivated his plot all year round, providing much of the food for Tenochtitlan and planting many acres in flowers as well.

Through careful planning the state reclaimed thousands of acres of swampy land, transforming them into a myriad of rectangular plots, some often only 10 feet (3 m) wide and 60 feet (20 m) long. Each grid of gardens had a house mound associated with it where the farmer and his family lived. Much of the agricultural population was dispersed among the chinampas, and these people communicated with their neighbors and with the cities travelling by canoe along the artificial drainage canals that served as watery roads as well. Chinampa agriculture is now a dying art—modern settlement has reduced the water table too drastically over most of the Basin.

Aztec life was founded on highly productive agriculture. When conditions favored it, the intensive nature of cultivation meant not only healthy food surplusses that released many people from food-producing activities and allowed them to divert their energies elsewhere, it also meant a great deal of specialized agriculture. The Mexica used their diverse environment to the full. Where flower production was advantageous, the local people specialized in flowers. Others in drier areas concentrated on maguey farming, selling its many byproducts in urban markets. In those markets crops such as maize, beans, and cotton were often differentiated according to the area they came from. Sahagun tells us that cotton from irrigated lands was the most prized, followed by that from the tropical lowlands. Even chilis were classified by their place of origin. The great markets of Tenochtitlan, Tlatelolco, Texcoco, and other cities contained foodstuffs from every corner of Mexico. "There were sellers of kidney-beans and sage, and other vegetables and herbs in another place, and in yet another they were selling fowls, and birds with great dewlaps [turkeys] . . . . Then there were fruiterers; and the women who sold cooked food, flour and honey cake, and tripe, had their part of the market" (Diaz, 1963, p. 232–233). The cultivation, harvesting, distribu-

tion, and marketing of food was an organized, centuries-old tradition that the Aztecs developed to a high pitch.

ANIMAL RESOURCES

Unfortunately, too few archaeologists have identified the fragmentary animal bones found in Basin sites, so our knowledge of the domestic and wild animals exploited by the Aztecs is tantalizingly incomplete. Unfortunately, too, most game species found in the area in prehistoric times have become extinct through the destruction of their natural habitats and overhunting. We do know that the Mexica lived mainly on grains and vegetables. With meat in short supply, most protein came from beans, maize, and squash.

Turkeys and dogs were the only domesticated animals kept by the Aztecs. They raised the raucous and unruly turkey both for eggs and meat, the latter apparently a highly esteemed dish. Although valued as companions, dogs were eaten, too. Domesticated animals may have become more important as the game populations of the Valley were overhunted. Plentiful in the widespread pine-oak woodlands of the Basin, the white-tailed deer (*Odocoileus virginianus*) were the most important game eaten, and these account for over 90 percent of the animal bones at many sites. Deer also flourished on fallow agricultural lands near human settlements—which may account for the preponderance of

The bean seller. From the Florentine Codex. Courtesy, University of Utah Press, Salt Lake City. Drawing, Sally Black.

deer bones in archaeological sites. The Aztecs did eat thousands of cottontail rabbits *(Sylvilagus),* trapping them in large numbers on the alluvial plains of the valleys.

The freshwater and saline lakes of the Basin lay on the fall migration routes of ducks flying south from the prairie swamps of western Canada. The Indians probably netted them throughout the winter, although few bird bones have been found at their sites. As recently as 1952, over 33,000 migratory ducks spent the winter on Lake Texcoco. One technique for snaring large numbers of waterfowl involved setting nets on posts in the water, then scaring the sleeping ducks at first light. The startled victims would become entangled in the waiting nets. The fowlers also took cranes, geese, pelican, quail, pigeons, and other local species, but most of this quarry went to the dining tables of the nobility.

In estimating the absolute contribution of meat to Aztec diet, the archaeologist has little more to go on than bone counts, and these are normally too fragmentary to gauge an ancient diet reliably. Using a spectrum of data derived from archaeological surveys and modern investigations, William Sanders has calculated that deer meat accounted for 13 percent of all calories consumed before the second millennium B.C., a figure that compares quite well with figures for modern hunter-gatherers in Botswana's Kalahari desert. The shift to agriculture increased population densities per square mile, pushed consumption of game meat to new highs, and carried with it the threat of overhunting. After 1000 B.C. meat eating is believed to have declined sharply, with consumption levels falling below 1 percent after A.D. 100—just the time that Teotihuacan was rapidly expanding. By this time in that locale hunting was no longer important in the food quest, and beans and domesticated animals provided most of the protein in Basin diet.

The Valley lakes teemed with fish, both large and small, that were taken with nets, spears, and lines. In spite of this abundance, fishing appears to have been an individual, relatively small-scale enterprise. The lakeside

villagers took turtles, salamanders, frogs, mollusks, and crustaceans. "The fishermen lie in wait as the turtles come out [of the water] arranged in order. When they have emerged, the fishermen quickly pounce on them to throw one on its back. There it lies. They run; they go to sieze another; they run to throw another upon its back .... Later they gather them without haste, for once they have fallen upon their backs, no longer can they right themselves again" (Sahagun, 11, p. 60). A bag of fifteen to twenty turtles was not uncommon. But beans remained the staple for most people.

WILD VEGETABLE FOODS

The gathering of wild vegetable foods has been vital to human life since the very earliest times, and it was once important in the Basin, too. Sanders estimates that the unmodified, natural vegetation of the Basin could have supported 15,000 collectors and 1,000 hunters—or a population density of about 1.04 persons per square mile, a figure comparable to that for prehistoric California. The population of the Basin in the late fifteenth century was at least a million people. Gathering was an insignificant activity in a heavily agricultural economy, but it played its role. The fruit, grasses, and tubers gathered ranged from figs to reeds, acacia nuts, foxtail grass, and reeds. The Aztecs collected an algae known to them as *tecuitlatl,* and to botanists as *Spirulina geitleri,* which flourishes in salt lakes. Collected in nets,

Net fishing from a canoe. From the Florentine Codex. Courtesy, University of Utah Press, Salt Lake City. Drawing, Sally Black.

91

then dried in the sun, it was cut into bricks that tasted like cheese bread. This seemingly exotic and prized food had several important advantages: it could be stored easily, grew abundantly and rapidly, and had a high protein content. Moctezuma Xocoyotzin's tax list in the Codex Mendoza lists tecuitlatl as a tribute item. The Mexicans still collect the algae—for export to Japan.

With such relatively insignificant contributions from wild sources, Aztec subsistence sat squarely on the shoulders of irrigation agriculture, an environment in which every hydraulic resource—floodwaters, springs, perennial water supplies, humid lands—was fully utilized. Thirteenth-century Basin farmers did not rely on irrigation. Sanders estimates that, using simple technology, 70 to 150 man-hours per hectare would be required to produce between 880 and 1760 pounds (400 to 800 kg) of maize per hectare, a figure based on modern races of corn. An extended family of seven Mexica (a figure documented from the codices) required about 2464 pounds (1120 kg) of grain for their basic needs, a minimum requiring about 200 man-days of agricultural labor. Add irrigation, however, and the agricultural yields almost double with only a slight increase in labor input. Chinampa agriculture, for example, yields four times the crop per acre that dry cultivation does. This development enormously enhanced the ability of the farmer to support a non-food-producing population. Once the southern lakes became vast chinampa plantations, the economic significance of irrigation agriculture was overwhelming.

The growth of Tenochtitlan clearly depended on the expansion of drainage agriculture on the lake shore and on the colonization of the lakes themselves. The state served as the entrepreneur for the development of the chinampa system. Once the system was in place, it drastically modified the Aztec political system, its economic institutions, and the organization of its society. We know from sixteenth-century demographic records that some 40 percent of the Basin population was concentrated in an area of some 400 square miles (650 sq km) around Tenochtitlan in 1519. The chinampa and drainage agriculture systems filled most food needs and led to temporary political stability. The highly organized subsistence economy of the Valley of Mexico also freed thousands of people to divert their energies into a multitude of specialized occupations—artisans, merchants, officials, or priests—and to create a sophisticated urban society. Above all, it allowed them time and opportunity to create and run the intricate webs of trade, tribute, and marketing upon which the Aztec empire and Tenochtitlan depended.

Cochina, cochina, cocatu ie njcnia
ololonjcanj, ie cihoatl njcochinay
teo. oaies yho. yia, yia.

q Xippe icuje, tatze iovalla
vana.

Ioalli Havana, i3teican, timone
nequja xjiaquj mjtlatia tcucuj
tlaqueinjtl, xjcmoquenti quetlonjia.

Noteuhoa chalchimmana tlacoa
pana itzmola, oiquetzallavcvcl,
ay quetzal xiujcoatl nech taiquj no
cauhquetl orjia.

Manjiaryia, njia, njia polivis
njyoatzin, achalchiuhtla noiollo,
atcucujtlatl nocoiaittas neiolce
visqujtlacatl achtoquetl tlaqua
vaia otlacatquj iautlatoa quetl
orjia.

Noteuhoa centlaco xaiaiiiviz co
noa yioatsin nietepeiocpa mjtz
valitla motzuhoa, visqujntla
catl achtoquetl tlaquavaia cha
catquj iautlatoa quetl orjia.

q Chicomecoatl icuje.

Chicomolotzin, xaia mehoa,

CHAPTER 4   Tenochtitlan

We saw cues *[pyramids] and shrines in
these cities that looked like gleaming white
towers and castles: a marvellous sight. All
the houses had flat roofs, and on the
causeways were other small towers and
shrines built like fortresses.*

Bernal Diaz, *The Conquest of New Spain,* 1963, p. 235.

*The Song of Xipe. From
Volume 2, Appendix, of Sahagun's General History,
beginning, "O loualluan, why
doesn't thou mask thyself? Put
on thy disguise. Don thy
golden cape. . . ." Courtesy,
University of Utah Press, Salt
Lake City.*

"The city of Mexico was so well fortified that it seemed
no human power would be able to take it. Not only
was it strong in troops and munitions, it was also the
queen and mistress of the entire land. Its lord Moteuc-
zoma, vaunted his dignity, the right of his city and the
number of his vassals. From this city he sent envoys
throughout the land, who were fully obeyed and highly
respected" (Motolinia, 1951, p. 272). Even after the
Spanish Conquest, Tenochtitlan was remembered as a
great and powerful city. In 1519 the Aztecs presided
over an empire that extended, at least in name, from
northern Mexico to the frontiers of Guatemala, and
from the Pacific Coast to the Gulf of Mexico. Their
ever-expanding conquests had created a bureaucratic
and economic machine of enormous complexity that
fed on a diet of tribute, trade, and a constant supply of
sacrificial victims from near and distant lands. The affairs of the empire were controlled by a handful of
powerful rulers. The numerous Aztec nobles below
them in turn fell into two parallel hierarchies: the secular bureaucracy of officials, judges, and soldiers, who
depended on the bounty of the ruler; and the tiered

organization of the priests, united by common religious faith and close family ties, servants of the gods and the ruler as well. This powerful class had its roots in the center of the Aztec world, the great city of Tenochtitlan in the Basin of Mexico. We must now describe that capital and examine the workings of an empire that catered to the insatiable tribute demands of its rulers and gods.

TENOCHTITLAN

The name Tenochtitlan, "the Place of the Fruit of the Prickly Pear Cactus," commemorated the site of the first temple of Huitzilopochtli. By the sixteenth century this great city served as the hub of the Aztec world, a vast metropolis that dwarfed its neighbors, the centripetal center of the Valley of Mexico and most of Mesoamerica at the time of the Conquest. Tenochtitlan was probably founded by a community of several thousand Mexica between 1325 and 1345. One-and-a-half breathtaking centuries later, the tiny swamp hamlet had become the largest community in pre-Hispanic America.

The rapid expansion of Tenochtitlan began after 1385 during the reign of Acamapichtli, who ruled "in peace and quiet. He had built the city, he had organized its houses and canals, and had done other things necessary to the good order of the state" (Duran, 1964, p. 38). By 1385 Tenochtitlan was no mere village, but a rapidly growing regional center with a substantial urban population. Acamapichtli and his successors embarked on large-scale irrigation schemes and developed hundreds of acres of chinampa gardens in and around the city. They developed a formal policy of population growth, encouraging not only farmers but artisans with special skills and merchants to join their urban labor force. The large immigrant population soon included soldiers, craft workers such as lapidaries and manuscript painters, war refugees, and thousands of unskilled workers, who found homes in the city precincts where members of their lineage lived. Tenochtitlan became the dominant city of the Valley largely because it was a trade and craft center that required the services of huge labor forces, as well as the home of a political and economic organization that secured raw materials and found the markets in which to trade the city's products. This was a cosmopolitan capital visited by thousands of people each year—delegations of foreign rulers, traders, pilgrims, casual visitors, perhaps even tourists. From its very earliest days Tenochtitlan had a social, political, and economic organization flexible enough to integrate large numbers of outsiders into its already large permanent population. Aztec society reflected a state, and a city, that depended not only on military strength, but also on its ability to organize large numbers of people to achieve its ends.

The twentieth-century tourist will have trouble finding Tenochtitlan. The ruins of the Aztec capital lie under the buildings of Mexico City. Cortes and his men razed much of Tenochtitlan as they fought their way to the central temple precincts, then used the stone blocks of the shrines and public buildings to erect a new city on the ravaged foundations. Even if Tenochtitlan were accessible, the archaeologist would face formidable technical problems. The city sank its foundations in the middle of a swamp. The Mexica erected their homes on bases of compacted mud, consolidated by driving wooden piles into the underlying earth. El Templo Mayor, the greatest temple in the city, was first dedicated when Tenochtitlan was founded. As was the custom throughout Mesoamerica, the shrine was periodically rebuilt in the same spot. Here, and elsewhere in the city, the archaeologist is confronted with damaged basal sections of later structures, and has to excavate earlier buildings by digging below the water table with the help of pumps. The archaeological finds from Tenochtitlan have come to light mainly during the digging of Mexico City's Metro system, and during recent, much publicized excavations on the Templo Mayor of Huitzilopochtli and Tlaloc in the heart of the city. Another view of the former capital can be glimpsed in the Plaza of the Three Cultures,

where a Spanish church and monastery overlook the exposed ruins of the pyramid of Tlatelolco, the temple where the doomed Aztec army made a last stand against the conquistadors.

Our knowledge of Tenochtitla ı comes almost entirely from scattered historical sourc s, especially from eyewitness accounts written by the conquistadors. In the main, these sources describe the more imposing public buildings and say little about the organization of Tenochtitlan or about its vast residential quarters. Edward Calnek has used colonial archives, as well as the chronicles and standard histories, to fill in some of the gaps. He worked with land titles, legal papers, wills, even bills-of-sale covering the ownership of individual residential sites and chinampa gardens situated within the city limits. He recorded the data from these documents on a scale map of the city made from air photographs so that he could plot the major street changes that had taken place since 1521. In some cases Calnek traced genealogies of land owners spanning as many as five generations and pieced together land titles from pre-Hispanic times right up to the seventeenth and eighteenth centuries. This laborious research has sketched out at least a provisional layout of an island city that covered between 5 and 6 square miles (8–9 sq km).

Reconstruction work on the Templo Mayor, Mexico City. Photo, Lesley Newhart.

CITY LAYOUT

The city originally consisted of two autonomous communities, Tenochtitlan and Tlatelolco, which maintained close ties even before the former annexed its sister city in 1473. Each had once had a large ceremonial precinct, an administrative palace, and a market. By 1519 the center of religious and secular power had moved to Tenochtitlan, but the major city market was still at Tlatelolco. Tenochtitlan was divided into four great quarters that intersected at a point at the foot of the stairway to the Temple of Huitzilopochtli within the walled central plaza. This lay north of the Zocalo of modern-day Mexico City, which was once a marketplace. The rectangular plaza was a walled enclosure perhaps 500 yards (450 m) square. Cortes wrote that this vast area could have contained "a town of fifteen thousand inhabitants." Diego Duran (1964, p. 75) wrote of the plaza that "it must have been immense, for it accommodated eight thousand six hundred men, dancing in a circle. This was the scene of the great public ceremonies, the feasts and festivals that punctuated the Aztec year.

The Templo Mayor dominated the north side of the plaza. In 1519 the west-facing temple rose some 150 feet (46 m) above the ground, a stepped pyramid with two steep stairways running up the front. Two shrines sat atop the pyramid, Huitzilopochtli's red chapel to the right, the rain god Tlaloc's blue one to the left. The temple was built of stone, covered with lime stucco, and decorated with brightly painted sculptures and murals. Blue bands, symbolic of water, decorated the facade of the rain god's shrine, while skulls adorned that of Huitzilopochtli. Both shrines had roof ornaments in the form of sea shells. The houses of high officials bounded the west side of the plaza, the front of Moctezuma Xocoyotzin's imperial palace, the east. A canal brought canoes right up to the southern border of the city center.

The plaza was a bright and busy place, surrounded by white palaces with lush gardens, and dominated by

General view of excavations at the Templo Mayor in the heart of downtown Mexico City. Photo, Lesley Newhart.

the carved walls and double stairways of the Templo Mayor. The entire precinct was ablaze with bright colors, a pageant of serpent-studded walls, feather banners, and brilliantly plumed capes and uniforms. Perhaps as many as seventy-eight buildings were situated within the walled enclosure, among them temples to Tezcatlipoca, and to the mother goddess Coatlicue. A cylindrical shrine to Quetzalcoatl stood on a pyramid 100 yards east of the Templo Mayor, its door modeled in the form of the gaping jaws of a serpent. "I always called that building Hell," wrote Bernal Diaz (1963, p. 239). The pyramids of the gods rose like small mountains around the central area, giving a profound impression of stability, majesty, and overwhelming power.

The Templo Mayor was almost certainly located on the spot where the very first temple of Huitzilopochtli stood. Its foundations have long since vanished deep into the swamps. Eduardo Matos Moctezuma's recent excavations have peeled off the remains of the original stone and mortar facades to reveal at least seven building phases and a number of minor additions to the facade and sides of the Templo Mayor. Successive rulers vied with their predecessors in embellishing it, "stacking" the facades of their enlarged pyramids against those of their predecessors. Eleven times the builders simply put new facades on earlier shrines that were slowly sinking into the mud. But on five occasions they constructed an entire new temple on the exact site of its predecessor. The first two buildings were completed before the Aztec war of independence in A.D. 1428. Fortunately, one of the earliest structures, that perhaps built around 1390, is preserved almost intact. It yielded the original sacrificial stone which faced the entrance to Huitzilopochtli's sanctuary, exactly where sixteenth-century chroniclers described another such stone lying in a later temple built on the same site.

Tlaloc's shrine alongside was guarded by a seated Chac Mool figure, brightly painted in red, blue, and white. The Chac Mool was a divine messenger, perhaps a symbolic intermediary between humans and the rain god. Two stone columns decorated with Tlaloc's eyes and red, blue, black, and white stripes stood at the entrance. The fourteenth-century temple was eventually covered by later shrines that followed the same general design, culminating in the Templo Mayor visited by Cortes. There were one hundred fourteen steps to the summit, and the view over the city from the two shrines on top was magnificent. The conquistadors examined the idol of Huitzilopochtli. "He had a very broad face and huge terrible eyes. And there were so many precious stones, so much gold, so many pearls and seed-pearls stuck to him with a paste ... that his whole body and head were covered with them. He was girdled with huge snakes made of gold and precious stones, and in one hand he held a bow, in the other some arrows" (Diaz, 1963, p. 236). The scent of copal incense pervaded the shrines, "and all the walls of that shrine were so splashed and caked with blood that they and the floor were black. Indeed, the whole place stank" (Diaz, 1963, p. 236). A great drum on the pyramid summit sounded so loudly that it could be heard six miles away, "like some music from the infernal regions." Almost nothing remains of Moctezuma's temple. The conquistadors pulled it down to build the neighboring cathedral.

The Templo Mayor excavations have yielded a superb array of Aztec ceremonial artifacts. More than a hundred offering caches were found buried in stone-walled chambers, boxes, and unlined cavities on the temple site. The caches contain figurines, idols, vessels, a wide range of miniature objects, and sacrificial remains. Recurrent themes in the caches are water and human sacrifice. Strangely, Huitzilopochtli is never modeled, but the goggle-eyed rain god Tlaloc is depicted on dozens of effigy vessels, together with the corn goddess and other deities.

Many of the masks and figurines were probably tribute objects, for they came from areas outside the Valley, from Guerrero, Mixteca country, and Veracruz. There were also antique specimens from places nearer home, from Teotihuacan and Tula, artifacts with special meaning because they came from two intensely

Ceramic effigy urn from the Templo Mayor, perhaps that of Moctezuma Ilhuicamina. Drawing, Sally Black.

sacred locations. One greenstone Olmec mask found in the temple precinct is more than 2,000 years old. Hieroglyphs list the places where the offerings came from. Other finds include braziers still containing copal incense, obsidian and silver necklaces and decorated sacrificial knives with obsidian blades, along with serpentine figures, shells, stone beads, bundles of coral, copal incense, and distinctive, often ceremonial, artifacts from all over Mesoamerica.

Human remains are abundant near the Templo Mayor. Rulers and other honored people were cremated and their ashes buried in special urns. The excavators recovered magnificent clay and obsidian funerary urns, two of them buried near a cremation pit and inscribed with the year 3 House (A.D. 1469), perhaps the urns of Moctezuma Ilhuicamina. One of these in the Veracruz style is adorned with the image of the war god Tezcatlipoca.

Many of these remains resulted from less natural deaths. The priests carefully displayed and adorned the skulls of prominent sacrificial victims, their eyes represented by shells or haematite, the stone sacrificial knives still embedded in nose or mouth. Sacred idols lay alongside some of the victims' skulls. There were signs of mass sacrifice as well. One offering consisted of a stone-lined pit filled with eleven painted stone effigies of Tlaloc, jade beads, copal incense, and the skulls of thirty-four children between three months and eight years old sacrificed to the rain god. Their bodies were dismembered before going into the pit.

The Templo Mayor was the heart of the Aztec empire. One can only guess at the symbolism of this remarkable monument. Eduardo Matos Moctezuma, director of the Templo excavations, believes that the pyramid with its two shrines may have represented two mountains, one dedicated to Tlaloc, who was worshipped on mountain tops, and the other recreating the peak of Coatepec, where Huitzilopochtli was born and where he conquered his sister Coyolxauhqui and her four hundred brothers. The temple itself, with its great serpent carvings, became the Serpent Mountain. Huit-

zilopochtli stands at the summit in triumph, his sister's
dismembered body—in the form of a great stone depicting her dismembered body—at the base. When the
priests sacrificed a human victim, they ripped out the
heart and cast the still quivering body down the steps
in a constantly repeated reenactment of the triumph of
day over night, of light over darkness, and of the birth
of the sun.

An Aztec hymn describes:

Huitzilopochtli, the young warrior,
he acts above, he follows his path.
"Not in vain did I adorn myself
with yellow plumes,
for I am the one who caused
the sun to shine."
(Garibay, 1958.)

The shrines of Huitzilopochtli and Tlaloc were focal
points in the great walled ceremonial precinct that included not only temples but the residential quarters for

*The Stone of Coyolxauhqui,
sister of Huitzilopochtli, found
at the Templo Mayor. Drawing, Sally Black.*

members of the religious communities. Lesser shrines flanked the great pyramid, including a round temple dedicated to Quetzalcoatl. The precinct also housed the *tlachtli,* the ball court, along with military arsenals, musicians' schools, and guest accommodations for visiting dignitaries. Fray Diego Duran wrote that the eight or nine temples in the precinct were all close together within a large enclosure. "Within this compound they all stood together, though each had its own staircase, its special courtyard, its chambers, and its sleeping quarters for the priests of the temples . . . . How marvellous it was to gaze upon them . . . . All stuccoed, carved, and crowned with different types of merlons, painted with animals [covered] with stone figures . . ." (Duran, 1971, pp. 75–76).

The ruler's palace, the *tecpan,* which served as the seat of secular government, stood outside the compound walls, sharply differentiated from the temple areas. The palace of Moctezuma Xocoyotzin, the last ruler, occupied a rectangle some 220 yards (200 m) on each side, on the site of the modern Palacio Nacional. Almost a small town in itself, the palace contained not only private living quarters and personal shrines, but a network of two story buildings, courtyards, and gardens. The Codex Mendoza tells us that Moctezuma lived on the upper floor. Government offices, council chambers, tribute storerooms, and courts occupied the lower stories. Here skilled artisans crafted gold and feathers, prisoners were sentenced and jailed, and caged wild animals were kept for Moctezuma's pleasure. "They were fed on deer, fowls, small dogs, and other creatures which they hunt and also on the bodies of the Indians they sacrificed, as I was told," wrote Bernal Diaz (1963, p. 229). He also describes the palace aviary, which contained "everything from the royal eagle, smaller kinds of eagles, and other large birds, down to multi-coloured small birds." The brilliantly plumed parrots and quetzals provided bundles of feathers. A large team of keepers supervised the feeding, breeding, and plucking of the birds.

Every day the city leaders assembled at the palace to receive orders from high officials and from the ruler, orders they transmitted to lesser functionaries in their own wards. This was the starting point of the civilian and military chain of command that extended from the palace into the remotest village. The facades and terraces of the palace were brightly painted in reds, blues, whites, and other hues and adorned with bas-reliefs, statues, and sculpture of all kinds. The tecpan was a secular building, a simple but luxurious administrative palace covering about 6 acres (2.4 hectares). The secular quarter also contained older palaces, among them that of Moctezuma's father where Cortes was lodged.

The city stretched southwards from the northern edges of Tlatelolco and merged into the marshes of the lake. At least five major canals flowed through the city from east to west, a sixth south to Lake Xochimilco. Secondary canals formed rectangular patterns that divided the city into large blocks. The layout of individual house sites and districts was carefully coordinated with that of major and minor waterways and with the small streets and thoroughfares that separated individual dwellings. This urban layout was so standardized that the sizes of residential plots and chinampas were predetermined by the authorities throughout the city.

Four large avenues, major land thoroughfares, extended in the cardinal directions from the gates of the ceremonial precinct and delineated the four great quarters of Tenochtitlan—Cuepopan, Teopan, Mototlan, and Aztacalco. Each had its own temples, markets, and public precinct. Each quarter was in turn subdivided into neighborhoods, known as *tlaxilacallis,* that bore the same names as individual *calpullis.* Sahagun refers to the calpulli as a form of corporate, social group (see Chapter 8), and there were at least eighty of them in Tenochtitlan at the time of the Conquest. Every citizen belonged to a calpulli and resided in a tlaxilacalli that served, as it were, as one's address. There is abundant reason to believe that the city grew through immigration and the deliberate importation of foreign artisans, among other means. Entire communi-

106

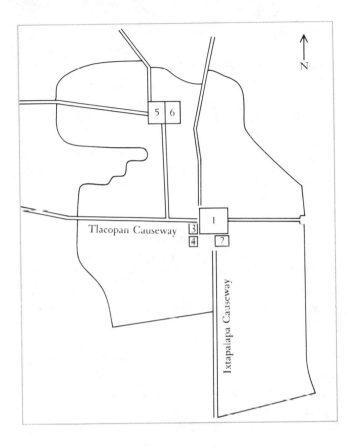

N

Tlacopan Causeway

Ixtapalapa Causeway

Simplified plan of Tenochtitlan showing (1) the central plaza; (2) Moctezuma Xocoyotzin's palace; (3, 4) other palaces; (5) ceremonial precinct of Tlatelolco; and (6) the adjacent marketplace visited by the conquistadors. The boundaries of the city are still uncertain, but its four quarters met at the central plaza. Redrawn from Edward Calnek, "Settlement pattern and chinampa agriculture at Tenochtitlan," American Antiquity, 1972, 37, 1, pp. 104–115.

ties of expert craftspeople, such as lapidaries or carvers, may have moved to the capital with the active encouragement of the ruler. War refugees may also have fled to the comparative security of Tenochtitlan.

The city precincts were divided in turn into groups of houses and households known to us only from tantalizingly incomplete archival descriptions. Many residential sites lay inside a walled compound that enclosed a number of separate dwelling units opening onto an open patio. Genealogies show that each dwelling was occupied by a family that included an elderly couple, their married children, and their grandchildren. Each married couple occupied a one- or two-room dwelling within the compound. Unlike the packed apartments at Teotihuacan, the Tenochtitlan compounds enjoyed direct access to the streets and canals and stood free rather than being joined to their neighbors. This free-standing architecture and the adornment of houses to commemorate personal achievement may indicate that the citizens of Tenochtitlan had more opportunity for initiative and individual advancement than had been the case in earlier settlements.

A map compiled from archival sources suggests that chinampa districts, residential quarters which included carefully integrated swamp plots, surrounded a more densely occupied urban core with its market and cere-monial precinct. But even the large chinampa plots within these districts were probably large enough to support only a single family group for part of the year. Most of Tenochtitlan's population depended on food supplies imported by water from the countryside to the great markets of the metropolis.

Tenochtitlan was a teeming city of closely packed roofs, single-storied houses, high pyramids, wide streets, and canals spanned by wooden bridges. "There are also great streets where there is water and nothing else; and these are used only for boats and barges, ac-cording to the custom of the country; for without these no one could move about the streets nor come out of their houses" (Cortes, 1928, p. 145). This was a city within a lake, joined to the shore by three carefully constructed raised causeways, as much dikes as road-ways, fabricated of stones and earth packed between two rows of wooden piles. Wooden bridges spanned gaps which let the fast-flowing lake currents through. The southern causeway extended for more than 5 miles (8 km) and "ran so straight that it bent neither little nor much." The twin city of Tlatelolco also had a large ceremonial precinct, but apparently it was not divided into quarters. The largest market in the Valley of Mex-ico lay close to the center of this merchant community, a market described by the conquistadors as rivalling those of Rome and Constantinople.

The building of Tenochtitlan was an organized, pro-digious undertaking such as only a highly organized people with a strong sense of mission and a chronic shortage of agricultural land would begin. The Aztecs created the land for their capital with wooden piles and sludge, with canals and embankments. When drinking water became a problem, they brought in fresh water by means of stone and mortar aqueducts. The original one, built by Moctezuma Ilhuicamina in the mid-fifteenth century, brought spring water from Chapultepec and extended for more than 3 miles (4.8 km). It had two channels, one of which was used while the other was cleaned. Because Tenochtitlan was in constant danger of flood, Moctezuma Ilhuicamina also built a great 10-mile (16 km) dike that ran from Atzacoalco to Ixtapalapa to protect the city from the overflows and from the salt water of the northern lakes. Every problem, however large, was tackled with the most plentiful commodities at the rulers' disposal: human ingenuity and an unlimited supply of organized, unskilled labor.

THE ORGANIZED LANDSCAPE

By the end of the fifteenth century, Tenochtitlan was an imperial capital known the length and breadth of Mesoamerica. As many as 200,000 people lived in its densely packed residential areas, and at least 400,000 city and country dwellers occupied a 230-square-mile (370 sq km) zone of foothills, alluvial plains, and lake bed areas near the capital. Archaeologist William Sanders has estimated that about 1,000,000 people lived within the confines of the Basin of Mexico at the Conquest, a figure at least four times that of the thirteenth century. The Aztecs settled everywhere in the Basin: their abandoned sites occupy every type of arable land and every variety of local environment in the region, the population density reflecting the type of agriculture practiced.

Tenochtitlan stood at the center of an organized landscape, a system of land use that provided the solid subsistence base for its rulers' imperial endeavors. The fifteenth century saw the authorities committing themselves to hydraulic schemes so vast that at least 24,700 acres (10,000 hectares) of chinampas were created in the southern Basin alone. The rulers created an agricul-

tural industry capable of supplying the basic food needs of at least half a million people. The settlement pattern around Tenochtitlan reflects a highly centralized transportation system that not only had to move vast tonnages of foodstuffs to the capital, but other essential commodities, such as salt, to markets where they could be accessible to farmer and nonfarmer alike. The capital may have been a city of artisans and merchants, with a population perhaps of 2 to 1 or 3 to 1 nonfood producers to agriculturalists, but these ratios are pure guesses, especially since historical accounts tend to emphasize markets and exotic products at the expense of prosaic activities like feeding people. In many respects, Tenochtitlan was identical in economic and subsistence terms to other large cities like Texcoco, where more than 30,000 people lived. As many as fifty or sixty city states may have existed in the Basin in the sixteenth

The environs of Tenochtitlan in the early sixteenth century. Data from Nigel Davies, The Aztecs, *p. 275, and other sources.*

century. What set Tenochtitlan apart was its sheer size, its sheer economic and political power that left it nothing to do but dominate the Basin and its surroundings.

We suspect that most production, specialization, and trading throughout the whole Basin of Mexico was ultimately oriented towards the needs, priorities, and constraints set by the rulers of Tenochtitlan, a city so strategically placed that it could obtain its basic subsistence needs by economic use of water transport.

The economic interdependence between the various Basin communities, large and small, had been a reality since the days of Teotihuacan, if not before. The movement of foodstuffs and other essential commodities probably continued, whatever the changing political fortunes of individual cities and rulers. The Mexica simply enlarged the scale of the entire endeavor in the fifteenth century as part of a push toward economic and political supremacy in the Basin and beyond. The Aztec empire was founded on meeting subsistence needs, but its expansion depended on imperial considerations, on the political ambitions of its rulers. They patched together an empire that was based on carefully calculated diplomatic moves and well-timed marriages, on the constantly changing tides of conquest and transitory alliances, on tribute gathering, and on long-distance trade. Such shifting factors were the realities that held the Aztec hegemony together and forged the links between the different, loosely knit parts of the empire and the great capital. But the empire would never have been possible had not Tenochtitlan been supported by a fertile, well-organized landscape and massive hydraulic works. From this sound economic base, the single-minded Aztec rulers conquered the Mexican world.

CHAPTER 5   Government and Empire

*All of these men brought offerings so great
in value and quantity that the enemies,
guests, and strangers were bewildered,
amazed. They saw that the Aztecs were
masters of the entire world and they realized
that the Aztec people had conquered all the
nations and that all were their vassals.*

Fray Diego Duran, *History of the Indies of New Spain*, 1964, p. 195.

"And all this tribute shows the magnificence and strength of the Aztec nation and how they came to be called and held to be lords of all created things, upon the waters as well as upon the earth." Fray Diego Duran (1964, p. 130) lists the vast tribute inventories that sustained Tenochtitlan and its gods, the taxes paid by vassals, the assessments that the Aztec armies of conquest made the penalty of surrender and defeat. By the time of the Conquest, the Aztec rulers were presiding over a patchwork of vassal states and uneasy political alliances that kept their armies in the field every year. Moctezuma Xocoyotzin presided over the affairs of thirty-eight provinces, each of which gave up sizable proportions of its agricultural and craft production to Tenochtitlan.

One is tempted to think of the Aztec empire as a monolithic, highly centralized state like that of imperial Rome. In fact, the empire is best described as a sophisticated tribute-gathering machine. The Triple Alliance of Tenochtitlan, Texcoco, and Tlacopan tightened its

Moctezuma's palace. From the Codex Mendoza. Courtesy, Bodleian Library, Oxford. MS. Arch. Selden A.1. folio 9.

113

hold on its neighbors by lightning wars of conquest, then assured a regular supply of tribute by a carefully orchestrated campaign of systematic taxation, political marriages, and veiled threats of armed force. Aztec imperialism was carefully tied to trade. Each successful conquest brought the Mexica territory, additional labor, and other important economic resources, often spied out in advance by their merchants acting as fifth columnists. All of these resources were placed in the service of the state as tribute.

As a result, the Aztecs' hold over many areas of the empire was loose at best, indeed it could be nothing else, given the great logistical difficulties of maintaining armies in the field far from the relatively secure heartland. They left many areas unconquered and allowed their vassals considerable political freedom and autonomy, provided they paid their tribute on time. The ubiquitous *calpixque,* the "tax collectors," were stationed in every province to ensure prompt delivery. Delinquent vassals were punished with doubled assessments, not so much of quantity, but in terms of sheer value and difficulty of supply. Jaguar skins, for example, were at a high premium on account of the labor that went into their collection and curing. The Aztec armies stood ready to pounce on rebellious tribute payers and to impose harsh punishment for delinquency. Indeed many of their harshly treated vassals later joined the Cortes' side in the hope that their tribute burden would be lightened.

IMPERIAL GOVERNMENT

From very humble beginnings the Mexica evolved the bureaucracy to run their empire as they went along. Their kingdom began as a tiny city-state, one of many in the Basin of Mexico. In the early fifteenth century, Tenochtitlan was a small polity, with its own dependent villages, just like dozens of other towns, each with their own temples, gods, and markets. Their separate villages and agricultural areas provided labor and produce for the rulers of the largest community. Before the

114

Aztecs threw their imperial blanket over Mexico, each city-state was an independent entity, linked to its neighbors by shaky alliances, trading arrangements, and sporadic warfare—a veritable political quicksand. During the mid-fifteenth century, the Aztecs and the Triple Alliance simply welded these smaller alliances into a vast imperial network of near and distant city-states. Each petty state had its own ruler, some of them independent leaders, others mere vassals of the imperial machine. These rulers, called *tlatoque* (sing. *tlatoani,* "speaker"), were responsible for the religious and economic life of their domains. They administered justice and supervised land holdings. A successful tlatoani had to combine all the virtues of a Mexica gentleman. He had to be a brave warrior, a discreet and successful diplomat, and a mellifluous orator. By the time of the Conquest, the more powerful rulers, among them Moctezuma Xocoyotzin, whose family claimed direct ancestry from Quetzalcoatl himself, were practically hereditary monarchs. The supreme ruler and his four advisers were all related and a *de facto* dynasty.

Only a highly select group of nobles, priests, and warriors were involved in the selection of a new ruler from this tiny group. Above all, he had to be brave, competent, and politically astute. The choice was always a vital one. For instance, the fourth day after the tlatoani Tizoc died in 1486, the Mexican leaders gathered to select a new ruler. They had to select just the right person, for Tizoc had died prematurely and many vassal chieftains were restless. Some counselors argued for an older man, "because the greatness of Mexico required someone old and venerable, whom the nations would hold in awe, and whom they would themselves respect" (Duran, 1964, p. 184). But the other electors held out for a younger man and wanted to follow the normal custom of passing the throne from one brother to another, rather than from father to son. They pressed for Ahuitzotl, the younger brother of Tizoc, already one of the army commanders. After prolonged debate and lengthy orations, the counselors duly appointed this gifted man, a ruler with brilliant gifts of leadership and a streak of ferocity that made him a general of genuis.

Following a series of elaborate religious ceremonies, the new ruler was expected to embark immediately on a war of conquest both to demonstrate his military skills and to collect sacrificial victims for his coronation. The ruler Ahuitzotl, for example, (1486–1502) was but a teenager when he ascended to the throne. But he was dressed in the correct royal insignia and given weapons, whereupon he marched into battle at the head of his armies. They attacked seven cities to the northwest of Tenochtitlan in a province that had been showing signs of restlessness. The soldiers captured the temple pyramids and "took all the priests prisoners, together with the other officials, and having tied their hands, they set fire to the temple" (Duran, 1964, p. 186). The conquered cities were ordered to pay tribute in "maize, beans, and other cultivated seeds, lumber and other things. The vanquished were ordered to bring workers to Mexico for the building of the houses of the nobility, together with slaves for sacrifice . . . . And so Ahuitzotl, accompanied by his chieftans and great nobles, returned to the city of Mexico, where he and the prisoners were received by the elders and priests. Great speeches were made to them, they were welcomed and congratulated for their successful venture" (Duran, 1964, p. 187). The coronation was set for the exceptionally auspicious day *Ce Cipactli,* "1 Alligator."

Ahuitzotl's coronation was not only an important ritual, it was a carefully planned political occasion designed to show Tenochtitlan's neighbors "the greatness of Mexico, . . . to bewilder them, fill them with fear, and make them see the grandeur and abundance of jewels and gifts that were exchanged on such an occasion. All of this was based on ostentation, vaingloriousness in order to show that the Aztecs were the masters of all the riches of the earth" (Duran, 1964, p. 188). Hundreds of human victims died on Huitzilopochtli's altar for the same reason. Every important official was ordered to attend, bringing a compulsory levy of provisions with him. Failure to appear meant immediate

Human sacrifice. From the complete facsimile edition of the series CODEX SELECTI, published by the Akademische Druck- u. Verlagsanstalt, vol. XXIII: CODEX MAGLIABE-CHIANO CL. XIII.3.

exile. Even the ruler's enemies and rivals were invited. Those who accepted were smuggled into the palace under cover of darkness to protect them from assassination attempts by zealous warriors. The entire panoply of feasts and human sacrifices was carefully calculated to impress both the Aztecs' allies and their enemies.

In the second year of his reign Ahuitzotl decided to complete the rebuilding of the temple of Huitzilo-pochtli started by his predecessor, and he ordered the vassal states to supply special tribute assessments to assist in the building. The dedication ceremonies were conducted on an even more grandiose scale than the coronation. Each neighboring ruler, received in secrecy lest the commoners suspect double-dealing, brought sacrificial victims and was showered with princely gifts. A huge line of prisoners was led in front of Ahuitzotl and his fellow rulers so that a precise account could be

kept. Duran claims that 80,400 were slain, but the actual figure must have been much lower. "King Ahuitzotl was greatly satisfied and he sat upon the royal throne, showing his grandeur to all the nations, the magnificence of his empire and the courage of his people" (Duran, 1964, p. 194). Next came the parade of each piece of the royal tribute from the highlands and the lowlands in front of the visitors. "All of these men brought offerings so great in value and quantity that the enemies, guests, and strangers were bewildered, amazed. They saw that the Aztecs were masters of the entire world . . ." (Duran, 1964, p. 195).

The tlatoani relied on relatively few advisers, among them the *cihuacoatl,* a vizier who took much of the burden of day-to-day government off his hands. Some were powerful men who influenced the ruler at every turn. Later appointees were apparently content to follow the orders of the tlatoani. All power flowed to the top. The ruler's character and personality, whether kind or militaristic, severe or easygoing, profoundly affected the nature of state government. For example, one of the best known characters of Mexica history is Nezahualcoyotl (1418–1472), the law-abiding, wise tlatoani of Texcoco. He was an engineer, and much interested in justice and the creative arts, so much so that Texcoco became a center of jurisprudence and artistic accomplishment, while the militaristic rulers of Tenochtitlan led their city to supremacy in war.

By the late fifteenth century, imperial power was firmly consolidated in the hands of these supreme rulers. But for all this consolidation, the empire was loosely administered. In most cases the tlatoani was content to appoint high-ranking tax collectors to each conquered province, officials who supervised the delivery of tribute levies. Veiled threats of reprisal and condign punishment were considered sufficient to keep defaulters in line. Only rarely did the ruler order the garrisoning of a dangerous frontier or colonize an underpopulated region, although Ahuitzotl did once recolonize the depopulated cities of Oztoman and

Alahuiztlan with two hundred Mexica families sent to work the valuable fruit, cacao, and cotton plantations.

A secular bureaucracy of judges, officials, and warriors administered the empire. Apart from the military establishment, there were tax collectors, judges, stewards, provincial governors, quartermasters, scribes, and many lesser officials. The justice system was closely supervised and highly structured. The state appointed all judges, from the lowly magistrates who presided over the commoners' neighborhood courts to the *teccalco,* the state court where major cases were tried. "Calmly and prudently they [the judges] heard the plaints of the vassals; in the picture writing which recorded the case, they studied the complaints" (Sahagun, 8, p. 42). Offending nobles and the most serious cases involving commoners were committed to the *tlacxitlan,* a panel of thirteen senior judges. Criminal cases could be appealed to the vizier, and on occasion to the ruler himself; civil disputes could not be appealed.

Punishment was swift and severe. One could be imprisoned, pierced with maguey spines, banished, or deprived of one's titles. Adultery, theft, and homicide were savagely punished by hanging or stoning. Sometimes the offender was given to the victim in slavery. Disobedience on the battlefield and offenses against the sumptuary laws—those regulating personal moral behavior—were punished by death. As for corrupt judges, the ruler "seized them and jailed them in wooden cages, exacted the penalty, and slew them, so that the judges might walk in dread" (Sahagun, 8, p. 42).

Paid out of tribute levies, this elaborate hierarchy of officials presiding over day-to-day affairs oversaw the administration of courts, the collection and storage of tribute, and the organization of people in the service of the state. Everyone, whether bureaucrat or commoner, had a role and perceived place in this stratified society. In a hauntingly modern aside, Duran adds: "The good order was such that no one dared to interfere with the job of another or express an opinion since he would be rebuffed immediately" (Duran, 1964, p. 183).

The administrative mechanism of the empire revolved around two main preoccupations: military conquest and the economic power, the collection of tribute, that went with it. The same wars provided not only tribute, but the human victims demanded by the insatiable gods.

THE TRIBUTE MACHINE

The expenses of the Aztec state were met almost entirely from tribute, whether that from Tenochtitlan's own citizens or levies from the provinces. Tribute was essential: it supported not only the tribute-gathering apparatus itself, it also paid the operating expenses of the Aztec armies, the priesthood, and the entire royal establishment—state artisans, diplomats, and royal officials. Special assessments paid for the necessary costumes and mantles for major religious festivals. Sometimes, too, the leader levied special tribute to pay for a major public project like a new temple or for a state funeral. Moctezuma Xocoyotzin's coronation in 1502 was so lavish that 1,000 villagers from up to 450 miles (725 km) around were drafted to the capital to prepare huge consignments of food every day. The noble guests departed loaded with lavish gifts, with "jewels, sumptuous and rich gifts, weapons and shields with their insignia done in fine feather work" (Duran, 1964, p. 226). To judge by conquistadorial accounts, a staggering quantity of goods was consumed at the palace alone. Bernal Diaz remarked that "they cooked more than three hundred plates of the food the great Moctezuma was going to eat, and more than a thousand more for the guard" (Diaz, 1963, p. 227). Thousands of tortillas and many baskets of chilis and vegetables came in from nearby farming communities to feed the ruler and his establishment every day.

This was only a small part of the tribute that poured into Tenochtitlan every month of the year. The labor of thousands of provincial commoners, farmers, artisans, fisherfolk, and laborers supported a collection system that reached into every household. Sometimes the tribute burden almost overwhelmed the farmers: "This gave rise to much distress; it caused much anguish; it affected them. And some therefore fled; they went elsewhere. And many cast themselves in the midst of war, they cast themselves to their deaths" (Sahagun, 3, pp. 6–7).

The array of tribute offerings astounded Diego Duran (1964, pp. 127–131):

Great quantities of gold, in dust and worked as jewels.

Large amounts of green stones ... besides many other types of stone which these people love greatly. The basis of their idolatry was the adoration of these stones together with the feathers which they called, "Shadow of the gods." These feathers were multicolored or green, blue, red, yellow, purple, white, and striped.

Vast amounts of cacao.

Cotton in large bundles, both white and yellow.

A bewildering amount of cloth; strips twenty, ten, five, four and two yards long, according to the wealth of each province.

Exceedingly rich mantles for the lords, differently woven and worked, some of them had rich fringes done in colors and feather work . . . .

Also mantles of maguey fiber given as tribute by the Chichimecs—most delicately worked and painted in different colors . . . .

Live birds, too, sent by the Chichimecs—green, red, blue; parrots large and small . . . .

Wild animals such as ocelots, jaguars, wildcats. All of these fierce animals were brought in cages.

Duran lists serpents, even spiders and scorpions on his tribute list, together with sea shells, "curious fish bones," turtle shells, pearls, colors and dyes. Some provinces sent mats, decorated gourds, even timber, stone, and other building materials. Pineapples, avocados, and guavas came from the lowlands, firewood and charcoal from those cities that "had woods." Some states sent delicately embroidered womens' clothing,

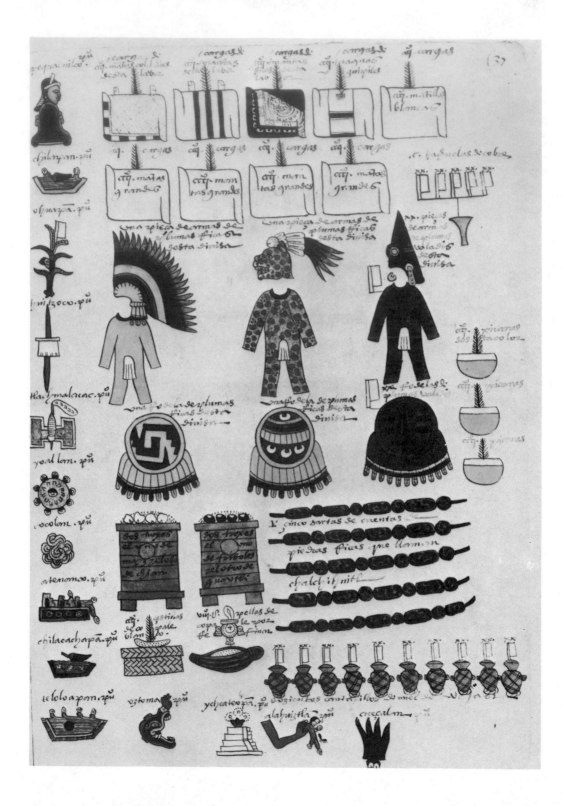

Left: A tribute list showing the tribute paid by the province of Tochtepec to the Triple Alliance cities:

The number of towns of the hot and temperate countries drawn and named on the next page is twenty two and the things they contributed are as follows:

1,600 rich mantles, 800 striped red, white, and green mantles, 400 warrior's tunics and shirts. Also one war dress with "bird device in the colors as depicted." Gold headbands, beads, also jadeite, amber labrets.

800 bundles of rich green feathers called "quetzalli"
8,000 little bundles of rich blue feathers
8,000 little bundles of rich red feathers
8,000 little bundles of rich green feathers
200 loads of cacao, 16,000 balls of oli, which is the gum of trees, and these balls when thrown on the ground bounce very high, all of which were contributed once a year.

From the Codex Mendoza. Courtesy, Bodleian Library, Oxford, MS. Arch. Selden A.1. folio 46.

others supplied cotton-quilted armor "so thick that an arrow or dart could not penetrate it." Featherwork shields, bows, and maguey slings came from the same areas, while others sent honeycombs or "great loads of flowers of a thousand varieties, all dexterously arranged." Some were brought with their roots, all ready to be planted in noble gardens. "Provinces that lacked foodstuffs and clothes paid in maidens, girls and boys, who were divided among the lords—all slaves."

Few statistics on the volume of tribute that reached the capital have survived. The *Codex Mendoza*, written twenty years after the Conquest, contains a pictorial record of tribute sent from the thirty-eight provinces of the empire. The record shows, for example, that mantles were brought to Tenochtitlan every eighty days, 5,200 of them of maguey fiber, 2,400 of palm fiber, and the figure does not seem unreasonable. The tribute was minutely inventoried and stored in central warehouses under the supervision of tribute officials. It was eventually distributed, not only to support armies and to feed officials, but to reward the brave and support Tenochtitlan's huge urban population.

Tribute foodstuffs were important in the capital, for everyday staples like maize and beans were sometimes insufficient in the markets, especially at times of famine. The state's food surplus fed people in times of disaster and supported the large labor forces needed to erect temples and repair canals, causeways, and ditches. The rulers also used tribute goods as gifts and as signs of official recognition for bravery in battle. The feather-decked warrior was adorned from tribute supplies. Large quantities of valued commodities, such as capes, were bartered by the state, using professional merchants as intermediaries. These same transactions also served as a front for political activities and spying.

Conquered peoples groaned under their vast tribute burdens. Cortes met a Totonac chief in Veracruz who, Bernal Diaz tells us in what is probably a rather self-serving account, "heaved a deep sigh and broke into bitter complaints against the great Moctezuma and his governors, saying that the Mexican prince had recently brought him into subjection, had taken away all his golden jewelry, and so grieviously oppressed him and his people that they could do nothing but obey him" (Diaz, 1963, p. 108). Soon afterwards the conquistadors met a group of Aztec tax collectors about their work, stalking through the villages with insolent confidence. "They wore richly embroidered cloaks and loincloths . . . and shining hair that was gathered up and seemed tied to their heads. Each one was smelling the roses he carried, and each had a crooked staff in his hand. Their Indian servants carried flywhisks" (Diaz, 1963, p. 111). The tax collectors did not deign to acknowledge the Spaniards' presence and fined the chief twenty sacrificial victims for entertaining them. Such officials were so confident of their safety that they travelled almost unarmed.

The ruler rewarded key officials and high nobles by granting them their own tribute privileges—land, for example, and the right to the labor of the *mayeques,* or serfs, who lived on it. The mayeques were commoners, without land of their own, who labored for the noble by providing domestic service as well as goods and produce—mantles, maize, firewood, even salt. This tribute was purely for the benefit of the landowner, rendered by people who had no obligations to the state except for military service. Very often, mayeques were commoners whose communally owned land had been alienated into private ownership as a result of conquest.

Those who labored to provide tribute received little benefit other than vague promises of assistance in times of famine or warfare in exchange for their work. Only those commoners living close to the Triple Alliance capitals occasionally shared allocations from the state granaries and benefited from the higher yields fostered by their own labors in the ever-expanding chinampas and on irrigation works. The Aztecs' intricate trade and tribute systems brought foodstuffs and other essentials within reach of most citizens who could afford them. But only a very few highly privileged rulers and nobles enjoyed their full fruits.

WARRIORS AND WARFARE

A preoccupation with warfare dominated every facet of Aztec life. Male infants were dedicated to it at birth, women who died in childbirth were revered as brave warriors. This preoccupation is hardly surprising. Conquest and war ensured a regular supply of the tribute for the state, so inevitably war was a more or less continuous activity. This same tribute was used to reward brave warriors, and it provided the necessary motivation for ever bolder military adventures. Clearly the battlefield was the best place to get ahead in Aztec society. Every young man was trained in warfare. Each was expected to take at least one captive in battle, and the unsuccessful soldier who took no prisoners was an object of derision. Even noble recruits could only wear a humble maguey cape until they had proven themselves in battle. The taking of prisoners was one of the greatest services a person could perform for the state.

We go to war for what politicians tell us are high-minded motives, and we justify military actions that give us economic and political advantage "fighting for freedom," or the "preservation of civilization." Theoretically, the Aztecs made war for similarly noble reasons: for religious purposes, to appease the gods with the hearts of prisoners of war. In fact, the rulers rejoiced in war for war's sake and picked all manner of excuses to go to battle: imagined insults, nonpayment of tribute, and, perhaps most common of all, assaults on Aztec merchants. Sometimes they triggered warfare by making intolerable demands for tribute, demands carefully calculated to emphasize the victim's subordinate position.

A declaration of war was a highly ritualized, formal business. Prolonged diplomatic courtesies also gave the attackers time to spy out the land and plan their strategy. A delegation of diplomats from Tenochtitlan would approach an intended victim and invite its leaders to join forces with the Triple Alliance. The conditions of this alliance were access to the other city's markets by Aztec merchants, the provision of some goods and services to the imperial capitals, and the erection of an image of Huitzilopochtli in their temples. The victim had twenty days to respond. Then a group of Texcocan ambassadors arrived to negotiate and to remind the leaders of their need to respond. Now the honeyed words became warnings and threats. Another twenty days grace would be allowed before emissaries from Tlacopan, the third city of the Alliance, arrived with gifts of weapons. They repeated the warnings and spelled out the terrible consequences of resistance and conquest, directing their predictions at the local warriors who would bear the brunt of the Aztec attack. After another twenty days, a state of war existed. Sometimes the ruler simply dispatched messengers with symbolic gifts—a feathered shield, an obsidian-bladed

Four priest-warriors in their military finery. From the Codex Mendoza. Courtesy, Bodleian Library, Oxford. MS. Arch. Selden A.1. folio 65.

club, and feathers—to announce that the recipients were at war with him. The pretexts for war were often flimsy in the extreme, merely an imagined insult that served as an excuse to pick a fight or obtain control over needed resources.

Every Mexica male, whatever his birth, wanted to become a warrior. Everyone received training in the basic martial arts. When a boy was about ten years old his hair was cut, leaving a *piochtli,* a lock on the nape of the neck, that was not shorn until he had taken a prisoner in battle. If several youths took a prisoner together, their locks were cut and the body was divided among them after the sacrificed death: "The first, who was the real captor, took his body and one of the thighs —the one with the right foot. And the second who took part [in the capture] took the left thigh . . ." (Sahagun, 8, p. 75). The partition of the body went right down to the sixth captor. The unfortunate youth who did not take a prisoner after several tries became known as "Big tuft of hair over the back of the head

. . . . Wherefore he cast himself [into the fray] in order to take a captive with others' aid" (Sahagun, 8, p. 76).

Once a young man had taken his first prisoner, he became an *iyac* and grew his hair so that it fell over his right ear. An ambitious and brave soldier could rise very high in the military hierarchy. Once he had captured or slain four of the enemy, he became a *tequiua,* "one who has a share of the tribute." This entitled him to a share of the booty of war and allowed him to wear special capes and regalia. A tequiua was entitled to attend key war councils and was qualified for high military and civil office. "And then in truth was when they placed him on the mat and stool of the warriors' house —there where were gathered the great, brave warriors . . ." (Sahagun, 8, p. 77). From there, an ambitious military man could become a high-ranking officer, a *tlacateccatl,* a "commander of warriors," for example, or a judge. Brave commoners could aspire to very high military rank and become one of the exclusive *quauh-pilli,* the top war commanders. Such men were given land by the ruler, but were not qualified to hold serfs to work it. They could also run *telpochcalli,* the schools for commoners. Only the bravest and most unruly soldiers, those considered too violent for administrative office, became members of the elite *otomi* and *quachic* warrior societies. They might join the band of select fighters who became the jaguar knights, outfitted in jaguar skins in battle, or eagle knights, caparisoned in eagle's head helmets, the true soldiers of the sun god.

These were the professional military men, and their elaborate uniforms and regalia proclaimed their bravery. The professionals were supported by thousands of humble soldiers, often recruits, who learned the fundamentals of warfare under the protection of experienced fighters. Military service was a compulsory obligation for every free man. In a campaign army, hundreds of bands of twenty men each were organized into companies of two to four hundred soldiers. The companies were raised by calpulli leaders, the officials responsible for the draft and for training. The trained companies took to the field in larger regiments organized accord-

Aztec Eagle Knight, andesite sculpture. From the Valley of Mexico, exact location unknown. Height: 14.8 inches (38 cm). National Museum of Anthropology, Mexico City. Photo, Lesley Newhart.

ing to the four quarters of the capital, each with its professional divisional leader.

One reason for Aztec military success was their ability to raise a huge army at short notice. But not all of these soldiers came from Tenochtitlan, nor were they even necessarily Mexica. A typical army of conquest might include regiments from all three cities of the Triple Alliance and from vassal states as well. The marching host often added units from distant provinces during a campaign. But the Mexica invariably placed themselves in the most dangerous places, for it was there that elite warriors, fighting in pairs, could take the most prisoners and attain the greatest honor.

They also suffered grievous losses. The Aztec armies were by no means invincible, and they sometimes suffered catastrophic defeats. In 1478 the tlatoani Axayacatl marched against the Tarascans of what is now the state of Michoacan. He found his army of some 24,000 men confronted by a rival force of more than 40,000. A ferocious battle went on all day. After nightfall, the nobles and warriors conferred with Axayacatl. Duran tells us that their faces were so covered with sweat and dust that they were barely recognizable. "Those in the most unhappy state were those who had sworn not to retreat; some of them were badly wounded, some by arrows, others by stones, others by sword thrusts, others pierced with spears" (Duran, 1964, p. 167). The ruler ordered that they be given a restorative broth known as *yolatl*, "heart water." The next day the battle resumed with a frantic Aztec assault. The warriors fell "like flies that fall in the water." The Aztecs were forced to retreat with the loss of many elite warriors. It is said that more than 20,000 men died or were captured on both sides. Only two hundred elite Aztec warriors out of more than a thousand survived the battle.

Supposedy a highly drilled military machine, in fact the Aztec army consisted of little more than unruly hosts of men armed with wooden clubs edged with obsidian and javelins hurled with *atatls,* or throwing sticks. They wore quilted cotton body armor soaked in brine that gave effective protection against clubs, arrows, and spears. This armor was so much cooler than steel plate that the Spaniards adopted it during the Conquest. Feather-decorated wicker shields covered with hide were used in hand-to-hand combat. Everyone wore insignia that distinguished their tribes and clans, and the knights donned elaborate wooden helmets and feathered plumes that set them apart from the common soldiers.

Military campaigns were short-term, logistical nightmares. Most culminated in a single battle before supplies ran out. The army lived only in part off the land for fear of inciting revolt among the more-or-less independent local people. Everyone carried his provisions on his own back. The military authorities demanded supply areas from communities near the battle zone where the army could assemble beforehand. Sieges were almost unknown, for most centers were well-defended. The lakes sufficed to protect Tenochtitlan which was only accessible by water or through a network of causeways that could be severed in a few minutes by removing wooden bridges. Temples were natural strongholds, and the roofs of the densely packed houses were ideal for harrying soldiers in the streets below. For all these reasons, opposing armies preferred to fight in the open. Tactics were rudimentary except for occasional ambushes or surprise attacks. One common ruse was to retreat across a stream in apparent disorder, leaving a select regiment in hiding to attack the advancing enemy at the moment of their apparent triumph.

The actual engagement itself was a vicious brawl. In most cases a howling mob attacked an opposing host, everyone took prisoners, and the first to be routed lost the battle. The victors burned some temples, imposed heavy tribute assessments, and retired with their captives. Looting was generally discouraged because it reduced future tribute levies. The conquered city not only had to pay tribute, it had to acquiesce to Mexica leadership and agree to honor Huitzilopochtli. More interested in tribute than annexation, the Aztecs were normally content to leave the conquered state with its own leaders, system of government, and local language and customs.

The secret of Aztec military success lay neither in the training and bravery of their soldiers nor in their superior tactics. It was their patience and political acumen that enabled them to solve the complex logistics of long-distance campaigns. Not least among their weapons were their merchants, who mingled incognito in the enemy's marketplaces and cities long before a campaign began. These merchants assessed the local political climate, watched for signs of rebellion, and calculated the value of an intended victims' resources. The authorities at home richly rewarded such spies.

War had molded many of the Aztecs' most cherished institutions, and it fascinated them. War, they believed, had been created as a means of feeding the Sun with blood and hearts. They called it *yaoyotl,* "the warriors' business." War, they believed, was a passion awakened by the Sun: "He awakens it on earth as something strong and valorous, all so that warriors and brave men, men powerful and turned towards war, will find great content and pleasure in it," recorded Sahagun (6, p. 22). The poets spoke of the battlefield with passionate euphemisms, as if battle were a rain of blossoms wherein warriors in all their finery fall and die like tree blossoms in the spring time. This was the famous *xochimiquiztli,* the "flower death," the cherished fate of the most elite of all Aztec warriors, the *teteuctin.* Their traditions dated back at least to the Toltecs, perhaps earlier, and membership was gained by prowess on the battlefield, by capturing prisoners, or by other valiant deeds. The teteuctin were the ultimate shock troops, called into action only in dire emergencies. Subject to vows of austerity, these knights contemplated death in battle with equanimity. The true techutli was conditioned and trained to long for *itzmiquiztli,* death by the obsidian knife. Every prisoner taken expected to be sacrificed, never contemplating escape lest his fellow warriors accuse him of cowardice.

The annual wars began once the harvests were in. When the Aztec armies moved out on the campaign of terror and conquest, the warriors were treated like gods —every town tried desperately to entertain and feed an army quite capable of wiping them out. "The earth trembled beneath them," wrote Diego Duran. The army returned with long lines of captives, their hands tied behind them and their necks locked in wooden collars. The prisoners received a rapturous welcome in the conquering city where they were divided among the various quarters for fattening. Meanwhile a formal lamentation for the dead was made to the Sun, complete with elaborate speeches. "I thank the creator that he has allowed me to see these many deaths of my brothers and nephews," cried one such orator (Duran, 1964, p. 171).

Sometimes the cities of the Triple Alliance fought carefully planned wars with peoples like the Huexotzincos and Tlaxcalans almost as ceremonial tournaments. The objective of *xochiyaoyotl,* the "War of the Flowers," was not conquest, but to capture prisoners for the Sun. City was pitted against city in tournaments that not only fed the gods but kept the martial spirits of the warriors at fever pitch. We know that the xochiyaoyotl was waged as early as the late fourteenth century, and both Tenochtitlan and Texcoco claimed it as their own invention, a festival of war that locked rival cities into chivalrous battle at regular intervals.

A War of the Flowers was declared when either side issued an invitation to combat, an invitation which was usually accepted. A party of volunteer warriors from each city set out for the regular battlefield accompanied by a priest bearing an image of Tezcatlipoca, the god who presided over the battlefield. Only a small number of knights fought at first, but others joined in as the battle progressed. Valiant warriors engaged in single combat while other bands of men fought it out to the death. The rivalry could become so intense that a flower war sometimes developed into real hostilities. The great vizier Tlacaelel once referred to the flower war as a form of military fair where the god, with his army, of course, went to shop for his food and drink: "Each of you, when he goes to war to fight, must think that he has journeyed to a market place where he will find precious stones," he cried (Duran, 1964, p. 142). All captives automatically became sacrificial victims, and their deaths on the temple altar kept the gods gorged with human blood.

The flower wars probably had more pragmatic purposes as well. Tlaxcala and Heuxotzinco were both powerful rivals whose economic resources were of little value to the Aztecs compared with those flowing to them from richer, easier-to-manage polities. The flower wars provided opportunities for keeping the political power of these rivals in check through elaborate, ceremonial contests.

Every aspect of Aztec imperial government, whether commerce, internal organization, or warfare, was focused to two ultimate ends—the perpetuation of the Fifth Sun by the feeding of the gods, and the maintenance of the power and prestige of the tlatoani and the tiny band of nobles, priests, and warriors that formed his closest advisers. For generations, the Aztecs achieved these single-minded objectives with astonishing brilliance.

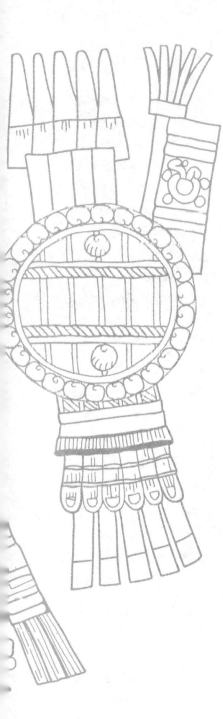

III

THE CONFORMING SOCIETY

Y esta astrologia, o nigroman
cia fue tomada, y ouo origen
de vna muger: que sellama
Oxomoco, y de vn hombre que
sellama cipactonal. Y los ma
estros, desta astrologia, o nigro
mancia: que contauan estos
signos, que sellamauan to
nalpouhque: pintauan a esta
muger oxomoco, y a este hõ
bre cipactonal: y los ponjã
en medio de los libros: don
de estauan escritos, todos los
caracteres de cada dia; por
que dezian: que eran seño
res desta astrologia, o nigro
mancia, como principales as
trologos: porque la inuenta
ron, y hizieron esta cuenta,
de todos los caracteres.

oan, iaopen concaeaia: velon
can mecahoa, intlaiecoalo,
y ixaxem iacan contocaia. Auh
intlaieoatl ellaeat: ynjc eatlaia
imalac, icheaioh, itzaoalcax,
ioan ipopouh, icchpanoaz ipan
contemaia ynjncaltilax, inj
nealtilapaz: ye qujnextlia, m.
iiampa ianj cioazintli, ean ealt
ichan: ic canmeHatitlan, Hecujl
nacazco contocaia ynjxic Auh
mm tonalpoalli, iuh mjto aia: te
hoam intlanexhl, ichoom qujte
macaque, m vmentin tencoalo
mtoca Oxomoco, ioan cipactonal
m Oxomoco cioatl micqujcujilo
aia: auh in cipac tonal oqujch
tli: in tonalpouhque catca, ymn
tonal amauh qujiollotivia, yn
myxiptla ynepantla qujntlalia
ia, injc quj nijcujiladia: caiuh
mjto aia, oncan tlatoque muchi
oa ynjpan ixqujch tonalpoalli

Injc vine capitulo: itech
pa tlatoa, injc vntetl, me.

CHAPTER 6 The Exemplary Life

The good old man [is] famous, honored, an
adviser .... He tells, recites ancient lore;
he leads an exemplary life.
The good old woman [is] a supervisor, a
manager, a shelter.

Fray Bernardino de Sahagun, *General History,* 10, p. 11.

Page 134: Tezcatlipoca. From
original drawing by Alonso
Caso. Courtesy, Fondo de
Cultura Economica, Mexico
City.

Left: A page from Volume 4
of Sahagun's General History,
beginning, "And this count of
days, so it was claimed, was
an invention of the two called
and named Oxomozo and
Cipactonal . . . ."

"Peacefully, quietly, tranquilly, deliberately art thou to
go ...." Fray Sahagun found that every member of
Aztec society, however lowly, lived according to clearly
laid out social rules that stressed moderation, conformity, and the need for exemplary behavior. Everyone had
a well-defined place in society. As in other complex,
hierarchical, and state-dominated societies—the Sumer-
ians of Mesopotamia, or the Maya of the Mexican lowlands— the Aztecs adhered to social and personal
behavior norms that were inculcated constantly, literally
from the moment of birth. One way to begin to understand Aztec society is to explore its definition of "an
exemplary life."

The primeval Mexica were probably a tribal society,
closely knit by ties of family and lineage. As new and
pressing needs for individual leadership made themselves felt, however, a much more hierarchical society
rapidly evolved, one with distinct social rankings of
chieftains, priests, and warriors. At first, people acquired rank through their own achievements and individual efforts, not through inheritance. Eventually birth
became the overriding factor. But even those who inherited high rank had to prove themselves and validate

137

their status. Diplomatic skills or prowess on the battle-field could promote upward mobility. But, the close ties of family and lineage—the reality of birthright—were the fundamental cement of Mexica society, the basis for social control for a sense of community, and for high position.

Aztec social organization was based on two principles: a strong sense of rank, a passion for hierarchy, as it were, and an understanding that a highly diverse society made up of peoples with different cultural backgrounds required very effective social controls. The system worked, established and reinforced as it was by ubiquitous educational systems that inculcated moral values and taught specialized skills. Everyone, however humble, passed through a life marked by well-defined signposts, the major events in one's life, conscious of his or her role within wider society. Aztec life existed not for the individual but for the group. Each member conformed to social norms and contributed to the preservation of the community and the state, in times of peace through tax labor and tribute, and in war through military service. This group interest overrode everything else, giving society a strong cohesion and the ability to endure under most normal circumstances. But, as we shall see, Aztec society could not long survive the erosion of divine and state authority that followed on the heels of the Spanish Conquest.

Aztec noblewomen engaged in animated conversation. From the Florentine Codex. Courtesy, University of Utah Press, Salt Lake City. Drawing, Sally Black.

THE PRUDENT LIFE

Highly explicit cultural codes set out appropriate behavior and the basic obligations of every member of
society. They defined and governed interpersonal relations and daily activities, making allowance for sex differences, age, and social rank. Everything rested on the
philosophical abstraction of what constituted the exemplary life: a combination of obedience, honesty, respect,
and above all, moderation. If two words can express
this ideal, they are "moderation" and "discretion."
This Aztec ideal was a far cry from the placid notion of
ma'at, "rightness," the prized virtue that the ancient
Egyptians based on their certainty that death was merely an incident on the way to eternal life. The Mexica,
with their strong sense of fatalism, lived their lives dis-
creetly and moderately to avoid falling from grace, to
ward off the doom that everyone knew was around the
corner. This was, perhaps, the ultimate in anonymous
societies, a society where it was easy to fall from grace
and the individual person mattered for little in the face
of the gods and the forces of doom.

The sixth book of Fray Bernardino de Sahagun's
General History quotes a nobleman advising his son on
the eight rules of modern living:

"First: thou art to be one who riseth from sleep, one
who holdeth vigil through the night. Thou art not to
give thyself excessively to sleep, lest ... thou wilt be
named a heavy sleeper ... a dreamer ....

And second, thou art to be prudent in thy travels;
peacefully, quietly, tranquilly, deliberately art thou to
go .... Do not throw thy feet much, nor raise they
feet high ... lest thou be named fool, shameless ....
Nor art thou to go trampling; thou art not to seem like
a firefly, not to strut, not to bustle about ....

Third: thou art to speak very slowly, very deliberately; thou art not to speak hurriedly, not to pant, nor
to squeak, lest it be said of thee that thou art a groaner,
a growler, a squeaker .... Moderately, middlingly art
thou to carry, to emit thy spirit, thy words. And thou
art to improve, to soften thy words, thy voice.

Fourth: thou art to pretend not to dwell upon that which is done, that which is performed. Especially art thou to depart from, to forsake evil. And thou art not to peer at one, not to peer into one's face . . . much less at someone's wife, for it is said he who stareth at, who peereth into the face of another's wife, with his eyes committeth adultery . . . .

Fifth: Guard, take care of thy ears, of that which thou hearest. Do not gossip; let what is said remain said. Ignore it . . . . If thou canst not ignore it, respond not . . . .

Sixth: when thou art summoned, be not summoned twice, be not called twice. The very first time, thou art to arise responding, to arise quickly . . . . Thou art to be diligent, and thou art to do things at only one bidding, for if thou art twice summoned thou wilt be considered as perverse, lazy, languid, negligent, or thou wilt be considered as one disdainful of orders, as a haughty one. This is the time when the club, the stone should be broken on thee.

Seventh: as thou art to array thyself . . . thou art not to dress vainly . . . thou art not to place on thyself the gaudy cape, the gaudy clothing, that which is embroidered. Neither art thou to put on rags, tatters, a loosely-woven cape . . . . Moderately art thou to tie it [the cape] on. Nor art thou to expose thy shoulder . . . be thou always prudent as to the cape, the sandals; place on thee that which is always good, proper, all fine.

Eighth: Listen! Above all thou art to be prudent in drink, in food, for many things pertain to it . . . . Furthermore, the courtesy, the prudence [thou shouldst show] are in this wise: when thou art to eat, thou art not to be hasty, not to be impetuous; thou art not to take excessively nor to break up your tortillas . . . ."

The wise father ends with more words of caution:

"Our forefathers, the old men, the old women, the white-haired ones . . . went saying that on earth we travel, we live along a mountain peak. Over here there is an abyss, over there is an abyss. Wherever thou art to deviate, wherever thou art to go astray, there wilt thou fall, there wilt thou plunge into the deep."

The only safe course was to live an exemplary life.

"Continue with caution on earth, for thou hast heard that moderation is necessary" (Sahagun, 6, pp. 121–126).

These general rules barely touch on the proliferation of precepts for a good and cautious life which governed one's roles as an individual person, as a family member, and as a man or a woman.

MALE–FEMALE ROLES

Men were expected to work hard, to labor in the fields, at their skilled trades and crafts, and on public works. They were the family providers whose wisdom and experience came with age. In the fullness of a man's years, he became a repository of ancient lore, and was expected to lead an exemplary life. The ideal family head was thrifty and an advisor and teacher of his children and any orphaned offspring of his relatives.

Aztec women were expected to work just as hard. Their lives revolved around household chores, child-rearing, and weaving. The noblewoman was "patient, gentle, kind, benign, hard-working .... She governs, leads, provides for one, arranges well, administers peacefully" (Sahagun, 10, p. 46). She had to cook well and to manage servants who did the marketing and food preparation. A hard-working common woman had to be vigorous, long-suffering, calmly accepting of reprimands, "pious, chaste, careful of her honor" (Sahagun, 10, p. 51). Above all, every woman strove to be a skilled weaver: "The good weaver of designs is skilled—a maker of varicolored capes, an outliner of designs, a blender of colors, a joiner of pieces, a matcher of pieces. She weaves designs. She selects. She weaves tightly" (Sahagun, 10, p. 96).

The ideal Aztec woman was a paragon at the loom, a capable cook, and, like her husband, a critical influence on her children. She could own property, take

cases to court, and enter into business contracts, but her legal rights were inferior to those of men. A husband was expected to respect his wife's rights, however, and an individual woman could exercise great personal influence and power.

Children were expected to be well-behaved and respectful. A good son was "obedient, humble, gracious, grateful, reverent;" a daughter, "untouched, pure, a virgin . . . obedient, honest, . . . well taught, well trained" (Sahagun, 6, pp.12–13). Often, of course, the ideal of a perfectly obedient child was not attained. Some sons never listened: "Training, teaching, reprimands, corrections go in one ear and out the other." The greatest sin was to be disrespectful, vain, and "given to pleasure" (Sahagun, 6, p. 13).

This was a society of conformers, and it expended much energy in reinforcing the notion of conformity. Not everyone, of course, trod the straight and narrow path of moderation and sobriety. There were those who drank to excess, who failed to cultivate their fields, who stole from their neighbors, and women who took

An Aztec woman teaching her daughter to weave. From the Codex Mendoza. Courtesy, Bodleian Library, Oxford. MS. Arch. Selden A.1. folio 60.

to prostitution for all the usual reasons. Parents, priests, and teachers pointed awful, warning fingers at those who deviated from the straight and narrow pathway of righteousness. They inveighed against drunken old men, lazy farmers, thieves, and dissolute youths. Just to be uncooperative, to act "without consideration," was a particular sin. Gaudy, wicked women came in for their share of derision, especially courtesans, the "bad maiden . . . who yields herself to others—a prostitute, a seller of herself . . . she goes about shamelessly presumptuously . . ." (Sahagun, 10, p. 55). (No one knows who patronized the harlots, but their services were in demand at the markets, and, presumably, at feasts.) Only a prudent and conforming people could have supported the ordered hierarchy of Aztec society, and prudence and conformity were the precepts handed on from parents to children within the family circle.

KINSHIP AND MARRIAGE TIES

The daily life of every Mexica resembled a complicated skein, not only of social classes, but also of kin ties and

A harlot exhibiting her wares. From the Florentine Codex. Courtesy, University of Utah Press, Salt Lake City. Drawing, Sally Black.

marriage rules. Kinship ties were traced through both the mother and father, so any family member had, say, aunts on both the father's and mother's side. With men marrying in their early twenties, and women in their mid- to late-teens, immediate, living kin ties could extend back perhaps five or more generations, to great-great grandparents who had "reached extreme old age" in their eighties or nineties.

The rules of inheritance governed not only the handing down of personal and household property, but membership in a social class and sometimes the titles that went with it. One inherited membership in a social class. If born a noble, for example, that made one eligible for various political, religious, and even military appointments. But that eligibility also depended on personal ability. By the late fifteenth century, there were far more nobles than there were official positions, so military or other achievements gave one the edge among a pool of theoretically qualified applicants. Therefore the highest positions of state were jealously guarded by the families that held them and passed to the most eligible son rather than the one most purely qualified by inheritance. The goal was not only to find a legitimate heir, but a competent successor as well.

We know little of the rules whereby the Aztecs inherited property, but it passed from father to son or daughter, or from mother to children. There seems to have been considerable flexibility of choice. Usually, lands and house sites were divided between several close relatives, even to distant connections like in-laws, rather than being passed to a single person. Household things like pots and grindstones were passed from mother to daughter, while prized jewelry and such prestigious items as feathered shields went from father to son, or from brother to brother. One could even inherit tribute rights, with the most promising and capable descendents receiving the lion's share of the inheritance.

The Mexica married within their social classes, and tended to select mates within their own lineage groups, but they were forbidden to marry immediate members of their nuclear family. Polygamy was permitted among the nobility, although commoners were apparently monogamous, and some rulers fathered dozens of noble children by many wives. Political marriages were commonplace for rulers and nobility, for such alliances were vital to solidifying relationships with powerful neighbors. By marrying his daughter to a neighboring, but subordinate, ruler, a shrewd leader could ensure close ties with a lesser state through the offspring of the marriage. Such relationships sometimes extended through many generations, and they were common in the Valley of Mexico during the fifteenth and early sixteenth centuries.

A newly married couple decided where to live based not so much on strict residence rules, perhaps, as on perceived advantage: land available to the family, population density, and whether a nuclear or joint family was practicable. These relatively flexible residence patterns enabled households to make maximum use of scarce agricultural land. Most households occupied a house that opened on to an enclosed patio, where most household activities took place. The size of one's residence depended on one's social class, affluence, and occupation. Many newly married couples lived with either the bride's or the bridegroom's parents, an arrangement that often upset one side of the family or the other. Many joint households consisted of between two and six nuclear families, formed by brothers, fathers, and sons, or more distant male relatives. The head of the household was invariably a married man, normally the elder brother, who was "bearer of all the burdens" (Sahagun, 10, p. 9), even if married daughters brought their families to live with their parents. Then, as now, great tact was needed on the part of in-laws: "The bad father-in-law [is] a sower of discord . . . , a divider, a scatterer of others," writes Sahagun (10, p. 7).

THE CALPULLI

Every Mexica was a member of a *calpulli,* or "big house," a group of families that claimed descent through the male line from a common ancestor. The calpulli was an ancient institution and a vital mechanism for state organization. Indeed, calpullis were basic to the entire economic, military, political, and religious organization of the empire. The four quarters of Tenochtitlan were organized into neighborhoods based on them. Even the smallest village, with its houses grouped around a central plaza and market, was founded on the pervasive calpulli organization. Commoners never dealt individually with the state. Rather, the calpullis served as the interface between citizens and government, paying taxes in labor and produce and allocating people to carry out public works. Depending on its size, each calpulli was expected to raise a company of two to four hundred soldiers in wartime. Each had its own temples and ran its own school.

Of equal importance to the smooth functioning of society, the calpulli provided stability of land ownership. Each controlled a territorial unit and each administered a land distribution system.

From the family point of view, the most important functions of the calpulli revolved around land ownership. The sixteenth-century Spanish judge Alonso de Zorita wrote in 1585 that "the lands these barrios possess they obtained in the distribution made when these people first came to this land. At that time each lineage or group obtained its shares or lots of land with their bounds, which were assigned to them and their descendants" (Zorita, 1963, pp. 106–107). The calpulli held its land communally, and no individual person could dispose of that land although he or she could enjoy its use for life and pass it on to his or her heirs.

The *calpullec,* the calpulli leader, was an elected head man who assumed the vital responsibility of allocating, guarding, and defending calpulli lands. A calpullec in Tenochtitlan attended daily on the chief tribute collector at the palace to receive orders for labor and other services. He carried out his duties with the assistance of a group of influential elders. The office was not hereditary, although, on the death of a calpullec, the elders often selected the son or another close rela-

146

tive, if he were a suitable candidate. The electors looked for wisdom, experience, and diplomatic ability in filling this critical post, for a capable man could be a powerful advocate with the central government and would carry out his duties of land stewardship with sensitive care.

The calpullec maintained the carefully updated maps that showed the boundaries of the calpulli's communal land, the individual plots, and the allocation of gardens to individual families. He kept close track of what land was vacant or badly cultivated. The calpullec and his advisers parceled out acreage, basing their allocations on changing family needs and on a family's capacity to work it. "He [the calpullec] has pictures on which are shown all the parcels, and the boundaries, and where and with whose fields the lots meet, and who cultivates what field, and what land each one. . . . The Indians continually alter these pictures according to the changes worked by time," wrote Alonso de Zorita (1963, p. 107). Once allocated, the land was treated as the property of that family. It could be taken away from them only if they failed to work it properly for two years. And they could apply for substitute lands if their present fields were unproductive or too small. Each family made a contribution in produce and labor to the calpullec to defray the cost of his office. Even so, it was an expensive office to hold, for the obligations of hospitality for elders and household heads were heavy and unrelenting.

No one knows exactly what size a large urban calpulli could reach, but it is likely that some contained many thousands of members. The largest ones had organizing officials known as *tequitlatoque,* men responsible for collecting tribute and organizing labor levies. They in turn worked with individuals responsible for groups of a hundred men or up to twenty households. Like everything else in Aztec society, the calpulli acted as channels of goods and services to the state.

In Tenochtitlan, a city of artisans and traders, the term *tlaxilacalli* was often used to refer to an urban calpulli. Often craftsmen or merchants lived within a well-defined neighborhood. Seven such areas in Tlate-lolco were occupied by merchants alone, while feather-workers had their own quarters there as well. The latter usually worshipped their own dieties and often came from areas outside the Valley of Mexico like the Gulf Coast or Oaxaca.

The calpulli was probably the most important social institution in Aztec society. It provided a mechanism by which people cooperated with one another and gave a large measure of security to everyone. The state used it not only to govern a teeming and diverse urban and rural population, but to recruit large numbers of people at short notice for public works or armies of conquest. The conquering Spaniards totally failed to comprehend the workings of the calpulli and the communal system of land ownership that went with it. They assumed that every family owned the land it cultivated simply be-cause Spanish peasants did so. Until this assumption quickly reduced many Mexica to abject poverty and starvation, the closely knit ties of family and calpulli provided a framework for an evolving and well-ordered life cycle that began with pregnancy and continued through birth, childhood and education, right through to the grave.

THE LIFE CYCLE

Pregnancy

An Aztec woman gained prestige and honor by bearing children. A pregnancy was a gift of the gods, an occa-sion for a celebratory feast and many congratulatory orations. The mother-to-be was exorted to be humble and hardworking, to "be a guardian of the treasure of our lord." She was advised not to "make too much sport with the one who is with thee. Especially are ye not to be excessive in the carnal act. . . . It will cause it to be feeble; it will come forth with lamed fingers [and] toes" (Sahagun, 6, p. 142). No pregnant woman walked abroad at night lest the baby be exposed to ghosts. Again, the virtues of prudence and moderation would prevent accidents.

During the seventh or eighth month, the family consulted a midwife. After some preliminary orations, the midwife "put the maiden in the sweatbath, where she massaged the pregnant woman's abdomen to set the baby correctly in the womb" (Sahagun, 6, p. 155). And she gave strict instructions. The mother must eat well and avoid lifting heavy weights, working hard, and taking fright. Violating these directives could result later in birth defects, even death during childbirth. The sweatbath was also used to accelerate labor. So were herbal expectorants, even ground up opossum tails. (No one knows how successful these remedies were). During labor, the midwife shook the mother and kicked her in the back to aid the birth. Babies who died before delivery were dismembered *in utero* with an obsidian knife and removed limb by limb. If the mother died in childbirth, she was revered as a goddess and buried with great ceremony. Relatives had to guard her body carefully because soldiers sometimes tried to cut pieces off the corpse. Warriors going into battle cherished the hair and middle fingers highly as talismans to bring them courage and success against the enemy.

Birth and Infancy

The midwife cut the umbilical cord of the newborn child, then washed it and wrapped it in swaddling clothes. (A boy's cord was dried and later abandoned on a battlefield so that he was dedicated to war; a girl's was buried by the hearth to symbolize her devotion to the household.) Meanwhile, the midwife praised the mother as a brave warrior returned victorious from the battlefield. Then she addressed the infant: "Precious necklace, precious feather, precious green stone, precious bracelet, precious torquoise, thou wert created in the place of duality, the place [above] the nine heavens. . . . Thou hast come to reach the earth, the place of torment, the place of pain, where it is hot, where it is cold, where the wind bloweth. It is the place of one's affliction . . ." (Sahagun, 6, p. 176).

From the moment of birth, an Aztec child became aware that the world was a place of hard work and

suffering. This ethic was reinforced by the constant greetings and orations of visiting relatives: "Thou wilt work like a slave, thou wilt labor, thou wilt suffer weariness here on earth. For this reason wert thou sent" (Sahagun, 6, p. 177). Directly after the child's birth the parents consulted a soothsayer who predicted the child's fate by referring to the *tonalamatl,* the Book of Days. The day and time of birth determined whether the child would be honorable or dishonorable, rich or poor. An auspicious day was chosen for the ritual bathing and naming of the child. A male child received a shield and miniature bow and arrows, as well as a cape and loin cloth. Such was the importance of textiles in Aztec life that a girl received spindle whorls and other items that symbolized her destiny as a skilled weaver. Most commoners named their children after the day they were born, but the nobles often chose more flamboyant names. Moctezuma, for example, means "Angry Lord." The birth of a child was one of the most special days in a family's life, and it was celebrated with much feasting and speech-making.

Bathing an infant. From the Florentine Codex. Courtesy University of Utah Press, Salt Lake City. Drawing, Sally Black.

Childhood and Education

Exhortations to live a respectable and honest life continued unabated from the moment of birth. Infants and children below the age of about five were not expected to work. They remained close to home and were praised for being happy, strong, and healthy. Commoners' children started to carry out household chores, carrying firewood and water, as early as age four or five. Slightly older children would carry goods to market and help with fishing or farming. If the family had a craft, such as feather-working or metallurgy, the child now began to learn that. The parents and immediate family assumed the responsibility for inculcating basic morality and behavior. Young children listened to constant admonitions and formal orations reminding them that moderation and hard work were the keys to success in a dangerous, uncertain world—the basic rule for the exemplary life. Little children were scolded, but the punishments became more severe as they entered their teens: beatings with maguey spines or sticks, or being forced to inhale the smoke of burning chilis.

While boys of noble birth were prepared for a life of military and public service, girls—both aristocrats and commoners—learned most of their skills at home. They began spinning cotton as early as age four, were cleaning house by the time they were twelve. A girl of thirteen could grind maize, make tortillas, and cook palatable meals. She learned the basics of weaving at much the same time. All these skills were regarded as essential preparation for marriage. Girls received little formal education outside the home, but, along with the boys, they did attend the "House of Song," which was attached to every temple, between the ages of twelve and fifteen.

The time spent in the *cuicacalli,* the "House of Song," was a critical period in Aztec education, for here everyone, noble and commoner, went through a highly structured curriculum of singing, dancing, and music. Each calpulli had its own cuicacalli where el-

Training and punishing children. At top, (left) boy of eleven being punished with chili smoke; (right) girl of the same age being threatened with chili smoke. Second row, (left) boy of twelve tied hand and foot and stretched out on damp ground; (right) girl of twelve sweeping. Two lower rows, (left) boys of thirteen and fouteen carrying rushes, paddling a loaded canoe, and fishing; (right) girls of the same ages grinding maize, preparing food, and learning weaving. From the Codex Mendoza. Courtesy, Bodleian Library, Oxford. MS. Arch. Selden A.1. folio 60.

derly men and women assembled the students an hour before sunset for long sessions of dancing and recitation. Here everyone, however humble, learned the correct songs and orations for every major religious ceremony on the Aztec calendar. These incantations spoke of the Aztec cosmos, the creation, and the great migrations of the ancestors. They dealt with the roles of mortals on earth, and of the relationships between gods and humans. At the cuicacalli everyone learned about their cultural heritage and about the mystical and highly symbolic world that surrounded them.

Beyond this, formal education was for young men, and especially for the sons of nobility. When they were between twelve and fifteen, noble boys attended the *calmecac,* temple schools which trained them for a variety of responsible roles. Every calmecac stressed manual labor. The students spent long hours at hard physical work and in basic military training. Long before they entered school, young nobles grew tufts of long hair on the backs of their heads, tufts that would not be shorn until the youth captured a warrior in battle. Great was the shame for a young man who failed to secure a

Teenage boys entering a temple school (above), and a "House of Song" (below). From the Codex Mendoza. Courtesy, Bodleian Library, Oxford. MS. Arch. Selden A.1. folio 61. Drawing, Sally Black.

153

prisoner promptly, for the girls would insult him for his cowardice. Part of the military training included practical experience on the battlefield, where seasoned warriors protected the boys and taught them "how one fought; how a spear was fended off with a shield...."

Calmecac training varied from school to school. Each was dedicated to a particular diety. Some prepared young men for the priesthood. The students acquired a great deal of specialized knowledge depending on the school—whether legal, military, or mechanical. Whatever they learned, however, they learned most of it by rote, memorizing orations and "songs they called the gods' songs. They were inscribed in the books. And well were all taught the reckoning of the days, the book of dreams, and the book of years" (Sahagun, 3, p. 65). The calmecac was the place where all of the sophistication and intense symbolism of Aztec civilization came together and was passed on to future generations. Since only a handful of people could read the codices, all of this information had to be memorized and transmitted orally. And it had to be learned well. The student who misbehaved or deviated from the norm, the ideal of conformity, was harshly punished. Drunkards and other serious offenders were shot through with arrows or even burned to death. Even minor peccadillos were punished with sharp and very painful pricks from a maguey spine.

Male commoners in their midteens received a more limited formal schooling in the *telpochcalli,* a military school run by their calpulli. They left home to work and sleep at school, spending long hours digging canals, sweeping streets, making mud bricks, or tending the fields. The main thrust of instruction was weapons training, for every young adult male was expected to go to war when calpulli levies were called up. Some religious instruction completed the curriculum. The supervising elders made sure that everyone fasted at the appointed times, maintained rigorous discipline, and meted out drastic punishments to nonconformers.

Once graduated from the calmecac or telpochcalli, the young man of twenty was deemed an adult, ready to assume the responsibilities of marriage and society. The average free citizen spent the rest of his life as a farmer, or engaged in trading or a craft occupation. Noblemen could embark on any number of careers—as soldiers, lawyers, priests, or officials of the state.

Marriage

Theoretically at any rate, Aztec marriage ceremonies were elaborate and time-consuming. The father decided that his son was ripe for marriage. "Let us seek a woman for him, lest he somewhere do something. He may somewhere molest a woman; he may commit adultery. For it is his nature; he is matured" (Sahagun, 6, p. 127). The parents threw a feast of chocolate, tamales, and sauces. His teachers were summoned to the festivities to release him from their care, and then discussions as to a suitable teenage wife could begin. Once the youth's kin had agreed on a candidate, professional matchmakers were engaged to negotiate the details. (We do not know how much say, if any, the boy and girl had in the matter). The old women shuttled back and forth from the girl's house for several days until agreement on the bride's dowry was reached. Then the family consulted the soothsayers about an auspicious day for the marriage ceremony. "Thereupon there were preparations; the ashes were prepared, ground cacao was prepared, flowers were secured, smoking tubes were purchased . . . all night they were occupied; perhaps two or three days the woman made tamales . . ." (Sahagun, 6, p. 129).

Received in order of their precedence, the guests at the bride's house included not only "those who were illustrious," but the bridegroom's teachers and contemporaries, as well as kin from both families. The guests ate and drank all day. Towards sunset the bride was bathed and decked out in red feathers by her family. Her face was painted red and she was placed on a reed mat before the family hearth. The bridegroom's elderly relatives now addressed her, admonishing her to "forever now leave childishness, girlishness," to be respectful, to fulfill her household obligations, and never to

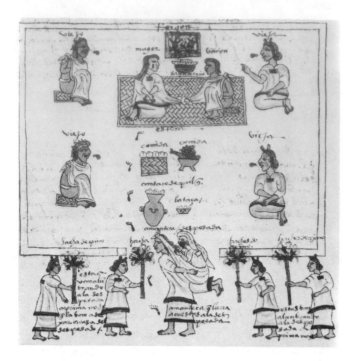

embarrass her elders. When the girl had protested her inadequacies, she was carried to the bridegroom's house in a ceremonial, torchlit procession. There the young couple were placed on mats in front of the hearth. Gifts were exchanged, and the matchmakers tied the man's cape to the woman's shift to symbolize the union. The couple were then fed tamales and escorted to a private room in the house of the groom's family where they remained in seclusion for four days, closely guarded by the matchmakers. The fifth day saw more elaborate ceremonies and feasting during which both bride and bridegroom were constantly reminded of their marital duties. "Go diligently; go covering thyself with dust; for it is our way of doing things on earth . . . for already we abandon thee . . . ," counselled their families (Sahagun, 6, pp. 132–133). Only after this was the marriage consummated and normal life for the couple begun.

Relatively few families could probably afford such a highly elaborate marriage ceremony. More likely, most

A marriage ceremony. At top, the couple's garments are tied together in front of the hearth as the elders exhort them to "go diligently." At center, a turkey stew and a pitcher of pulque. At bottom, the bridegroom's female relatives carry the bride to the groom's home. From the Codex Mendoza. Courtesy, Bodleian Library, Oxford. MS. Arch. Selden A.1. folio 61.

commoners enjoyed less formal weddings. But once the ceremonies were over, the couple set out to raise a family and to live the carefully monitored exemplary life that custom prescribed. Most people lived well-regulated, humdrum lives, rising before dawn for a long morning of toil before a light snack of maize or chocolate in mid-morning and a heavy meal at midday. Everybody rested during the heat of the day before going back to work in the afternoon. Many farmers, traders, and fishermen varied their activities with the season, so some patterns of daily life changed. But always most people retired early after a light meal, probably a short time after sunset. Like most big cities, however, Tenochtitlan was always busy—with priests conducting ceremonies and shifts of watchmen guarding against surprise attacks.

While everyone worked hard, people had plenty of diversions as well. Nobles and commoners alike enjoyed the ball game *tlachtli*. Hundreds of spectators watched important matches and wagered everything from precious stones to slaves, even houses and land, on the outcome. Tlachtli was played on a special ball court between 100 and 200 feet (30.48–61 m) long. A line was drawn across the center to divide the court in half. Two rings were erected at either end of the divider. Specially trained players dressed in gloves, gir-

Tlachtli, the ball game. Two players face one another, with wagers of feathers and a jade necklace lying at the corners of the court. Redrawn from Diego Duran.

dles, and deerskin hip guards to protect themselves against injury from the fast-flying rubber ball. The players propelled the ball back and forth with the aid of hip or knee. Hitting the ball with any other part of the body was a foul, and so was failing to hit the ball across the center line. The team that managed to score a goal by hitting the ball through one of the two rings was the immediate winner. Tlachtli was played on important ritual occasions, but also to settle wagers, and simply for entertainment.

Everyone played *patolli,* a dice game played with marked white beans. The players moved six pebble counters around a board according to the fall of the beans. Even in this conformist society, some people gambled compulsively on patolli, and as in every urban society, their antisocial habits got them into trouble: "The gamblers addicted to this game always went about with the mats under their armpits and with the dice tied up in small cloths." The addicts would croon and speak to their dice, begging them "to be favorable, to come to their aid in that game" (Duran, 1971, p. 304). Patolli tournaments attracted dozens of big-time gamblers who wagered enormous sums on the outcome. Compulsive gambling reduced many people to penury: "They were forced to gamble their homes, their fields, their corn granaries, their maguey plants. They sold their children in order to bet and even staked themselves and became slaves" (Duran, 1971, p. 318).

Beyond recreations like these, and, of course, the interruptions of family celebrations, the even tenor of the daily round was also punctuated by occasional bouts of public service and by regular religious festivals. Eighteen monthly ceremonies took place during the solar year involving fasting, singing, dancing, and sometimes human sacrifices. Some of these were for everyone, and others were for particular members of the community —merchants, children, or farmers, for example. As the secular and religious calendar ticked along, less important sacred rituals also took place, some of which involved everyone in ritual penance and blood-letting to the sun god. Each segment of the community had its special religious duties and ceremonies in which offerings were made to patron gods or goddesses.

Old Age

Many people did not survive their adult years. They succumbed to disease, died in battle, or ended up as sacrificial victims. Those that did live into old age occupied an especially privileged place in society.

"The revered old man, the aged man [is] white-haired ... hardened with age ... experienced ... a successful worker." Such men were the pillars of the Aztec family, honored as repositories of ancient lore and as counselors. "The revered old woman, the noble old woman [is] one who never abandons the house ... a shelter" (Sahagun, 10, p. 11). It was the old, people over fifty, who delivered many of the orations that guided the young. They were determined to leave a respected legacy behind them. Many elderly people devoted their later lives to advising and training the young, assuming the roles of "reprehender" and "indoctrinator." They played an important part in school life and supervised many public ceremonies. As respected elders, they were accorded many special privileges. People over fifty were permitted occasionally to drink pulque to excess, a remarkable indulgence in a society that considered drunkenness a public offense among the young. Even then, moderation was expected. Sahagun records the low esteem in which habitually drunken and "luxurious" old men were held. As always, the expectation was that all citizens would live moderate, prudent lives.

The oldest people of all were in their seventies and eighties, great-great-grandparents, those "who tremble with age, [the] cougher[s], [the] totterer[s]." They enjoyed high esteem for originating "good progeny." As death neared, the dying person sometimes chose to make a last confession for sins of "evil and perverseness, debauched living," or perhaps for some serious, undetected crime. Such a confession could only be made once, in front of a reader of the sacred books

who would order penance such as blood-letting or fasting to expiate the sin before death.

Death

The Aztecs believed that warriors and women who had died in childbirth would have the most glorious afterlife. Brave soldiers killed in battle or sacrificed were thought to journey with the sun from the moment it rose until it reached its zenith. Then they rested. After they had travelled with the sun for four years, they returned to earth as hummingbirds. The women took over at the zenith, carrying the sun in a feathered litter to its setting after which they delivered it each night to *Mictlan,* the place of the dead. They would then roam about as *cihuapipiltin,* female goddesses.

The manner of one's burial depended on how one died in a society where the infant mortality rate was probably very high and considerable numbers of women died in childbirth. Some people were buried with great ceremony, among them lepers, victims struck by light-

Elders drinking pulque. From the Codex Mendoza. Courtesy, Bodleian Library, Oxford. MS. Arch. Selden A.1. folio 71.

ning, and women who perished giving birth. These last were revered like goddesses, a woman's unsuccessful struggle to deliver a child being comparable to the hero's death in battle. Those who died by drowning were also interred with honor because they had been chosen by the water gods. They enjoyed a life of ease in the happy gardens of Tlalocan, a divine paradise.

Most people had a tougher time. Dressed in their finest clothes, their bodies were carefully wrapped in a bundle of cloth and displayed for four days while the mourners feasted and chanted funeral dirges. Then they were cremated and their ashes buried in a container along with their prized possessions. These possessions and ample food supplies were vital, for the Mexica believed that the dead set out on a four-year journey through the nine layers of the underworld until they reached Mictlan, the dark void inhabited by the ancestors. The surviving relatives assisted the journey by making periodic offerings at the grave to sustain the soul on its descent. The long trip took the travellers past high mountains and through eight deserts. They braved a serpent and a green lizard, crossed the terrible "place of the obsidian-bladed winds," and "the place of the nine rivers." Like so many journeys to the underworld, the wealthy and those who had lived strictly and prudently according to the rules of life had a relatively easy passage. But woe betide those who had lived lazy and useless lives or had few worldly possessions! Their passage was fraught with horror.

From birth to death, the Mexica lived within a framework of cultural rules that compelled people to serve the gods, to cooperate with one another, and to tread carefully along the narrow footbridge that led safely across the hazardous abysses of life on earth. Admonitions and orations reminding the Aztecs of their proper roles, of proper and appropriate behavior, marked every stage of life from one's first weeks on earth. The same process of admonition and counseling ensured that the institutions and the lore of earlier generations, the very fabric of their civilization, were perpetuated for as long as the Fifth Sun shone.

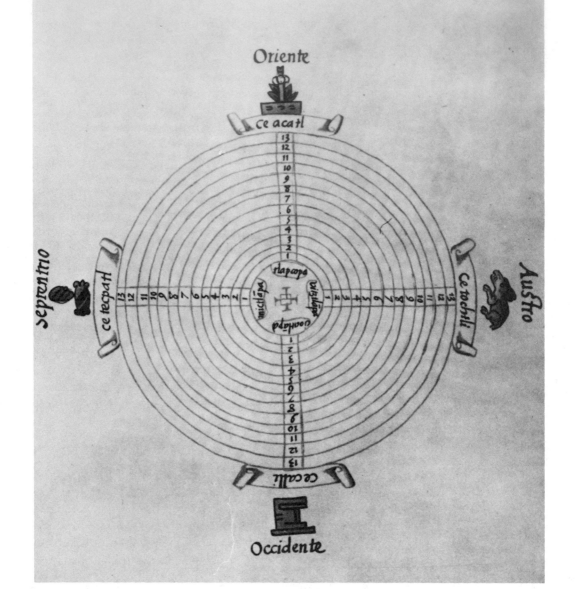

Oriente

ce acatl

septentrio

ce tecpatl

Austro

Ce tochtli

ce calli

Occidente

CHAPTER 7   Nobles and Commoners

*It is said of some ruler who enters the house
of some poor commoner ... "This ruler—
living is not with the poor"; that is to say,
he is not to enter the house of a poor man,
but he should enter the house of a ruler ..."*

Fray Bernardino de Sahagun, *General History,* 6, p. 232.

"Behold what was customary in days of old. . . ." Time
and time again, the Aztec chronicles describe decades-
old precedents and rules that defined not only the exemplary life, but also the minute details of the complex,
ranked hierarchy of Aztec society. From the time of
Moctezuma Ilhuicamina in the mid-fifteenth century,
the Mexica lived within a carefully regulated system of
social classes superimposed on the traditional family
and kin ties. These classes were based on birth, occupation, and to some degree personal achievement.

NOBLES AND COMMONERS

A fundamental division in Aztec society—a vast social
and economic chasm—separated nobles from commoners, those who held valued positions and had social
status from the rest of the people. Sahagun (10, p. 1)
was told that "one's father [is] the source of lineage.
. . . A noble person [is] great, superior of lineage . . . a
descendent of nobles." At first the qualifications for
nobility were relatively flexible. Every noble had to
trace his or her genealogy back to the first Aztec ruler,
Acamapichtli (1372–1391), a complex task given the
prevalence of polygamy and inheritance rules that trans-

*The calendar wheel. From
Volume 7 of Sahagun's*
General History. *Courtesy,
University of Utah Press, Salt
Lake City.*

163

mitted social status through either fathers or mothers. Pure-born nobles were considered direct descendents of the Toltec royal lineage to which Topiltzin Quetzalcoatl had belonged as Acamapichtli had.

At first there were enough official positions for a rapidly expanding and polygamous nobility. But by the late fifteenth century there were thousands of nobles and not enough posts for them. Moctezuma Ilhuicamina addressed the problem in the 1450s. He promulgated strict sumptuary laws—that is, laws governing personal behavior—that dictated what ornaments and cape decorations everyone might wear. These regulations extended right down to sandal styles and appropriate gold ornaments. When Moctezuma Xocoyotzin came to the throne in 1502, the nobility was enormous. He set forth stricter, but undefined, criteria for claiming noble status. The last Aztec ruler insisted that only those of pure birth could serve him, "even though he be his own brother, son of his father Axayacatl, for he considered that anyone born of a lowly woman or a slave might take after his mother and be, therefore, ineligible for his service" (Duran, 1964, p. 233). He imposed other restrictions, too. Only nobles could build two-story houses. A commoner who visited the royal palace had to use different rooms from those of the nobility.

Above all, the ruler and his nobles controlled land ownership and had exclusive rights to make use of communal labor. Through birthright, tribute levies, and appointed position, the nobility also managed nearly every strategic resource in the empire, be that gold mines, quarries, or trade routes. Subject to the jurisdiction of different courts, they were, however, generally punished far more strictly than commoners. Rulers were known to sentence members of their own family to death for improper sexual relations, for adultery, for example.

The tribute and labors of tens of thousands of commoners supported these noble privileges. The systematized obligations of individual, family, and calpulli provided the food surplusses to feed thousands of non-

A page of the "Book of Days." This sacred book contained the ritual calendar and portrayed thirteen Lords of the Day, thirteen birds, and the nine Lords of the Night associated with the day count. Each of the major deities—Quetzalcoatl, Tlaloc, and so on—was associated with a species of bird or a butterfly. Each day was also attached to a Lord of the Night, again a major deity, who rotated in turn. No one knows what the exact meanings of the Lords and birds were. From the complete facsimile edition of the series CODICES SELECTI, published by Akademische Druck- u. Verlagsanstalt, vol. XLIV: CODEX BORBONICUS.

farmers, the labor to build temples, palaces, and other public works, and the soldiers to fight wars of conquest. The humble commoner, with his coarse cape and work-worn hands, supplied a very small number of people with an endless supply of food, firewood, water, fine clothing, and a host of luxury goods that came to the markets of Tenochtitlan from all over Mexico.

A "good" commoner was no descendant of Quetzal-

coatl but simply a hardworking citizen: "The good farmer ... [is] active, agile, diligent, industrious. ... [He goes] without his sleep, without his food; he keeps vigil at night; his heart breaks. He is bound to the soil" (Sahagun, 10, p. 41). The farmer, whose destiny was unremitting toil, was as praiseworthy as the potter, who was "wiry, energetic, active ... skilled with his hands" (Sahagun, 10, p. 42). Such ideals contrast sharply with those for the nobility. "The good one of noble lineage [is] compassionate, solicitous of others. He speaks calmly, peaceably; he is just," says Sahagun (10, p. 16). Moderation, status, prudence, discretion, and success were the desired qualities.

A great deal depended on the astrological characteristics of one's birthday in the *tonalamatl,* the Book of Days. This powerful document defined the future course of everyone's life, however high or low. For a noble to be born on the day 1 Alligator meant that he "would be a lord, a ruler, he would prosper; he would be rich and healthy" (Sahagun, 4, p. 2). A commoner born on the same day would fare well too: "He would be a brave warrior—a valiant chief, esteemed, honored, and great. He would always eat" (Sahagun, 4, p. 2). Alas for those born on 9 Deer. Anyone with such a birthday was "inconsiderate, not given to silence." They were lazy, ill-tempered. "All [their] acts and efforts were repeated adultery, thievery, absconding with tribute; making off with many things by trickery, coveting, and deceiving" (Sahagun, 4, pp. 50–51).

TLATOQUE ("RULERS")

The Aztec state was in effect a tightly organized oligarchy controlled by the tlatoque of the three capitals of the Triple Alliance. The supreme leader among them was the ruler of Tenochtitlan. Each of the three tlatoque had heavy responsibilities. Each owned extensive lands as his birthright. State-organized labor forces and tribute from conquered states fell under their direct jurisdiction. They also controlled all lands within the

Nezahualpilli, the famous tlatoani of Texcoco, dressed in his finery. From the series FONTES RERUM MEXI-CANARUM, published by Akademische Druck- u. Verlagsanstalt, vol. 9: CODEX IXTLILXOCHITL.

state's domain: palace fields, temple acreage, and land used for supporting the military. The supreme leader could appropriate lands and produce and allocate them to anyone at will.

But imperial tlatoque like Moctezuma Xocoyotzin had war and conquest as their primary responsibility. "His charge was war. Hence, he determined, disposed, and arranged how war would be made," writes Sahagun (8, p. 51). He alone was responsible for the defense of the capital and the realm, for the deployment of guards and watchkeepers. The supreme rulers also served as the ultimate appeals court in important law cases and played a leading part in major religious festivals. But above all, their rule depended not on draconian force or sheer terror, but on their personal qualities and exemplary life-style: "The ruler [is] a shelter— fierce, revered, famous, esteemed. . . . The good ruler [is] a protector; one who carries [his subjects] in his arms, who unites them, who brings them together. He rules, takes responsibilities, assumes burdens. . . . He governs; he is obeyed. . . . [To him] as shelter, as refuge, there is recourse . . ." (Sahagun, 10, p. 15).

By the time of the Spanish Conquest, the tlatoani of Tenochtitlan lived in magnificent splendor, wearing the finest cotton garments and elaborately decorated capes and sandals. Moctezuma Xocoyotzin lived in an imposing palace surrounded by fine gardens and aviaries. No one could look him in the face. Even great lords had to approach him barefoot and dressed in coarse clothes. Sahagun tells us that Moctezuma Xocoyotzin's cooks prepared over two thousand different foods for him: "Hot tortillas, white tamales with beans forming a sea shell on top; red tamales; the main meal of roll-shaped tortillas and many [foods]: sauces with turkeys, quail, venison, rabbit, hare, rat, lobster, small fish, large fish; then [all manner of] sweet fruits" (Sahagun, 8, p. 39). The few lords privileged to eat in the ruler's presence did so standing up, while the tlatoani drank chocolate from a gold cup. "Sometimes at mealtimes he was attended by hunchbacks and jesters, while others sang and danced for his amusement; to those he would give what remained of the food and cacao" (Diaz, 1963, p. 227). He amused himself by wagering heavily on ball games and patolli, with special deer and bird hunts, and by singing.

Always chosen from the same family, the tlatoani was often the son or brother of his predecessor. A council of four great lords normally advised the ruler. These four counsellors were also of the royal family and were eligible for the succession. Often, a dying ruler had some say in the appointment of his successor, concerned as he was with the future efficient government of his domains. In the event that he did not, the electors would make their choice and then seek the approval of the rulers of the other Triple Alliance cities. By the same token, the ruler of Tenochtitlan had a say in his neighbors' appointments. The *Tlatocan,* a council of twelve to twenty nobles, and a separate military committee also advised the ruler, and both bodies had some say in the election of a new tlatoani. For all the checks and balances inherent in these councils and advisors, the very nature of the Aztec state concentrated most power in the hands of the supreme ruler.

The coronation of a new tlatoani was an event of the utmost political and symbolic importance. The ruler-to-be was escorted to the temple of Huitzilopochtli by a large, silent crowd. He walked up the steps to the summit supported by two priests, there to have his nose pierced for golden ornaments and to receive the regalia of state. The priests clothed him in two capes, the one blue, the other black, decorated with white skulls and bones to remind him of his own mortality. They addressed him with flowery orations, reminding him of his duties and responsibilities:

Thou wilt take over the burden, thou wilt take thy bundle, thou wilt carry the carrying frame for thy progenitors, the lords, the rulers who departed bequeathing it to thee...." Thou art to devote thyself to the great bundle, the great carrying frame, the governed. On this back, on thy lap, in thy arms our lord placeth the governed, the vassals, the common folk, the capricious, the peevish.

For yet a while thou wilt fondle them as children; thou wilt rock the cradle. Thou art yet to place the city upon thy thigh, in thy embrace. . . .

Receive, speak to those who come in anguish, and those who come meeting their fate. Be not a fool. May thou not speak hurriedly, may thou not interrupt, may thou not confound . . . arrive yet at the truth, for, it is said and it is true, thou art the replacement, thou art the image of the lord of the near, of the nigh . . . (Sahagun, 6, pp. 47–55).

After the required penance and ritual blood-letting, the ruler descended from the pyramid to receive the homage of lesser rulers and nobles who plied him with rich gifts. Then he sequestered himself in a room where he fasted and prayed for four days in silence. The coronation ended with a procession back to the palace and lengthy feasting.

The supreme lords of the Triple Alliance received tribute from many lesser tlatoque, rulers of conquered states, small towns, and lesser communities. These leaders controlled the tribute of commoners within their jurisdiction and owned their own lands that were worked by serfs. Most such offices were passed from father to son. The official positions of the tlatoque were reinforced by political marriages and by the control of communally owned lands assigned to them.

TETECUTIN

The nobles—those who the Spanish judge Alonso de Zorita called "Lords of the second kind"—were termed *tetecutin,* or "chiefs" (sing. *tecutli*). Many of them served as top officials, provincial governors, generals, or senior judges, and many spent much of their time attending the tlatoani. Moctezuma Xocoyotzin and his predecessors needed plenty of responsible officials. They presided over the fate of more than five million people who lived in at least thirty-eight provinces joined together by uneasy alliances. Itzcoatl was the first tlatoani to grant his nobles official titles. Duran records how the great official Tlacaelel petitioned the ruler to give them "titles of distinction according to their merit." Moctezuma Ilhuicamina appointed his own four closest advisers as tetecutin, giving them additional titles like *tlacochcalcatl tecutli,* "Chief of the Spear House." Tlacaelel himself was awarded both this title and that of *cihuacoatl,* "Woman Serpent."

Tetecutin held office for life, having achieved their positions by ability, especially on the battlefield. The ruler did, however, often favor a son of proven ability to succeed his father. Because their decisions were a major instrument of social control, judges were among the most influential tetecutin. Sahagun lauds the good magistrate as "just, a hearer of both sides . . . a listener to all factions, a passer of just sentences, a settler of quarrels, a shower of no favor" (Sahagun, 10, pp. 15–16). He listed no less than thirteen different types of magistrate, and every judge was expected to be dignified and "stern-visaged."

Far more than merely honorific, the tecutli title carried important privileges with it. The ruler granted estates to most of these men, so each became the head of a *teccalli,* a chiefly household to which were attached both lesser nobles and a number of commoners, either distant kin of the lord or people allocated to him. Under an appointed supervisor, the commoners living on teccalli lands worked them for the lord, provided tribute in clothing, farm produce, and labor, and supplied fuel, water, and household services. Theoretically at any rate, the lord looked after his peoples' interests and protected them. Each chief's estate housed a minor hierarchy of nobles and commoners, most of them linked by loose kin ties. (Sometimes the lands of a teccalli coincided with those of a calpulli, but the distinction between the two is obscure.)

PIPILTIN

The word *pipiltin* really means the "sons of nobles,"

but it came to stand for all of the nobility, the sons and daughters of rulers and chieftains. The pipiltin served in many capacities, and they were trained in the calmecac in all manner of esoteric subjects designed to prepare them for service to the state. Some became warriors; others, priests or petty officials supervising water rights or agricultural production; a select few, tax collectors. Many served as courtiers in Tenochtitlan or undertook diplomatic missions. Moctezuma Ilhuicamina and his successors invariably used nobles as messengers to neighboring states. The hierarchy of officialdom was carefully defined and closely supervised. "The nation has a special official for every activity, small though it were," wrote Diego Duran (1964, p. 183). "Everything was so well recorded that no detail was left out of the accounts. There were even officials in charge of sweeping...." Many were *pilli,* young nobles gaining experience and serving the state before being elevated to a higher rank. *Pipiltin* enjoyed many privileges. Not only could they wear more elaborate clothing than commoners, they were exempt from tribute and could own land.

THE PROPER ATTIRE

The age-old adage that clothes make the man applied with a vengeance to the Mexica who used raiment as a definitive guide to rank and status. One could tell the social position of a Mexica from his or her dress in the marketplace.

It was Moctezuma Ilhuicamina who promulgated the sumptuary laws that governed Aztec attire. Diego Duran enumerates some of the requirements:

Only the king and the Prime Minister Tlacaelel may wear sandals within the palace. No great chieftain may enter the palace shod, under pain of death. The great noblemen are the only ones allowed to wear sandals in the city. . . . But these sandals must be cheap and common. . . .

Only the king is to wear the fine mantles of cotton embroidered with designs and threads of different colors and featherwork.

The common people will not be allowed to wear cotton clothing, under pain of death, but only garments of maguey fiber. The mantle must not be worn below the knee and if anyone allows it to reach the ankle, he will be killed, unless he has wounds of war on his legs.

Only the king and the sovereigns of the provinces and other great lords are to wear gold-arm bands, anklets, and golden rattles on their feet at the dances . . . (Duran, 1964, pp. 130–133).

The sumptuary regulations were tightened and elaborated in later years. By the time of the Spanish Conquest, a person's clothing displayed not only rank and status, but his tribal affiliation as well. Moctezuma Xocoyotzin's first gifts to Cortes at the Gulf Coast, perhaps the most critical diplomatic gesture of his career, included the prescribed regalia for the returning god Quetzalcoatl: "Thereupon they arrayed the Captain. They put him into the turquoise [mosaic] serpent mask with which went the quetzal feather head fan . . ." (Sahagun, 12, p. 15). At this supreme moment of crisis in Mexica affairs, strict rules regulated what should be worn, what should be offered as gifts. Protocol demanded that everyone—god, ruler, noble, warrior, or commoner—had to wear the correct attire on all occasions.

Few areas of the world are dry enough, or cold enough, to preserve prehistoric textiles. The famous wool and cotton garments of coastal Peru have survived in an area where no rain falls for years on end. No early textiles have withstood the damper climate of the Aztec homeland, so archaeology can tell us nothing of the cotton raiment that dazzled the conquistadors. Our only insights into this vital aspect of life come from the codex paintings that depict properly attired gods and humans engaged in a variety of activities. They provide us with a revealing picture of the complexities of Aztec society.

Textile and costume expert Patricia Anawalt has recently completed a remarkable study of Aztec clothing based on twenty-four codices and a few surviving wall murals. After minute examination of hundreds of paintings, she discovered that each class and occupation in this tightly controlled society had its own prescribed garments and insignia of rank. Far more than mere badges, these marks of position served as actual incentives for further service to the state. Anawalt used nine pictorial documents from the Valley to compile an inventory of Aztec clothing. For example, the Codex Mendoza, drawn in about 1541–1542, includes many paintings of people wearing elaborate regalia.

Most Aztec garments were draped lengths of cotton cloth, just as they came off the loom, knotted over the shoulders as cloaks, tied at the waist as hip-cloths, or wrapped around the body to form women's skirts. Every male, whether slave, commoner, or noble, wore a *maxtlatl,* or loin-cloth. Those of the *pipiltin* were of fine cotton, decorated with a wide variety of embroidered designs. Priests and their helpers also wore distinctive loin-cloths of markedly different design from the secular garment. Many people wore hip-cloths, simple garments still worn in remote parts of Mexico to this day.

The major status garment was the *tilmatli,* the cape. Commoners and slaves wore mantles of maguey-, yucca-, or palm-fiber. Only the upper classes could wear cotton capes. The decorations, the colors, and the amount of adornment were precisely specified for every grade of noble and warrior. Capes were awarded for prowess in battle. The Codex Mendoza tells how warriors who captured two prisoners were awarded orange-bordered mantles, those who took three, finer garments. There must have been hundreds of different designs: Sahagun records at least ten different coarse maguey cape styles alone. And every part of the rectangular cape had meaning. Official regulations prescribed not only the length, fabric, and decoration of the cloak, but even the way it was knotted. So important were capes in Aztec society that they were a major tribute item. One list records that no less than 51,600 mantles were brought to Tenochtitlan every eighty days.

The most elaborate costumes were worn by war leaders and knights. One such garment was the *ehuatl,* a tunic made of feather-covered material. The color and kinds of feathers on the ehuatl identified the wearer's rank. Sahagun tells us captains wore red parrot feathers and turkey-hen feathers. The most prestigious type of Aztec military attire was the *tlahuiztli,* a complete feather-covered garment made in a variety of colors and styles. Various body colors, headpieces, and attached insignia established further differentiations in rank. Feather-covered headdresses and suits represented the coyotes, jaguars, and death-demons. Others were in the form of gods. Some headdresses matched the body garment; with others the warrior gazed out from between the open jaws of his disguise. Some fitted body suits were equipped with a ladder-like frame attached to the back and covered with feathers. The tlahuiztli was worn over the standard quilted armor, and, with the shield, headdress, and back device, symbolized that warrior's valor. An ambitious warrior literally fought his way up the clothing ranks until he achieved the coveted coyote costume or a long, feathered staff, the prize for a soldier who captured many prisoners.

Every detail of Aztec clothing reflected the intricate secular and religious protocol of a hierarchical society. The elaborate feathered uniforms of great warriors,

The various grades and uniforms of Aztec warriors. From the Codex Mendoza. Courtesy, Bodleian Library, Oxford. MS. Arch. Selden A.1. folio 67.

even the subtle nuances of commoners' capes, all conveyed intricate social messages. The most spectacular costumes were reserved for the worship of the gods, of course, and were just one more way to ensure the continuity of the Fifth Sun.

MACEHUALTIN

Most of the Mexica population was made up of *macehualtin,* free commoners: farmers, fisherfolk, and artisans. All paid tribute to the nobility in produce or manufactures and labor. Peasant levies also formed the ranks needed for massive armies of conquest. Sahagun describes their impoverishment: "Among the poor folk, among the workers of the fields and the water folk . . . only miserably, in poverty and want, were receptions and invitations made. . . . Many things were omitted or spoiled. . . . Perhaps only old withered flowers could be

175

found or come by; perhaps by leftover, bitter sauces, and stale tamales and tortillas were offered them" (Sahagun, 4, p. 124). Most macehualtin had but a handful of possessions—a tattered cape, a set of grinding stones, some cooking pots, and a sleeping mat. They lived mainly off vegetables cooked with chilis and maize products.

Relatively few commoners seem to have become well-to-do. The laws were restrictive, and it was difficult to acquire enough land and the people to work it. Those occupied in a craft needed less land than full-time farmers, but the allocation for any commoner appears to have been far from generous.

Most macehualtin were grouped into calpulli whose communally owned lands were allocated to individual families. Those who held onto larger allocations over several generations might well have done better than land-hungry neighbors. And allocations may have been more or less rigid in different areas. In some outlying regions local rulers may have assigned land on an annual basis to ensure intense cultivation of available acreage.

The state maintained its authority over every commoner, either through his or her membership in a calpulli or through the assignment of a person's services to a particular noble. This authority was reinforced by tribute normally paid in the form of service, labor on public works, and, of course, on the battlefield. The obligations for individual commoners must have varied according to their occupation, calpulli membership, and individual ranking. That there was some ranking among commoners seems unquestionable, but the details almost completely elude us. The one sure way to preference, advancement, and wealth, of course, was prowess in war. The bravest warriors could rise to the highest ranks of society and were permitted to wear finely ornamented capes.

MAYEQUE

The *mayeques,* "serfs," or "farmhands," may either have formed a class lower than free citizens, or, more

Commoners: (top) farmer; (middle) the seller of coarse maguey capes; (bottom) the clay worker. From the Florentine Codex. Courtesy, University of Utah Press, Salt Lake City.

176

likely, have been simply free but landless citizens bound to the service of a noble. Many mayeques had been deprived of their lands by economic stress or the vicissitudes of war. The Mexica would often conquer a defiant city and then allocate communally held lands to the ruler or victorious warriors, making mayeques of the previous owners, mere tenants who worked the land for new masters. The mayeques were menial laborers, deprived of the privileges of calpulli membership, many of whom served as farm laborers on the large estates of the nobility

Alonso de Zorita describes how a mayeque was forbidden to leave the land to which he was attached. "The sons and heirs of the lords of such lands succeeded to them; and the land passed together with the mayeques who lived on it, and with the same obligation of service and rent. . . . The rent consisted in payment of part of the mayeque's harvest to the lord, and in working a piece of land for the lord . . ." (Zorita, 1963, p. 183). The mayeques also provided domestic service, firewood, and water. Exempt from paying tribute to the state, they paid it instead to the noble to whom they were assigned. Mayeques were, however, liable for military service and subject to the same laws as commoners. As the Aztec nobility expanded, so the demand for laborers rapidly increased. Many people displaced by the Mexicas' constant military campaigns were drafted as mayeques, faceless bodies who fed and served the burgeoning class of pipiltin.

TLACOTIN

The buying and selling of *tlacotin,* "slaves," was a lucrative business throughout the empire at the time of the Conquest. The ever-increasing nobility required ever more laborers to serve in their households. Slave merchants operated from as far away as the Tabasco region of the Gulf Coast and frequented human markets at Azcapotzalco and Itzocan. "They bring as many slaves to be sold in that market [Tlatelolco] as the Portuguese bring Negroes from Guinea," wrote Bernal Diaz (1963, p. 232).

Any commoner had the option of becoming a slave. One could assume the status of *tlacoti* by exchanging one's services for the food to survive or to expiate a crime like theft. One could also sell oneself or a member of one's family into slavery to settle gambling debts or to pay off some other financial obligation. A merchant had the right to enslave members of a deceased debtor's family. But the most common reasons for becoming a slave were either failure to pay tribute or extreme poverty. Sahagun describes the distress of the poverty-striken commoner who had but the most threadbare capes and loin cloths. He "lived in poverty, in his house, exposed to inclement weather. Never was it warm; old, worn mats and seats were strewn about. No one swept. Rubbish was all about and surrounded him" (Sahagun, 4, p. 31). An indigent person could appear before at least four witnesses and declare his or her wish to become a slave. The successful applicant was granted twenty capes and sufficient resources for a year before the period of servitude began. The person who assumed the responsibility for the slave usually provided basic subsistence and clothing.

Some household slaves assumed positions of considerable authority in noble houses. Their owners might have the right to their labor, but slaves still retained the right to own land and could marry whomever they wished. Children born to slaves were free citizens. One could only acquire the status of a tlacoti, for slavery was a reversible condition, almost never an inherited one. Slavery was a popular institution in times of famine, when one could plead poverty, become a slave, and be assured something to eat at least. Many families sold their children into slavery during the great famine of Moctezuma Ilhuicamina's reign. "They would trade a child for a small basket of maize and the owner was obliged to maintain the infant while the famine lasted. If the father or mother wished to ransom him later they were obliged to pay for all his maintenance" (Duran, 1964, p. 147). Most of the state's *tameme,* or

178

porters, were slaves. They carried the thousands of burdens of food, merchandise, and tribute that reached the capital each year. Slavery was a valuable asset to the Mexica, but it never became the pervasive social disease that afflicted classical Athens or the Roman Empire.

People captured in war were the lowest of the low. These people, and those sent to Tenochtitlan and other capitals as tribute victims, lost even their right to life. As sacrificial victims, they were the property of the gods.

THE STRATIFIED SOCIETY

Aztec society was only a few centuries old at the time of the Spanish Conquest. When Tenochtitlan was founded in 1325, Mexica society was basically tribal, with only a handful of nobles as leaders. But fifteenth-century Aztec society was highly stratified, with a tiny elite ruling over thousands of humble commoners. The broad subdivision of Aztec society into nobles and commoners was an umbrella for a host of specialist occupations, described elsewhere in these pages. Some of these specialists, such as merchants, priests, and warriors, developed social hierarchies of their own that occasionally cut across the well-established lines of class and customary tribute-giving. The social hierarchy relied on a network of social and economic dependence that bound nobles and commoners to one another through obligations of service.

The changes in Aztec society coincided with the rapid growth of Tenochtitlan from a mere town into a large city. The material changes were obvious: more imposing ceremonial buildings; a rapidly expanding urban population; artisans and merchants flocking to Tenochtitlan's markets from hundreds of miles around. But even greater changes in social life marked the shift from a kin-based, tribal society into an urban civilization with distinct social classes based not so much on kin ties and common ownership of land as on status at birth, and, to some degree, prowess in war and economic acumen.

At the time of the Conquest, Tenochtitlan was still divided into quarters and residential areas where different kin groups lived. But the ultimate control over land had passed from these kin groups to the ruler. He acquired land by conquest and parcelled it out to worthy nobles as their private property. In the long term, this meant that land became a means for the nobility to strengthen their hold over the kin leaders, who had always been the traditional authorities on land ownership. These land awards strengthened the position of the nobility as a separate class in Aztec society, while commoners, organized in their kin groups, slipped into a lower order.

By 1519, Aztec society was embarked on a course of fundamental, even radical, change. Despite strong vertical kin ties between nobles and commoners, the trend was towards increased separation between the ruling class and the rest of the population. Communally held land taken through conquest was then farmed by its previous owners as mere serfs who paid tribute not to the state but to the aristocratic owner. Free commoners farming communally owned land did send tribute to the state. Theoretically at any rate, the volume of agricultural tribute flowing to Tenochtitlan would have dropped over time. But there is no real reason to expect that it did, partly because slavery—and we are guessing here—may have begun to play a more important role in Aztec society in the decades before the Conquest.

The number of slaves in Aztec society was probably relatively small. Many of them transported commodities and tribute to Tenochtitlan, for a civilization without draft animals places a heavy load on human backs. Other slaves worked for noble households. But an increasingly stratified society needs to maintain high levels of tribute—especially in agricultural produce—to feed more and more nonfarmers. So the state may have permitted commoners to own slaves as the extra farm laborers required to produce material for tribute, thereby offsetting the loss of tribute from acreage alienated to private use. The new fiat also served to encapsulate the common people and their corporate lands within an increasingly rigidly organized urban society where rank and military prowess counted for everything.

Fifteenth-century Tenochtitlan stood at the hub of an exploitative state with a stratified social system where every artisan, merchant, commoner, serf, and slave worked for the benefit of a tiny minority. Every exhortation, every law stressed prudence, order, and moderation, the need to conform to the established order. Alonso de Zorita (1963, pp. 186–187) realized this when he wrote of pre-Conquest times that "there was good order and harmony as concerns the kinds of tribute paid by the subjects, for each province or town gave tribute according to its climate, people, and lands. Each town or province paid tribute in the things that were grown there, so the people did not have to leave their natural surroundings to seek tribute." Authority and tribute flowed up and down a social pyramid that was erected on a solid base of close family ties, ancient lineage connections, and communal ownership of land among the commoners.

quechol ieheatl ipe pech mochioa,
ixaniençie italapachio tlauhque
chol. anoço tla tlapa lpalli ihuitl
auh mizjtli ipepech mochioa inaz
tlapalli ihuitl, cannoie quimope
pechtia intozcuicuil, inhuitl in
motenehoa coztlapalli, çan mopa,
mocoztieapa. mocozpa tleco icucie
ipan quaqualaca in tlapalli, çacatlas
calli, tlaxococtl monammetia: auh
eakpan motequisquiuia, inieoac in
omotequisquiui, inicomoçenauh,
inizquiuae icac tlapepech toztl, ini
huu tlaoatzalli: inienouan omote,
tecac, omotzacoaz, impan icheatl
mepan tlacuilolli, çatzpan mocokaa
Auh inicoac centeil momanacoa
paltontli ipan moçaloa ca amatl,
oceppa ipan micuiloa in omocru
cuic machiotl, intlacuituitl o
mochiuh. icheatl ipan iecaui im
huitlachioalli, ipan mocenealoa
inahuitl oapalli, aço suchitlacui
lolli, aço quilla cuilolli, anoço itla
tlaixiptlaiotl inmochioaz, inaço
quenapu tlamachtli, intlauelittaa
lli. Iniecac omicuilo, inomothu

CHAPTER 8 Artisans and Merchants

I suspect that if I said to a market woman accustomed to going from market to market: "Look, today is market day in such and such a town. What would you rather do, go from here right to Heaven or to that market?" I believe that this would be her answer: "Allow me to go to the market first, and then I will go to Heaven."

Diego Duran, *Book of the Gods and Rites*, 1971, p. 275.

A page from Volume 9 of Sahagun's General History, beginning, "Here is told how those of Amantlan, the ornamenters, perform their task." Courtesy, University of Utah Press, Salt Lake City.

"When we arrived at the marketplace ... we were astounded at the great number of people and the quantities of merchandise, and at the orderliness and good arrangements that prevailed. . . ." Bernal Diaz (1963, p. 232) and his fellow conquistadors marvelled at finding a non-European society capable of producing and marketing an astonishing array of products that they obtained from every corner of their world. The elaborate organization and channelling of creative energy required to achieve this depended far less on innovative technology than on the systematized labor of thousands of anonymous people, those who moved stone blocks, those who created exotic ornaments with feathers or metal, those who carried loads, those who drained swamps, those who designed canals, and those who laid out temples and palaces. The key to it all was occupational specialization. The Mexica honored and respected good artisans, people with detailed knowledge and special skills. These people lived within social hierarchies of their own in which their positions were measured as much by skill and technical expertise as they were birth.

The various experts, artisans and administrative specialists, such as scribes, depended on an intricately organized network of designers, producers, porters, buyers and sellers, tax-collectors, and so on. Most of them dealt in luxury goods—exotic substances and goods from distant places. Every village manufactured most of its own day-to-day requirements. Local workers produced simple agricultural tools, made looms and wove cloth, turning out maguey fiber capes for commoners. But the production of luxury goods had to be much more organized. Craft specialties were big business in the Valley of Mexico, and specialized artisans, each working in tightly controlled craft guilds, inhabited entire residential quarters of the Triple Alliance cities. More than thirty recognized crafts flourished in Texcoco alone. Among these were the metal-workers, the feather-workers, jewelers who worked with jade and turquoise, and dyers and embroiderers of fine cotton fabric.

The nobility measured power, prestige, and prosperity strictly in material terms—the construction of one's house, the quality and decoration of one's clothes, the beauty and productivity of one's estate—so artisans played a critical role in society. They worked for only a tiny minority at the apex of society. Rulers even competed with each other for the services of the finest artisans at their courts. Some crafts such as feather-working and metallurgy enjoyed unusual prestige, the most expert and esteemed workers ranking not far below the nobles. Many craftspeople worked directly for the ruler and the state, fabricating the luxury goods and magnificent cult objects that played an important part in public ceremonies. Others worked for their own profit, selling their wares in the great city markets.

BASIC TECHNOLOGY

Most people had but the simplest of possessions. The

average farmer relied on stone implements: axes, grinding stones, and other domestic artifacts little changed from Stone Age times. The most elaborate domestic artifacts were fabricated in clay. Every household used pottery, and styles varied from village to village. The Aztec potters built up their vessels with strips of clay, molding the pot to the desired shape by eye. With an abundant supply of fine potting clay that turned orange when fired, the potters created goblets for drinking pulque, graters for grinding chilis, platters, roasters for cooking tortillas, and storage pots decorated with painted curvilinear and naturalistic designs. The Texcocans in particular were expert potters and traded their wares throughout the Basin, thin, polychrome vessels ornamented with sophisticated designs. Texcocan products, along with painted Cholula vessels, graced Moctezuma's table. Clay was also used for the small weights that a spinner used to twirl her whorl before weaving cotton or wool, for fabricated temple roof ornaments, and for adobe bricks.

Many commoners worked as full- or part-time specialists, as potters, mat and basket makers, carpenters, or as masons or obsidian workers. Their workshops were in their own homes, often situated near abundant supplies of the raw materials that they needed. They sold their products or exchanged them for food stuffs in city and village markets. Each general category of artisan worshipped a common patron god. Nappatecuhtli, the deity of mat-makers, oversaw the production of most household furnishings, for example. Even the ruler sat and slept on woven mats much of the time.

Utilitarian craftsmen were often capable of very fine work. The carpenters, for example, fashioned flat-bottom craft made from planks tied together with tightly drawn fibers. They also made dugout canoes from logs hollowed out with fire. Although few houses boasted wooden furniture—the ruler sometimes sat on a simple wooden throne—some were decorated with chests and screens. Unfortunately none of these survived Cortes' onslaught. Some carpenters enjoyed reputations as wood-carvers. They fashioned cylindrical drums, often

Cholula polychrome vessel with a ring stand. Height: 10.5 inches (24 cm). Courtesy, Museum of the American Indian, Heye Foundation, N.Y. Photo, Carmelo Guadagno.

carved in the form of a crouched man or an animal. They hollowed out the instrument with a carefully regulated fire, then delicately chiselled the walls to achieve exactly the right tone. Carved wooden masks were vital to the public ceremonies in which priests reenacted the deeds of the gods.

Stone-workers produced not only prosaic objects like grinding stones, but ceremonial stone boxes for storing human hearts made by pecking out lumps of lava and decorating them inside and out with reliefs depicting the honors paid to the god. Obsidian was much treasured for mirrors, polished to produce eerie and murky reflections, and also for the sacrificial knives that opened the chest cavity and tore out the victims' palpitating hearts. Even today, obsidian tools are occasionally used by modern surgeons for delicate procedures such as eye surgery.

THE METAL-WORKERS

The most intense craft specialization occurred in the cities, where groups of artisans often lived within the same calpulli, each in its own residential quarter. This close-knit residence pattern enabled the artisans to organize their own people in ranked guilds and to train their successors in organized apprenticeships. The products of these skilled craftsmen—goldsmiths, silversmiths, painters, lapidaries, and feather-workers—were strictly reserved for the nobility. Perhaps the most highly valued of all were the metal-workers.

Metal-working arrived in Mexico during Toltec times, about the eleventh century, having been developed somewhere to the south—in Panama or coastal Ecuador and Peru. Only a few, relatively simple techniques spread north to Mexico. Because the smiths knew little of alloying tin or lead with copper to make durable bronze tools, they mostly made simple, soft-edged implements, dancing bells, and body ornaments from soft, lustrous metals. Gold and silver were widely used for ornaments and ceremonial objects, never for

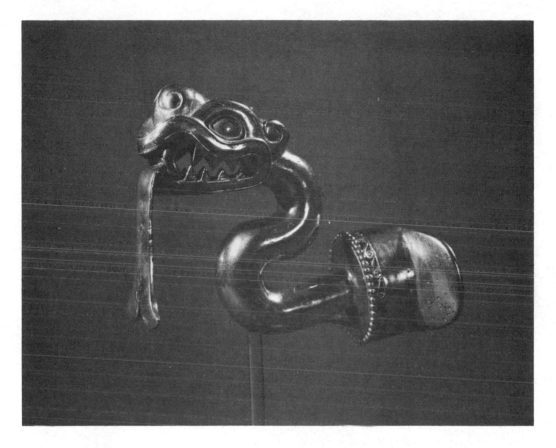

Gold lip plug made in the Mixtec style, so designed that the forked tongue moves within the snake's jaw. The Mixteca were esteemed goldsmiths whose products were in great demand among the Aztec nobility. Height. 2.75 inches (7 cm). Courtesy, American Museum of Natural History (negative number 2A7477).

everyday things. The ruler restricted the privilege of wearing gold and silver ornaments so carefully that many metal-workers enjoyed a special relationship with the palace.

No copper, gold, or silver was found in the immediate confines of the Valley of Mexico. Some came from mountain and coastal rivers and streams, some from mines deep in the mountains. Copper and gold were collected in nugget form, or traded as dust in quill containers. The smiths melted the ore in simple, charcoal-fired furnaces. Relays of workers blew on the flames through a tube. Regular supplies of ore and smelted metal flowed to the Triple Alliance capitals as tribute or in formal trade, and these cities became major metal-working centers. The Mexica also imported finished metal-work from other regions, Oaxaca, for example, whose ornate metal ornaments were much prized.

Toribio Motolinia described the artistry of the metal-smiths in almost lyrical terms in his *History of the Indians of New Spain,* written between about 1536 and 1543:

> ... they can cast a bird whose tongue, head, and wings move, and they can mold a monkey or other monster which moves its head, tongue, hands, and feet, and in its hands they put little implements, so that the figure seems to be dancing with them. What is even more remarkable, they can make a piece half in gold and half in silver and cast a fish with all its scales, in gold and silver, alternating ... (Motolinia, 1950, pp. 241–242).

To make such intricate objects required skillful use of the "lost-wax" technique. The artisan began by sculpting a mold of ground charcoal and clay in the likeness of the finished object. Then melted beeswax, rolled into a fine "skin," was smoothed carefully over the mold and covered with a thin layer of ground charcoal paste. The completed assemblage was encased in an outer, protective layer of more ground charcoal and clay, and allowed to dry out slowly. It was then heated until the beeswax melted and flowed out of holes left for that purpose. This process completed, molten gold or silver was poured into the mold, replacing the melted beeswax and producing a fine duplicate of the wax prototype. Every object made by this technique was unique, for the metalworker had to smash the mold to extract the finished piece.

This simple technology enabled the smiths to produce necklaces of fine beads, ear plugs, human and animal masks, plaques, and other elegant ornaments that excited the conquistadors to ecstasies of greed. Most Aztec gold was either lost during the siege or melted down by the Spaniards. But in 1932 the discovery of a Mixtec ruler's tomb at Monte Alban in Oaxaca yielded an extraordinary treasure of ornaments which proved that Cortes did not exaggerate the achievements of Aztec craftsmanship. When Albrecht Durer visited a public display of looted Aztec gold in the City Hall at Brussels in 1520, he saw "a sun all in gold as much as six feet in diameter and a moon all in silver," among the magnificent artifacts in the inventory (Conway, 1889, p. 15).

THE SCULPTORS

Sahagun (10, p. 27) tells us that Aztec sculptors were "of skilled hands, able hands, accomplished [after the manner of] Tula." The reference to the Tolteca is interesting, for the Aztec artists inherited most of their techniques and motifs from earlier cultures. They excelled at sculpture, creating both massive works nearly 10 feet (3 m) high and tiny figurines only a few centimeters long. Whether they worked in relief or in the round, almost invariably they depicted military or religious motifs. The carved idols of such dieties as Huitzilopochtli were often of massive proportions, brightly painted, and adorned with gold, semiprecious stones, and amulets. But the sculptors were as comfortable with naturalism as with symbolic representation. They crafted realistic snakes, sometimes feathered in honor of Quetzalcoatl, jaguars, rabbits, eagles, and a host of other familiar beasts, even grasshoppers and flies. They created models of temple pyramids, ceremonial drums, and human figures—realistic representations of commoners and warriors. Fine masks carved in obsidian, rock crystal, and other precious and semiprecious materials often depicted skulls, for many masks symbolized the transformation of priests and sacrificial victims from mortals to gods. Dieties, along with elaborately caparisoned warriors, figured in temple and building reliefs, sometimes laid out in scenes of gods and humans which conveyed complex, mythical happenings or which commemorated historical events.

The Aztec sculptors were probably part of an organized guild, mostly city dwellers who sometimes worked in teams, working according to familiar, almost standardized formulae. This is hardly surprising, since most of their work fulfilled religious functions. They worked closely with palace and temple authorities, sometimes carrying out elaborate commissions, of which the famous Stone of the Sun from Tenochtitlan (see page 33) is surely an example. The sculptors used stone tools, but their approach to their work shows evidence of the long Mexican tradition of working in clay. They simply worked out their techniques in this familiar medium before translating the image into stone. Their grinding and polishing emphasized surface and contour just the way their clay modelling did. They pictured their gods as austere and passive, more often sitting than standing. There is no sense of Western beauty, softness, or emotion here. Aztec sculpture is gloomy and forbidding, even ferocious, with a monumental quality that is apparent even in the smallest object. It depicted gods and goddesses with an extraordinary balance of realism and esoteric symbolism, combining human and animal forms with the most macabre ornaments. The earth, for example, was symbolized as a monster with yawning jaws that swallow the setting sun, the remains of the dead, and the blood of sacrificial victims. The Aztec artist was capable of drawing the squat Mexica body with its short limbs in almost perfect proportion. But he also drew out sinuous curves of the feathered serpent with menacing horror, the fanged symmetry of the heaving snake faithfully portraying the mystery and horror that dominated the Aztec's sense of the world.

The Aztecs believed the gods grotesque and abstract, and the artist drew them so. Perhaps the most famous figure of all is the statue of Coatlicue, "Serpent Skirt," now in the Museum of Anthropology in Mexico City. She is decapitated, two serpents meeting nose to nose representing two streams of blood. Her necklace is made up of human hands and hearts. Writhing snakes form her skirt, her feet and hands are armed with claws. The artists conceived of their gods with horror, and they succeeded brilliantly in wrenching horrifying images out of intractable stone.

Diorite head of Coatlicue, symbolizing the struggle between the forces of day and night. Height: 27.3 inches (70 cm). Probably from Tenochtitlan.

The same grotesque gods were engraved in bone, in wood, and sometimes set in turquoise mosaic. The lapidaries and gold-workers reduced the images to tiny sizes, but they conveyed the same terrifying vision, whether they worked in obsidian, rock crystal, or jade. In general, sculpture was produced on a massive scale, but the smallest creation carried as much artistic authority as the largest piece.

191

THE FEATHER-WORKERS

Feather headdresses, shields, fans, and decorated war costumes were important rank insignia. Specialists either glued on feathers individually or tied their quills to the fabric during the weaving process, arranging the feathers to fashion animals or other decorative motifs in a delicate blend of colors that soothed and excited the eye. The feather-workers were skilled at matching and arranging feathers, using not only local feathers, such as those from herons or ducks and turkeys, but exotic tropical plumes from species such as the quetzal and the parrot. Thousands of bundles of feathers were bought and sold in Valley markets. Brightly colored plumes were a major staple of trade, and feather-workers maintained close relationships with the merchants who brought in their raw materials from the distant lowlands.

Feather-workers enjoyed a privileged status, for their products were the exclusive prerogative of the nobility. They provided the feather regalia not only of the ruler, but that of the gods as well. Their neighborhoods at Tlatelolco and elsewhere were known as Amantlan, hence their name, *amanteca,* "people of Amantlan," was applied to feather-workers generally.

The actual techniques of feather-working, handed down from parents to children, took many years to learn, and the process involved the entire family. Many hours of careful pattern design preceded the application of a single feather. The men began by taking a length of finely woven cotton, pressed out and smoothed onto flat maguey leaves. Meanwhile, their children prepared the glues. The craftsmen glued and reglued the surface until it became very glossy. Next they peeled the stiff, shiny cotton from the leaf and placed it over the intricate pattern design that a specially trained scribe had drawn on bark paper. After tracing the design onto the cotton, the feather-worker reinforced the cotton with a paper backing and further stiffened it with another piece of glue-hardened cotton, itself often backed with a maguey leaf. By now the women had prepared bun-

Featherworking. From the Florentine Codex. Courtesy, University of Utah Press, Salt Lake City. Above: Feather devices and their manufacture.

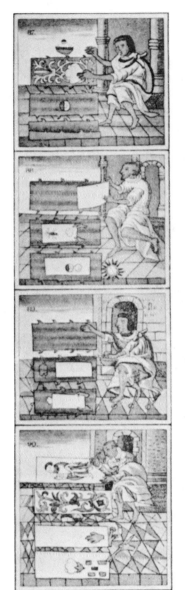

Cutting and designing patterns.

More pattern designing and cutting.

Hardening the glue and dyeing feathers.

dles of local and imported feathers and had dyed the cheap plumes to match the expensive exotics that would make up the final layers.

The men did the final assembly. First they glued the under-feathers to the design, cheaper plumes from local birds, dyed to match the bright colors of the more expensive outer feathers, that served as a soft backing for the exotic layers above. The final layer was a subtle, superb kaleidoscope of color, mingling quetzal, parrot, hummingbird, and other plumes in stunning mosaics. Sometimes gold and other ornaments arranged among the feathers heightened the dazzling effect. Glueing sufficed for rigid objects like shields or fans, but head-dresses, capes, and other ornaments where the feathers had to move were created by tying and sewing the quills to the fibers of the cloth or other backing. The plumes could then hang freely, giving a dramatic, qui-vering, shimmering effect on ceremonial occasions.

Feather-working was one of the ultimate artistic achievements of the Aztecs. Unfortunately, only a few fragments survived the ravages of the Conquest, and we have to rely on the codices for most of the details of this remarkable craft.

THE LAPIDARIES

Stone-working was also an ancient craft in Mexico. The lapidaries worked in many precious and semiprecious substances, including amber, amethyst, jade, obsidian, rock crystal, and turquoise. It was they who fashioned the necklaces and bracelets, the ear plugs, pendants, lip plugs, and earrings, that adorned the ruler and his nobles. Their techniques were slow and laborious. "The lapidary [is] an abrader, a polisher, one who works with sand; who glues [mosaic] with thick glue, works with abrasive sand, rubs [stones] with fine cane, makes them shine," writes Sahagun (10, p. 26). The vital sand and emery needed for the finest work came from the provinces of Tototepec and Quetzaltepec, areas added to Aztec domains specifically to ensure a steady supply of the correct materials to the lapidaries

*Quetzalcoatl in green porphyry.
Courtesy of Musée de
L'Homme, Paris.*

of the Triple Alliance cities. Like the feather- and metal-workers, the stone-crafters probably lived in their own calpulli and formed an exclusive craft guild with its own ceremonies and ranks based on skill and experience.

195

The most refined lapidary art was reserved for the turquoise and shell mosaics that adorned the wooden handles of obsidian sacrificial knives, masks, shields, and small ornaments. The mosaic designs were laid out and glued to wooden surfaces in intricate designs in which turquoise frequently played a leading part.

THE PAINTERS

Few examples of Aztec wall painting have ever been found, but those that have survived come from sites which have also divulged much fine sculpture. Apparently the painters' work never rivalled that of the artists of Teotihuacan or the Mayan frieze painters of the lowlands. Some experts believe that sculpture siphoned off the best Aztec artists.

The finest painting comes from the crabbed but colorful codices where it certainly did not exist as art for art's sake. Naturalism, perspective, and color values were subordinated to the requirement that ceremonial criteria be met to the letter. Many codices served as prompt books for orators, so this is hardly surprising. The pictographs in the codices depict Aztec life in curiously informal ways, as if the artists enjoyed drawing human figures for the pleasure of it. This may be one reason that Indian writing, unlike their sculpture, survived the Conquest. The scribes were still making faithful copies of Indian annals as late as 1560, and Sahagun and his scholarly contemporaries made good use of their skill.

THE SCRIBES

Because their work preserved the ancient traditions for future generations, Mexica scribes were an honored class. They were masters of the nonalphabetic glyphs that recorded the days, months, and years of the sacred and secular calendars, the clock by which the whole of society ran. (A glyph is a carved or painted symbol; a hieroglyph, a picture standing for a word or a concept.) Hundreds, if not thousands of codices from the scribes' libraries—priceless repositories of tribute, genealogies, land maps, and legal records—were burnt by the Spanish friars.

Most Aztec books, codices, and manuscripts were inscribed on *amatl,* a form of paper made from the inner bark of fig trees. They soaked the bark in water, beat it to separate and thin its fibers, then treated it to create a smooth surface. The resulting paper came out in long strips that were folded into accordion-like "books" or cut into single sheets. The scribe wrote on both sides of the paper, using red, yellow, green, blue, and other bright inks to form an intricate kaleidoscope of colors and glyphs. Color was so important, in fact, that Aztec hieroglyphs were known as *in tlilli in tlapulli,* "the red, the black."

Aztec writing was designed both as a record system and as a means of jogging an orator's memory, as a prompter for speechmakers and reciters. The glyphs give only the general sense of the message, and they were useless to a reader who had not memorized the text behind the symbols. Very often the scribe must have been an orator himself, a craftsman who knew much more than his glyphs could communicate on their face value.

The glyphs themselves were predominantly pictographic, a drawing of a rabbit, a bundle of reeds, a serpent. These simple messages were easily interpreted and understood because they were intended as keys. Then there were ideographs, stylized symbols that represented common phenomena—the scrolls found on so many pictures stand for speech, for example. Footprints implied travel; scrolls with flowers, poetry or song; a shield and arrows, warfare. A bundle of reeds depicted the "year-bundle," the clutch of reeds that symbolized the fifty-two years of the calendar cycle. Phonetic symbols were commonly used for personal names and places.

The shapes of the glyphs were only part of the system. The size of human figures and many other variations in detail conveyed all sorts of significant information. Important people were drawn on a larger scale than less significant people. Colors could depict rank; the arrangement of ornaments could communicate minute distinctions in the sumptuary codes; the correct regalia could depict the specific role of a deity.

In a sense, Aztec writing was not a transliteration of spoken words but an elaborate code that was reserved to those who had learned its intricacies and the orations behind it in the calmecac—to the nobility, to the highly learned, often wise men who were far more than mere clerks. Their function stood at the very core of Aztec philosophy and religion.

THE WEAVERS

"The good spinner [is] one who forms a thread of even thickness, who stretches it delicately . . ." said Sahagun (10, p. 35), and other sixteenth-century chroniclers leave us in no doubt that textiles were of vital importance to the Mexica. Capes and other regalia of rank were major tribute and trade items. The wearing of such garments, and of all textiles, in fact, was subject to strict sumptuary laws. Every Aztec woman, however humble, was expected to become a competent weaver, and she started learning the craft in childhood. Noblewomen and priestesses wove the finest capes and cotton garments for the nobility, as well as clothing for idols, temple hangings, and other religious offerings. Commoners turned out not only some fine garments, but wrappings for mummy bundles and prosaic household items, as well as thousands of maguey capes.

The simple weaving involved the so-called "backstrap loom," a simple and highly effective device that is widely used in Mexico to this day. The loom is attached to the weaver by a strap that passes around her hips. She sits or kneels on a mat so that she can open the sheds and beat down the weft of the cloth with a strong stick. The crossbeam for the rolled up, finished cloth lies across her lap, attached to the ends of the strap. An identical beam at the outer end of the loom, attached to a tree or post, holds the warp threads in place. The back-strap loom has the advantage of sim-

plicity, and it is easy to carry. Most weavers probably worked out-of-doors where the light was better.

The finished product from a loom of this type was a length of woven cloth with four finished sides that could be used as a draped garment without any further work. The size and nature of the loom, however, restricted the cloth to a more-or-less standard width, although the weaver could sew several lengths together to make a larger garment.

Aztec raiment may have been simply made, but it was brightly decorated with intricate designs and stamped motifs. The weavers used brocade motifs on their looms, as well as striped designs. Other workers applied designs to the cloth by stamping and by dyeing. Flower and vegetable dyes provided a variety of colors, some of them claimed to be fade-resistant. The dyers also used bright hues from shellfish and the female cochineal (an insect that thrives on prickly pears). Expert embroiderers worked on the finest garments using threads made from delicate plant fibers and the fine underbelly fur of rabbits. Fine embroiderers were highly prized, and it was said that if an especially skilled slave woman were destined for sacrifice, a replacement victim would be found.

The social importance of weaving was reflected in the regalia and symbols associated with various divini-

A backstrap loom and the tools of the weaver. From the Florentine Codex. Courtesy, University of Utah Press, Salt Lake City. Drawing, Sally Black.

199

ties. The fertility goddess Tlazalteotl often appeared with thread-filled spindles, while Xochiquetzal, the patroness of weaving, was frequently painted with looms, spindles, and textiles.

THE AZTEC MARKETPLACE

The Aztec economy produced so many different goods that intricate exchange mechanisms were needed to distribute not only foodstuffs but luxury goods throughout the empire. Every village, every town, every city had at least one *tianquiztli,* a marketplace where goods of every description were bought and sold. The open-air markets were lively, bustling places, as they are in Mexico today. It was here that people met to haggle over provisions, to dispose of surplus products and unwanted goods, to exchange the latest gossip, or just to enjoy their friends. Most markets were open at least five days a week, and they were carefully regulated by special officials who kept an eye on prices and brought cheaters into line.

The greatest markets were at strategic, central places like Tenochtitlan and Tlatelolco, vast emporia to which flowed all the products of the far-flung empire. The conquistadors were staggered by the size and orderliness of the great market at Tlatelolco. Bernal Diaz wrote that some of his companions, who had travelled as far afield as Constantinople, had never seen anything so large or well-regulated. Huge throngs of people crowded the stalls, "Some buying and others selling, so that the murmur and hum of their voices and words that they used could be heard more than a league [three miles] off" (Diaz, 1963, p. 235). An anonymous sixteenth-century chronicler estimated that between 20,000 and 25,000 people used the Tlatelolco market daily, and as many as 40,000 to 50,000 came on the scheduled market day that fell every fifth day.

The orderliness of the market included not only its cleanliness, but its layout as well. "Every kind of merchandise was kept separate and had its fixed place

200

marked for it." Bernal Diaz takes his readers on a tour of the great marketplace: "Let us begin with the dealers in gold, silver, and precious stone, feathers, cloaks, and embroidered goods, and male and female slaves who are also sold there. . . . Some are brought there attached to long poles by means of collars round their necks to prevent them from escaping, but others are left loose" (Diaz, 1963, p. 232). There were people selling coarse cotton capes, chocolate merchants, traders with sandals, and sellers of jackal and deer skins. Diaz described just a fraction of the merchandise offered in Tlatelolco's stalls: all kinds of foodstuffs, not only maize and beans, but turkeys, succulent young dogs, tender waterfowl. There were people selling pitchpine for torches, pottery, paper, medicines, salt, tobacco, even human excrement for use as fertilizer. All manner of services were provided, too, including those of procurers and whores. Sahagun roundly condemns them: "The carnal woman is an evil woman who finds pleasure in her body; who sells her body—repeatedly sells her body . . . a brazen, a proud, dissolute woman of debauched life; a fraud—gaudy, fastidious, vain, petty. . . . She paints her face, variously paints her face; her face is covered with rouge. . . . She arranges her hair like horns." (10, p. 55).

Everything was carefully regulated by the state: "There exists in this great square a large building like an audience hall, where ten or twelve persons are always seated and who act as judges in all cases and questions arising in this market. . . . And in the same place are other people who continuously walk among the people, observing what is sold and the measures with which it is measured; and we saw one measure broken which was false," wrote Cortes (1928, p. 55) after a long tour.

The Aztecs bought and sold goods using a standardized pricing system based on commodities such as cacao beans, cotton cloths known as *quachtli,* and small T-shaped pieces of copper. The quachtli came in standard sizes and were of greater value than cacao beans.

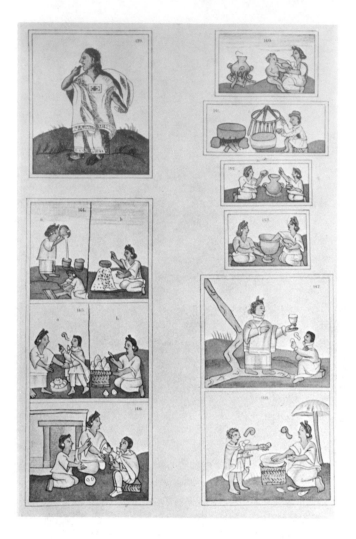

One cloth was worth between 65 and 300 beans, depending on the quality of both commodities. Cacao beans remained in use as a form of currency long after the Conquest. Gold dust stored in transparent goose quills was also a medium of exchange. Everything, whether a foodstuff or a slave, had its recognized value. Taxes were probably assessed on every stall, but we have no details on how they were collected or how much they were.

Marketplace characters: Left column, (top to bottom) the chicle chewer; the chocolate and salt sellers; chalk and limestone sellers; the procuress. Right column, (top to bottom) administering medicine; the candle seller; the herb seller; the atole seller; the prostitute; the tobacco seller. From the Florentine Codex. Courtesy, University of Utah Press, Salt Lake City.

Few markets were as comprehensive as Tlatelolco's. Many specialized in local products or specific wares. Azcapotzalco and Itzocan were famous for their slaves; Texcoco, for cloth, gourds, and pottery. Cholula provided jewels and feathers, while chilis and honey were sold in the neighboring countryside. Hundreds of merchants and small-scale entrepreneurs travelled from market to market buying and selling every imaginable form of commodity, especially popular and essential items like cacao beans, cloth, and salt cakes.

All of the intricate systems of production and exchange met in the hundreds of markets, large and small, that were found in every corner of the Aztec empire. Here luxuries were displayed and tribute gathered; here, too, vital political, social, and economic information was exchanged. The Aztec markets descended from earlier marketplaces that had linked peoples from highlands and lowlands through well-established trade routes from as early as 1500 B.C. Cities might rise and fall, political hegemonies wax and wane, but the long-distance trade route, the marketplace, and the honored profession of trader endured as one of the most characteristic features of Mexican civilization, whoever the masters of Mesoamerica.

THE MERCHANTS

Almost every Aztec family that grew food or manufactured something traded their household surpluses in city and village markets. Most people who sold their goods in the market were petty vendors of agricultural goods or crafts which met the everyday needs of every family, however eminent. Foodstuffs were brought from chinampa to market, cakes of salt piled up in small stalls, canoe loads of firewood paddled to the city. All of these humble, day-to-day activities together made up the distribution system for basic commodities throughout Aztec society.

The professional merchants, the *pochteca* (pl.; sing., *pochtecatl*), who dealt in goods in quantity and specialized in the luxury items that came to the Valley of

Mexico from afar, were something else entirely. Neither nobles nor commoners, the merchants were almost a society apart, a class below the aristocracy, with their own customs and laws and with immense power in Aztec society. The pochteca could own land and sacrifice slaves, and they had some sumptuary privileges at important festivals. They paid their taxes in luxury goods.

The entire city of Tenochtitlan depended on the activities of its professional merchants. The movement of foodstuffs by family vendors filled only part of the city's requirements. Her artisans constantly needed raw materials like obsidian from within the Valley and exotic stones, feathers, and other scarce materials obtainable only from the distant tropical lowlands. Many of these more valued luxuries came into the capital as tribute, but Aztec traders ventured even farther afield, far beyond the confines of the empire, in search of goods to buy and sell.

Traders had been important in Mexican civilization from its earliest days, maintaining trade contacts between highlands and lowlands as early as the second millennium B.C., carrying conch trumpets and other exotica from the Olmec lowlands to the highlands in exchange for precious obsidian. Cities like Teotihuacan and Cholula were famous trading centers for centuries, the latter right up to the Conquest.

But the Aztec pochteca were far more than mere traders, and they were a highly organized class within Aztec society. Many of Sahagun's informants, former merchants from Tlatelolco, told how the pochteca combined trading and war. They wandered everywhere, learned the local languages, dressed humbly, suffered the arduous conditions of the road. But to put it bluntly, the pochteca were also fifth columnists, reporting back to the ruler on local conditions in the state's territories, and often journeying through still unconquered lands. They always carried desirable trade goods on these expeditions: "Golden mountain-shaped miters, like royal crowns; and golden forehead rosettes; and golden necklaces of radiating pendants. . . . And

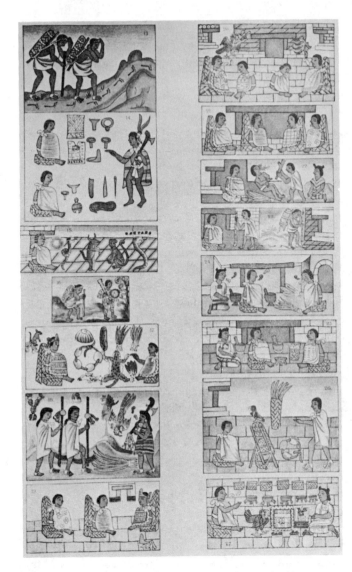

Merchants: Left column, (top to bottom) on the road; displaying their wares; merchants' favorable day signs; carrying wares; presenting goods to a local ruler; disguised merchants scouting out the land; appearing before Moctezuma Xocoyotzin. Right column, (top to bottom) merchants, courts, and punishments; returning merchant; listening to the admonitions of the elders; merchants' equipment; preparations for a banquet. From the Florentine Codex. Courtesy, University of Utah Press, Salt Lake City.

the things used by common folk were obsidian ear plugs, [or] tin, and obsidian razors with leather handles, and pointed obsidian blades, and rabbit fur, and needles for sewing and shells ..." (Sahagun, 9, p. 18). They ran dangerous risks, sometimes getting themselves involved in major military campaigns—or killed. One group of pochteca on an expedition to the Pacific Coast southeast of Acapulco was besieged for four years. Eventually they broke out of their fortress and routed their assailants, greeting a relief expedition with the news that their journey had not been necessary. It was said that pochteca never cut their hair while on an expedition. These merchants returned with hair down to their waists.

No merchant acted completely independently. The state supervised all trading activities and shared in the profits. The pochtecas' lives, like everyone else's, were bound by elaborate rituals. No trader ever set out from the capital on an inauspicious day, nor would he return on anything but a favored date. Every pochtecatl belonged to the merchants' community, a guild apart from the others with its own privileges and obligations. The pochteca had their own law courts and could send their children to the calmecac. Despite the legal restrictions on their social position, their political and economic power was considerable, so much so that the pipiltin sometimes resented them. The merchants were careful to feign humility, wearing humble clothes in public. The returning pochteca would enter the city swiftly, by canoe, at night. "And as to their goods, no one could see how much there was; perhaps they carefully hid—covered up—all the boats" (Sahagun, 9, p. 33). The cargo was secretly unloaded at a friend's or relative's house before daybreak. Everything was done to avoid any impression of great wealth or any hint of conspicuous consumption.

The pochteca lived within tightly knit hereditary guilds and guarded their trade secrets closely. Within their own residential areas, members were governed by strict rules and codes of conduct. The more senior merchants watched closely over their juniors. Orations to young men departing on their first expedition warned them to bear suffering and hardships without complaint and to be alert for ambushes and other hazards. When they returned, forcible reminders humbled them, and cut them down to size: "Where didst thou get that which thou gavest us to eat [and] drink? Perchance thou didst go somewhere to remove it from one's pot. . . . Thou hadst robbed someone. . . ." And ". . . they charged him not to be presumptuous, not proud, not to attribute his gains falsely to himself. . . ."

Prudence and the utmost discretion were the hallmarks of the successful merchant. "Only humbly, saddened, did they live. They did not seek honor [and] fame. They walked about wearing only their miserable maguey fiber capes. They greatly feared notoriety, the praise with which one is praised" (Sahagun, 9, pp. 28–30).

For all their subordinate status, successful merchants enjoyed considerable influence. They often carried out special missions for the ruler. It was said that Moctezuma Xocoyotzin especially prized the advice of "the old merchants, the disguised merchants . . . he made them like his sons" (Sahagun, 9, p. 32). They and their highly organized subculture were the eyes and ears of the ruler. Successful pochteca could influence affairs in ways that sometimes allowed them to assume positions in society they could never have attained through birth. Many of them acted on the ruler's personal behalf, returning with items bought with the tlatoani's own goods, luxuries destined for the palace, obtained as official tribute. The merchant who acted as such an agent was granted important privileges, virtual monopolies on trade areas. Whatever the ruler did not take became the pochtecatl's own: gold ornaments, feathers, and other exotic baubles traded with local rulers. Since all trade was carried out on foot, without the aid of draught animals or wheeled vehicles, most luxuries were small objects easily carried in inconspicuous bundles and on slaves' backs.

In the well-defined ranks of the merchants' guild, the elders supervised its affairs. Below them were the wealthiest traders, often slave dealers, and the so-called "disguised" merchants who acted as spies in foreign lands. Most members were ordinary pochteca or young merchants who had yet to prove themselves in the field. No one in the guild accumulated wealth for wealth's sake. One acquired renown by accumulating wealth and managing it successfully, by opening up new foreign areas.

One then cemented one's social position by displaying generosity to one's fellow guild members, acquiring fame and status by throwing bacchanalian ceremonies and feasts where dozens of expensive dogs and turkeys were consumed. The elders would inspect the host's goods and satisfy themselves that he had sufficient resources for a feast that would not discredit the guild. The feast was conducted with meticulous ceremony and protocol on an auspicious day chosen by the soothsayers. Protocol dictated that gifts of food, flowers, tobacco, and chocolate were distributed by specially chosen welcomers, "those of good bearing [and] appearance, not cowardly, nor bewildered, or shy." The guests ate numerous tamales, drank copious drafts of chocolate, and consumed hallucinogenic mushrooms: "He who eats many of them sees many things which make him afraid, or make him laugh. . . ." The host would make offerings of quails and burn incense to Huitzilopochtli, rituals that were followed by a night of singing and dancing. A generous and wealthy host gained great prestige by distributing the leftovers to his guests, for to be stingy on public occasions was a terrible stigma.

The greatest ceremonies for the pochteca were conducted at the festival of Panquetzaliztli, "the Raising of the Banners," a day that honored Huitzilopochtli. The feasts were an exercise in conspicuous consumption. A wealthy merchant often purchased a slave, had him or her ritually bathed, then sacrificed. All of the rituals were accompanied by an orgy of gift-giving and elaborate squandering of food and drink. Sahagun describes one festival where the participants consumed as many as a hundred turkeys and forty dogs, as well as twenty sacks of cacao beans. More than four hundred decorated loin cloths and between eight- and twelve-hundred richly adorned capes were distributed: "These were capes with plaited paper ornaments and with carmine colored flowers, made with eight blotches of blood, and with orange flowers; and netted capes; and capes with whorl designs; capes with spiral designs; and long, narrow ones, two fathoms long . . ." (Sahagun, 9, p. 47).

The powerful, close-knit merchants' guilds were laws unto themselves, with their own code of justice, the authority to mete out even savage punishments, and even some control over prevailing prices in the marketplace. Clearly the pochteca occupied a very strong position. They often bartered goods that were worth but a tiny fraction of the value of the luxuries they brought back to the capital. Their trading activities were backed by the constant threat of force, and much Aztec trade was little more than an expansion of tribute demands.

The pochtecas' rewards were not those of the noble or commoner. They achieved wealth and status within their own guild by using their personal riches to acquire higher rank and prestige. As they rose in the hierarchy, so their access to further sources of wealth increased. It was a self-perpetuating system that exercised so much subtle power in Aztec society that the pochteca had to be careful not to offend the influential, but sometimes poorer, nobility. One of Sahagun's informants described them as "those who had plenty, who prospered; the greedy, the well-fed man, the covetous, the niggardly, the miser, who controlled wealth and family" (Sahagun, 7, p. 23). But even the merchants had to conform to the ritual and symbolic customs of one of the most religious civilizations ever developed by humankind.

IV

FLOWER AND SONG

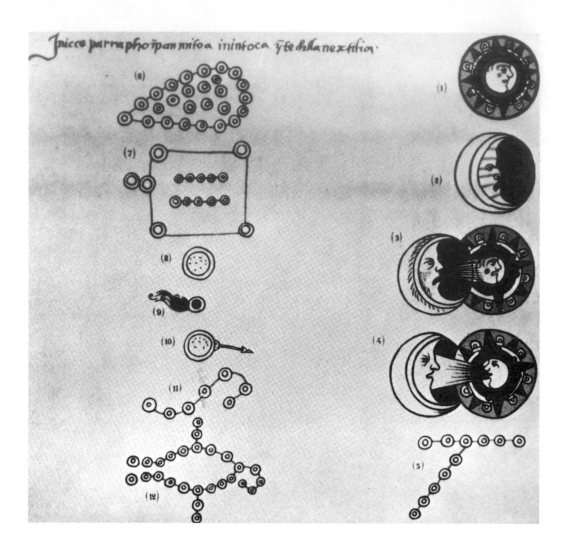

CHAPTER 9

Cosmos and Creation

Beyond is the place where one lives.
I would be lying to myself were I to say;
"perhaps everything ends on this earth;
here do our lives end."

Cantares Mexicanos, 61, V. Leon-Portilla, 1963, p. 130.

Now do I hear the very words of the *coyolli* bird
as he makes answer to the Giver of Life.
He goes his way singing, offering flowers.
Is that what pleases the Giver of Life?
Is that the only truth on earth?
(Leon-Portilla, 1963, p. 79.)

The richness and precision of Nahuatl language allowed the Mexica to express themselves in poetry and song, to communicate with the gods, and to cope with the intensely symbolic world they perceived around them. The wise men taught lofty ideals and philosophies that they believed had come down to them from the Tolteca. Every Aztec, whether noble or humble commoner, dwelt in a world that would be hard for Westerners to comprehend even if we knew all about their beliefs, which we do not. The Mexica world view reflected not only the martial ideals of a young warrior people, but a rich cultural heritage from earlier civilizations as well. The foundation of this world view was a collection of very ancient cosmic myths that the Aztecs revered but altered to serve their own militaristic ends.

The Mexica may have been tumultuous, bloodthirsty warriors, but they were tough, sophisticated thinkers,

Page 210: Tlaloc. From original drawing by Alonso Caso. Courtesy, Fondo de Cultura Economica, Mexico City.

Left: A page from Volume 7, Appendix, of Sahagun's General History, *beginning, "When the moon newly appeareth, he seemeth like a thin, little curve of wire...."*

too. Every activity, however ambitious or prosaic, had a symbolic content in a world where symbolism and ritual guided every deed. Their sacred places commanded such reverence that everyone, "whether noble or plebian, removed their sandals in the courtyard before they entered to worship their gods . . ." (Leon-Portilla, 1963, pp. 172–173). From a patchwork of documents that record poems, songs, and formal orations, we can piece together at least an impression of such metaphysical concepts as death, free will, good, and evil. Using written sources and sculptures like the Stone of the Sun and the famous monumental depiction of the mother goddess from Tenochtitlan, we can speculate on the nature of the Mexican cosmos as well.

TIME AND THE CALENDAR

The lore of the stars and the heavenly bodies played a vital role in Aztec culture, for the words of the gods and the procession of time could be read in the skies. The Aztecs isolated sacred time from secular time, and each kind of time had its own calendar. But time was also cyclical, with each unit repeating itself. Even the great Suns were cyclical, each destined to end in a fullness of years. With this repetitive view of time, the Aztecs certainly needed an accurate calendar to keep track of the passage of days, months, and years, to schedule the complicated rituals of their lives, and to foretell the future. They also believed that every person's destiny was closely tied to his or her birth date. All of these requirements caused them to use two separate but intermeshing calendars, calendars that had earlier precedents among the Tolteca, Maya, and other Mesoamerican peoples.

The secular calendar, known as *Xihuitl,* a "stem of grass," and by extension the "time of the new grass," marked off an annual cycle of changing seasons, of planting and harvest. The Aztec secular calendar was based on the number 20, *cempohualli,* "one full count," the twenty fingers and toes of a human being. Cempohualli gave a sense of totality, of completion—a perfect number that should never be exceeded. Each xihuitl was a total entity as well, consisting of eighteen twenty-day months, known as *metztli* ("moon"), making up a year of 360 days. The xihuitl, which was close to our solar year of 365 days, left five-and-a-quarter days to be accounted for. These days, the *nemontemi,* had no divine patron, were days of evil omen and dread significance.

Reflecting the actual length of the solar year, the secular year was divided into eighteen named months for spiritual purposes. The priests monitored the calendar, grouping every four secular years into a divine year with special rituals, some of which commemorated Quetzalcoatl, the god who created and maintained the calendar. Each month of the xihuitl had special religious significance and culminated in a festival where its god was honored. The new year started by honoring Tlaloc, the god of rain, subsequent months commemorating Xipe, the spring deity, and other figures associated with the remainder of the farming cycle. The seven months roughly correspond to September to March in our calendar were nonagricultural, the months of warriors, hunters, women, and other members of society. The xihuitl ended with a celebration of Xiuhteuctli, appropriately, the "Lord of the Year."

The secular calendar served to schedule planting, harvest, and other routine annual events, and to regulate market days at five-day weekly intervals. The priests who devised it had obviously based their calculations on astronomical observations, but we do not know how they accounted for the quarter-day discrepancy between the arbitrary 365-day year and the solar year of 365.24 days—if they did at all. (We, of course, add an extra day to our calendar every four years.)

The sacred, ritual calendar, *tonalpohualli,* consisted of 260 days, a day count formed by joining twenty signs with the numbers 1 to 13. Each day-sign could be associated with any one of thirteen numbers, giving two hundred sixty possible combinations. The sequence of numbers began with thirteen signs associated with

Day Name	Meaning	Glyph	Associated Numbers
cipactli	alligator		1 8 2 9 3 etc. 10 4 11 5
ehecatl	wind		2 9 3 10 (4) 11 5 12 6
calli	house		3 10 4 11 5 12 6 13 7
cuetzpallin	lizard		4 11 5 12 6 13 7 1 8
coatl	snake		5 12 6 13 7 1 8 2 9
miquiztli	death		6 13 7 1 8 2 9 3 10
mazatl	deer		7 1 8 2 9 3 10 4 11
tochtli	rabbit		8 2 9 3 10 4 11 5 12
atl	water		9 3 10 (4) 11 5 12 6 1
itzcuintli	dog		10 4 11 5 12 6 13 7 1
oxomatli	monkey		11 5 12 6 13 7 1 8
malinalli	grass		12 6 13 7 1 8 2 9
acatl	reed		13 7 1 8 2 9 3 10
ocelotl	jaguar		1 8 2 9 3 10 (4) 11
cuauhtli	eagle		2 9 3 10 4 11 5 12
cozcacuauhtli	vulture		3 10 4 11 5 12 6 13
ollin	movement		4 11 5 12 6 13 7 1
tecpatl	flint knife		5 12 6 13 7 1 8 2
quiahuitl	rain		6 13 7 1 8 2 9 3
xochitl	flower		7 1 8 2 9 3 10 4

the numbers 1 to 13. Then a new number sequence began, linking the second series of numbers 1 through 7 with the remainder of the signs. When all twenty signs combined with all thirteen numbers (260 days), the tonalpohualli began anew. Thus, the sign Alligator was first associated with the number 1, then 8, 2, 9, and so forth. By the time the 260-day cycle was completed, Alligator and all the other signs had been linked with every number from 1 to 13.

The originators of the sacred calendar centuries earlier had started with the number 20, then added another sacred number, 13, perhaps representing the thirteen layers of the world and the sky. The calendar progressed by revolving a set of digits from 1 to 13, like sprockets of a gear wheel, upon another set of twenty signs, each in fixed order and named after an animal, another object, or a natural phenomenon. There were twenty sets of thirteen days in each tonalpohualli, each beginning with the sign linked with the number 1. The priests used charts and poetry to teach people the order of years:

One Rabbit, this is the name of the annual sign, the year count for the region of the South.
Thirteen years it carries, guiding, carrying always on its shoulders each of the thirteen years.
And it goes along, guiding, beginning; it introduces all of the signs of the years: reed, flint . . . .
(Leon-Portilla, 1963, pp. 54–55)

The 260-day tonalpohualli—the word means "count of day-signs"—was divided into four sixty-five-day groups of five thirteen-day "weeks," each carrying a sign oriented toward north, south, east, or west. This orientation kept the sun in motion throughout the year. Each "week" had its own patron deity or deities, as did each of the twenty day-names, the patron giving the day its special characteristics. For example, the goddess Mayahuel, the deity of pulque and intoxication, was the patron of *tochtli,* or "rabbit" days, because the drunkard weaved and strutted about in the same erratic and unpredictable way as a rabbit. Each direction in

The tonalpohualli, *otherwise known as "the Count of Days." After Frances Berdan,* The Aztecs, *p. 146.*

the sacred calendar also had an allocated span of thirteen years within the Aztec "century" of fifty-two years.

The Aztec century was called *xiuhmolpilli,* "a bundle of years." The priests marked the passage of years by putting aside a peeled reed for each one until fifty-two wands were accumulated. Then they bound them together and buried them in a ritual designed to symbolize the start of a new count. The xihuitl and the tonalpochualli coincided every fifty-two years. In other words, the day was distinguished by the same tonalpochualli sign and the same position in one of the eighteen months every fifty-two years. At this moment, time was supposed to expire, either to be replaced or never to reoccur. The public ceremonies at the end of each cycle were filled with apprehension. Everyone expected demons to descend from the heavens to destroy the world. The people broke their idols and possessions and stayed awake in fear until the priests rekindled the flame symbolizing the start of the new cycle on a mountain top—in the heart cavity of a sacrificial victim. Only then might the Aztec world continue for another finite "century."

THE UNIVERSE

All Aztec philosophy was based on the assumption that everything concrete was ephemeral, transitory, and destined for oblivion. Convinced that the physical world was really a dream, the wise men turned to the metaphysical, to *topan,* the "world above and beyond us."

In the Aztec cosmos, the disc-like surface of the earth was at the center of the universe, encircled by a ring of water, so the world became *cemanahuac,* "that surrounded by water." The earth was thought of as a land mass, *tlalticpac,* surrounded by water on all sides. The ocean, *ilhuica-atl,* reached up vertically to merge with the skies, forming the walls, as it were, of the lowest heaven. The heavens were formed of at least thirteen layers of various colors, each associated with its own deities. These gods ruled over successive days of

The cosmological plan of the Aztec universe, laid out horizontally. The illustration shows the nine Lords and two hundred sixty days of the Sacred Calendar assigned to the four cardinal directions, the center of the Universe, and sacred birds and trees. From the Codex Fejervary-Mayer I.

the sacred calendar that repeated themselves in endless cycles. Originally there may have been only nine layers, with nine deities, but the evidence is uncertain. The underworld was also divided into layers, in this case, nine of them. They were more hazards than layers, however, stages through which a dead person's soul had to pass on its way to eternal rest in the ninth layer. (A similar layering of thirteen heavens and nine hells is found in the Mayan cosmos.)

The Aztec philosophers thought of the earth as supported by the universal, primeval sea, *teoatl.* In this sea floated a terrible monster that took several forms. One of its forms was the Earth Monster, Cipactli, the crocodile-like creature that had once been torn asunder to form heaven and earth. Another form was Tlaltecuhtli, a toad-like monster with snapping mouths, the creature that swallowed and disgorged the sun at dusk and dawn. Tlaltecuhtli also devoured the blood and hearts of sacrificial victims and the dead.

The center of the earth, *tlalxico,* was the point at which the four quadrants of the world converged. This notion of a center and four quarters was of vital organizational importance. Four gods supported the lowermost layer of the heavens at the four points of the compass. The details are somewhat confused, but it appears that the god of the planet Venus, Tlahuizcalpantecuhtli, stood to the East *(Tlapcopa),* the good and fertile direction associated with the color yellow. East was the region of light, depicted by the reed, the symbol of life and fertility. North *(Mictlampa),* which was associated with the color red, was evil, the cold desert, the land of the dead, supported by an unknown fire god. West *(Cihuatlampa),* whose color was blue-green, was too humid, an unfavorable direction associated with the ubiquitous Ehecatl-Quetzalcoatl, and with the land of women. South *(Huitztlampa)* was white and neutral, the concern of Mictlantecuhtli, an uncertain direction symbolized by the rabbit which leapt around in unpredictable ways. Other gods were associated with directions, too. The four year-signs and twenty day-signs of the sacred calendar were associated with the four directions, subtly blending the concepts of time and space. Birds and animals, like the quetzal, the hummingbird, and the jaguar, also had associations with the four directions.

The Aztecs organized their lives within a cosmos entirely controlled by a crowded and elaborate pantheon of several hundred powerful deities. Everyone felt the influence of the cosmic forces for good and evil. The success of human existence depended on understanding the cosmic forces that determined one's fate and on maintaining a harmonious balance among competing and unpredictable tensions.

HUMAN EXISTENCE

The cosmos was a vague, but well-ordered place, but what about the reality and value of human existence? The tlamatinime, the wise men, puzzled over the meaning of life and, probing tentatively into the nature of reality and the verities of life, wondered whether it was all a dream:

Do we speak the truth here, Giver of Life?
We merely dream, we are only awakened from dreams.
All is like a dream . . . .
No one speaks here of truth . . . .
(Leon-Portilla, 1963, p. 220.)

These same philosophers had more practical missions as well, among them an obligation to "place a mirror before the people, that they might become wise and prudent: to endow with wisdom the countenances of others . . ." (Leon-Portilla, 1963, p. 104). It was their task to give people born faceless a purpose and an identity. So they sought a meaning for human activities. Was there a truth to human existence? Were humans real beings, or just transitory illusions?

Perchance, is it true?
Did our Lord, our prince Quetzalcoatl, bring man back to life;
he who invents man, he who creates man?
Perchance, was it determined by the Lord and Lady of Duality?
Was not the word handed down?
(Leon-Portilla, 1963, p. 111.)

The tlamatinime speculated not only about human reality, but about human nature, its origins, its capacity to lay out and follow moral and social principles, and its existence, if any, after death. They believed that everyone had a soul, a *tetonal,* the spark that transformed them into artisans, artists, or warriors, and brought about all of their thoughts and actions.

The wise men taught that one's self attempted to fill its own emptiness by searching for wisdom and art, for its own image, the "face and heart," the Aztec image of the individual. So deeply traditional was this notion that the Aztec teacher was called *teixtlamachtiani,* "teacher of peoples' faces." The achievement of this "face" gave one a chance to arrive at his or her own truth and at an understanding of the mystery of human life. Part of this process involved predicting one's destiny, a task undertaken with the aid of the "book of days." The 260 days of the tonalpohualli were made up

of a magic combination of signs and numbers, convey-
ing omens of good and evil. The magico-religious pattern of the day-count determined one's destiny.
Everyone needed to know the meanings of the signs
for one's important days. Sahagun tells us that when a
child was born, the parents searched out a priest who
consulted the tonalamatl and attempted to balance evil
signs with positive ones. The readings were not absolute. The Mexica believed that a person's deeds on
earth could alter his or her fate, sometimes for the
worse. "And some conducted their lives wastefully even
though they had been born under a favorable sign.
They lived a wretched life," commented Sahagun's informants (1, p. 94).

Beyond attempting to influence their pupils' wills,
the tlamatinime taught self-discipline through strict education. They well knew the dilemma confronting a
people who have a measure of individual freedom while
at the same time confronting a world controlled by the
Creator. "We are but toys to Him; He laughs at us,"
speculated one wise man. Humans existed to serve the
gods. Their existence on earth was but transitory. With
death, one entered the world of "the beyond, the region of the dead."

The Aztecs enjoyed a rich system of belief about the
life after death. Sahagun records how most people went
to *Mictlan,* the nine-level region below the earth. After
four years of wanderings and repeated tests, they came
to permanent rest in *Chiconamictlan,* the "ninth place
of the dead." Here, at last, people were freed from
their bodies. Those favored by Tlaloc, the God of Rain,
went to an earthly paradise called *Tlalocan* where, Sahagun tells us, "never is there a lack of green corn,
squash, sprigs of amaranth . . . and flowers" (6, p. 122).
As god of water and lightning, Tlaloc called those who
died by drowning or by being struck by lightning, as
well as those who died from diseases like dropsy. The
finest fate of all awaited those who died in battle, the
captives who had perished at the hands of their enemies as sacrificial victims, and women who died in
childbirth. These privileged people went to *Tonatiuhil-*

huicac, the dwelling place of the Sun. There the warriors would sing war songs as they accompanied the
Sun to the zenith of his journey. After four years they
turned into humming birds who sipped from the
flowers of heaven and earth. The manner of one's
death, not, as Christians believed, one's behavior on
earth, determined one's final destiny. So the Aztecs
bent their energies toward obtaining the immediate approval of the gods for their earthly conduct, leaving
their fate at and after death in the hands of heaven.

Aztec philosophy and metaphysics defy our close understanding, separated as we are from their wise men
by four-and-a-half centuries and the disruptions of the
Spanish Conquest. We know that they derived from a
whole cosmology and were expressed in the language
of the ancient myths. Through the intuition of "flower
and song," the metaphor for inspiration, the poets revealed and explained the universe. The painter, the
singer, the sculptor, the poet, and all those worthy of
the title of artist (sometimes symbolically called Toltec,
the epitome of cultured civility), these were the vision-
aries empowered to create divine things. Such people
were often associated with the teachers in the calmecac
where students were taught to see the world and find
themselves. To know the truth was to understand the
hidden meanings of things through "flower and song,"
a power that emanated from the gods. In the metaphysical world of the Aztecs, beauty was perhaps the
only reality, an unreal world view by Spanish standards,
but one which led the Aztecs to invent their remarkable calendar, to acquire their astronomical knowledge,
and to achieve a level of self-understanding that perhaps exceeded that of their conquerors.

THE LEGEND OF THE CREATION

The reality of human existence began with the Creation, not only of "the world above and beyond us,"
but of humanity itself. The legend of the Creation, of
the five great Suns, was intimately connected with the
notion that human life was ephemeral and doomed to

extinction. The complex, symbolic creation legends blend into the historical accounts of the Toltec era so that it sometimes hard to know where legend ends and history begins. But the creation legends themselves are clearly fictional, based on the belief that Four Suns had preceded the present world, or Fifth Sun, a world destined to evaporate in a swarm of earthquakes and cataclysms. Some myths spoke of even earlier cosmic events, of two creative deities, Tonacatecuhtli and his wife Tonacacihuatl, who lived in the thirteenth, and highest, heaven. Self-created, eternal, the source of all life, these two great primeval deities gave birth to four sons: the red god Tlatlauhqui Tezcatlipoca (Xipe); the evil black Yayauhqui Tezcatlipoca; Quetzalcoatl, who was the white Tezcatlipoca; and the small, left-handed Huitzilopochtli, otherwise known as the blue Tezcatlipoca.

After six hundred years of limbo, Quetzalcoatl and Huitzilopochtli were ordered to create the world. They manufactured fire and a half-sun, then a half-moon. Next the gods created Oxomoco, the first man, and Cipactonal, the first woman, ordering them to till the soil and weave textiles. It was they who later gave birth to the *macehualtin,* the thousands of commoners who were to live on earth. The two dieties next designed the calendar and created Mictlantecuhtli and Mictecacihuatl, the gods of the underworld. Next came the heavens and the waters where the great crocodile-like monster Cipactli lived. The rain god Tlaloc and his wife Chalchihtlicue now emerged, while Quetzalcoatl and Huitzilopochtli created the earth from the parts of the dismembered Cipactli. Next Oxomoco and Cipactonal gave birth to their son Piltzintecuhtli who married a maiden created from the hairs of the goddess Xochiquetzal.

The creation myths now become a powerful, impelling epic of four world ages covering 2,028 years and divided into fifty-two year cycles. These famous Four Suns differed in length (the exact numbers vary with the different sources), and each had its own special characteristics and patron deity. Each terminated in a

The Aztec Suns. Top to bottom: Sun of the Tiger, Sun of Water, Sun of Fire, Sun of Air. Drawing, Sally Black.

224

cataclysm. The first Sun was 4 Ocelotl, an age assigned to the Earth. Tezcatlipoca presided over this world and its population of giants. A swarm of voracious jaguars ate them up and ended the first age. The age of the Air or Wind, Four Ehecatl, followed. This was Quetzalcoatl's Sun. He ruled over a population of nut-eating people who were turned into monkeys when their world was destroyed by fierce hurricanes. The third Sun, 4 Quiahuitl, was the world of Fire, the domain of Tlaloc. His people lived off aquatic plants and became butterflies, dogs, and turkeys when a fiery rain consumed their earth. During The Fourth Sun, 4 Atl, the world was populated by more seed-eaters and ruled by the water goddess Chalchiuhtlicue. Her subjects became fish when a great flood wiped out her domains. Primeval waters now covered the darkened earth.

THE FIFTH SUN

Tezcatlipoca and Quetzalcoatl were given the task of dispersing the floods and restoring the sunless earth. One legend has them pushing four roads through to the center of the earth, then raising the fallen sky by turning themselves into giant trees. Another tells how the two gods turned themselves into two great serpents and grasped the four limbs of the hideous toad-like earth monster Tlaltecuhtli (some versions say Cipactli) swimming in the primeval depths. Their prehensile coils split her in half. The upper half of Tlaltecuhtli formed the earth, her lower portion became the skies. Angered by this cavalier act, the other gods decreed that the earth monster was to be the source of all human food. They used her hair to create trees, flowers, and herbs. Her skin became grass and small flowers, her eyes wells and springs, the mouth rivers and large caves. The earth monster's shoulders were mountains. But she cried out and refused to bring forth fruit unless she was nourished with human hearts, yet to be created, and soaked in blood. All this was said to have occurred in the year 1 Tochtli—A.D. 978 in the European calendar.

Darkness still prevailed, so Tezcatlipoca brought forth fire to light humanity by twirling fire sticks in 2 Acatl, the second year of the first fifty-two year cycle of the new world. In subsequent years other gods created the stars, the night, water, rain, and Mictlan, the underworld. Next it was humanity's turn. The most common legend has Quetzalcoatl descending into the underworld to obtain the bones and ashes of previous human beings in order to recreate humanity. Mictlantecuhtli, the ruler of Mictlan, gives him the bones, but harasses the departing god so much that he drops them, a misadventure that accounts for the differences among people. Quetzalcoatl delivers the bones to the assembled gods in Tamoanchan, where the bones are ground into a powder and placed in a vessel. The gods then undergo mass autosacrifice, their blood drips into the sacred vessel, and this fertilizes the pulverized bone. After four days a male child emerges; after four more days, a female. These are the people who would form the basis of later society, the macehualtin, or commoners, "those who deserved and [were] brought back to life because of penance."

Now the gods turned their attention to feeding the newly created people. One version has Quetzalcoatl becoming a black ant. A red ant leads him to Tonacatepetl, the "Sustenance Mountain," where he obtains maize grains and brings them back to Tamoanchan. The gods taste them and decide they are suitable food for humankind. Eventually maize is stolen from the rain gods and given to mortals, together with beans, amaranth, and other staples. Many people believed another legend in which the gods buried Centeotl, a son of the primeval couple, Oxomoco and Cipactonal. His body brought forth maize, cotton, and many food plants. The maguey plant was created from the grave of the young maiden goddess Mayahuel. Quetzalcoatl stole her from her monster guardians and made her part of a great tree. When the angry monsters arrived to claim her, they dismembered her limb from limb. Quetzalcoatl gathered up her bones and buried them.

Maguey plants sprang from her grave to provide the pleasures of pulque for humankind.

The world was still without sun and moonlight. It took the gods twenty-six years from the beginning of the fifth world to create the sun. In the year 13 Acatl they gathered at Teotihuacan, where the gods Nan-auatzin and Tecuziztecatl volunteered to cremate themselves. They jumped into the sacrificial fire and became the sun and moon. The assembled gods now sacrificed themselves in the fire to provide nourishment for the sun, bequeathing their regalia and mantles to their retainers. These sacred bundles and the songs and musical instruments that survived the immolation were those used in the rituals for the gods.

But this act of supreme sacrifice was not enough. The Sun and the Earth had an insatiable craving for human blood. Inevitably humanity had to bear the burden of sacrifice as well. So war was established as a means of satisfying the Sun's needs. One legend says that Tezcatlipoca started it all fourteen years after the creation of the fifth sun by creating four hundred men and five women to stir up strife. Within three years all the men were sacrificed to the Sun. A year after the creation of the Sun, the god Mixcoatl-Camaxtli created four men and another woman to stir up trouble. The following year he struck a rocky cliff with his staff. Four hundred "Chichimeca" emerged. They were revellers and drunkards, so the god sent the original five to slaughter them. According to another legend, the survivors of this battle may have lived at Chicomoztoc, the fabled seven caves of early Mexican history.

The legends speak of the Fifth Sun as the last world, a world destined to be destroyed by great earthquakes, its peoples devoured by celestial monsters. The world would fall into darkness and become a void:

In the year 13 Reed,
So they say, it first appeared.

The sun that now exists
Was born then

This is the fifth sun,
Its date-sign is 4 Movement.

It is called Movement Sun
Because on that day it began to move.

The old people say
That in this age earthquakes will appear
And there will come starvation
And we shall perish.
(Leon-Portilla, 1963, p. 44.)

The Aztecs spent their lives awaiting the arrival of the fatal day *Nahui ollin* (day 4 Movement) that would end the Fifth Sun. In the meantime, they fed the sun daily with *chalchiuhuatl,* the vital sacrificial fluid from human hearts. To the Mexica, life was symbolized by the heart, *yollotl,* something that was inconceivable without *yolli,* movement itself. Their world involved unalterable sequences of direction and passing time, sudden transitions from good times to bad, and an inexorable destiny controlled by divine forces of good and evil. The rites of human sacrifice, the feeding of the gods, played a vital role in this ambivalent, tension-filled world.

HUMAN SACRIFICE

Just the mention of human sacrifice makes us blanch, yet the Aztecs regarded it as a deeply religious and sacred practice. The conquistadors' view of human sacrifice as the work of the devil astonished the Aztecs. Shock and revulsion did not prevent Diego Duran, however, from perceptively remarking "how cleverly this devilish rite imitates that of our Holy Church, which orders us to receive the True Body and Blood of our Lord Jesus Christ" (1971, p. 95). The Mexica did indeed offer up victims to the gods on a scale unparalleled in any other society, but they did so with the conviction that the continued existence of the cosmos depended on it. Why did they regard this symbolic custom as so important? Were the Aztecs cannibals, and if so why? These questions have fascinated anthropologists for generations.

The Spaniards may have been repelled by human sacrifice, but it would have been insane for an Aztec to consider it immoral. The offering of human blood was perhaps the most profound of religious acts. Human sacrifice was the touchstone of all Aztec virtue, the key to their understanding of the spiritual world. The gods themselves had originated the rite of sacrifice by immolating themselves to nourish the Fifth Sun. Humankind had an equal responsibility to feed the sun. The Aztecs believed that they had acquired the custom from the gods themselves, a lineage sufficient to clothe it with powerful divine sanction.

Sacrifice renewed not only the god to whom it was offered, it provided an ultimate test of manhood for the victims. Human beings counted in the cosmic order only insofar as their offerings nourished the gods. The more valorous the offering, the more the gods were nourished. It followed that the blood or the heart of an elite warrior was much more nutritious than that of a slave. Every captive was the property not of his captor but of the god to whom he was destined to be sacrificed. Often the victim was painted and dressed in the god's regalia so that he or she became a symbolic god sacrificed to the god himself or herself. Elaborate rituals surrounded the more important of these sacrifices. The flawless young man chosen to impersonate Tezcatlipoca assumed the role of the god for a full year. He walked around in divine regalia, playing the flute. A month before his death, he was married to four young priestesses who impersonated goddesses and who sang and danced with him as he walked around the capital. On the day of sacrifice, the young man climbed willingly and alone to his date on the sacrificial stone. His decapitated head was displayed on the skull rack that stood in the plaza below the temple. On occasions like this, human sacrifice was not an earthly, but a divine, drama.

The Aztecs knew of many varieties of human sacrifice, including death by arrows, burning, and beheading. Then there was autosacrifice, a form of blood offering involving self-mutilation, the piercing of limbs and other parts of the body with maguey thorns and/or sharp pointed bones and collecting the blood on slips of paper that were presented to the god. Sometimes the entire community indulged in such blood-letting rites in a collective orgy of self-offering.

The most common sacrifice was the extraction of the heart, a practice unique to Mexican civilization. The priests painted the sacrificial victims with red and white stripes, then reddened their mouths and drew black circles around them. They glued white down on the victim's heads. The priests then marshalled the victims at the foot of the temple pyramid steps before escorting them up the staircase one by one. At the summit, each prisoner was thrust backwards over the *techcatl*, the sacrificial stone. Four priests grasped the limbs, a fifth pressed down on the neck so that the doomed person's back was bent backwards under great tension. The high priest quickly opened the chest with blows of the *tecpatl*, the sacrificial knife with a chalcedony or obsidian blade, thrust his hand into the chest cavity and wrenched out the still-beating heart. This he held high as an offering to the sun before flinging it into a special bowl. The priests tipped the still-quivering body over the edge of the pyramid, sending it tumbling down the steps. The captor seized the corpse at the bottom and took it to his house. Some authorities speculate that the entire sacrificial rite was symbolic. The climbing prisoner was the young sun rising to his zenith at the moment of sacrifice. The tumbling body was the setting sun returning to the earth.

No one knows exactly how many human victims the Aztecs sacrificed. Cortes estimated that fifty people were killed at every temple annually, which would mean that some twenty thousand persons died for the gods throughout Aztec domains every year. Several early chroniclers agree that Tlaxcala sacrificed eight hundred captives in most years and a thousand every

Chalcedony-bladed sacrificial knife. Courtesy, Trustees of the British Museum.

Human sacrifice by cutting out the heart. From the complete facsimile edition of the series CODICES SELECTI, published by the AKADE-MISCHE DRUCK- u. Verlagsanstalt, vol. XXIII: CODEX MAGLIABECHIANO CL.XIII.3.

fourth year, the divine year. But the highest numbers were counted in Tenochtitlan, where as many as eight hundred victims for one festival alone have been spoken of. Sahagun describes how thousands of warriors went to their deaths at the consecration of Huitzilopochtli's great temple at Tenochtitlan. In truth, no reliable figures for human sacrifice are available, but it seems more likely the prestige of the victims, if only a handful, was often more important than sheer numbers.

Many Aztec temples boasted a *tzompantli,* a skull rack where the heads of sacrificial victims were displayed. The largest stood in the plaza at the foot of the Templo Mayor in Tenochtitlan, a lattice-like construc-

231

tion of long poles that displayed the defleshed skulls in long tiers. Two of Cortes' conquistadors estimated that at least 136,000 heads were displayed on this particular tzompantli, flanked by two towers made of more skulls cemented cheek-by-jowl on its macabre facade. Probably a gross exaggeration for propaganda purposes, archaeological findings help to put these figures in proportion. Only one hundred and seventy skulls perforated for stringing on poles have come from excavations at the important temple of Tlatelolco, a far cry from the 136,000 claimed for the nearby Templo Mayor.

Women too were sacrificed. A middle-aged woman impersonated the mother goddess Cihuacoatl at the festival of Tititl in the seventeenth month. She was induced to weep in imitation of the rain as she died by decapitation, and her severed head was then garlanded with paper decorations. A young girl died at the festival of "the Sweeping" in the eleventh month. Told that she was to be honored by spending the night with the ruler, the unsuspecting victim was led to a richly decorated shrine, where she was greeted by a priest who lifted her on his back. Another attendant promptly broke her neck. Her body was flayed and the head priest donned the fresh skin. Carrying the sacred double ears of corn and holding a quail in his lips, he processed to the steps of the Templo Mayor, there to don the headdress of the maize goddess Chicomecoatl.

Children also were important sacrificial victims. Tlaloc often preferred young victims, for their copious tears were the harbinger of abundant rains. They were painted black and adorned with paper ornaments, then decapitated or drowned.

The Aztecs certainly did not invent human sacrifice. The gods had fed off people during Teotihuacan's later heydey, and the Maya were experts at human sacrifice, too. But the Mexica developed the practice of mass sacrifice to new and obsessive heights. They institutionalized sacrifice and war as instruments of political policy. Human sacrifice was far more than a political device or a means for a brave warrior to obtain rich rewards. It embodied the effort of an entire nation to prolong the Fifth Sun, to keep the Sun itself in the heavens. It never occurred to an Aztec that sacrificing people was wrong. Quite the contrary, it would have been a grave sin not to do so.

CANNIBALISM?

Accustomed as they were to bloodshed and butchery and to the macabre teachings of their own faith with regard to death and Hell, the conquistadors were totally unprepared to understand the insatiable appetites of the Aztec gods for human sacrifice. Sahagun describes how the Mexica divided up the bodies of their captives "in order to eat them." A favorite recipe, we are told, was a stew of human flesh flavored with peppers and tomatoes. One special stew of dried maize, beans, and human flesh was known as *tlacatlolli,* "dried maize with human flesh." The Spaniards' lurid tales horrified and titillated everyone back home, and inevitably, the Aztecs were labelled as incorrigible cannibals by the world at large. Historian William Prescott embellished the stereotype even more when he turned Sahagun's sober descriptions into a "banquet teeming with delicious beverages and delicate viands, prepared with art and attended by both sexes" (1843, p. 421). Unfortunately, the custom of consuming human flesh, like exotic sexual practices, polygamy, and other alien habits, raises violent, distinctly unintellectual passions in the Western scholars who study them.

How important was cannibalism to the Aztecs? Was it a symbolic matter, or did the bodies of sacrificial victims form part of the regular diet? Many anthropologists believe that the Mexica ate human flesh as a religious rite, but Michael Harner of the New School of Social Research has recently argued that, beyond a mere matter of ceremony, human flesh provided a vital source of meat protein for a population living in an environment where meat was in short supply. He theorizes that while the nobles could enjoy delicacies such as turkey or dog meat, they organized mass human sacrifice not only as an instrument of foreign policy, but as a means of delivering convenient packages of protein-rich meat to their warriors and the common people. This provocative theory assumes that the Indians needed animal protein. In fact, the tribute lists show that the Aztecs obtained food stuffs from all over Mexico, commodities that enabled much of the population to enjoy a more than adequately varied diet. Harner may have confused the well-organized pre-Hispanic centuries with the chaos, disorganization, and malnutrition that followed the Conquest. In any case, there was no way that the priests could sacrifice enough victims to fill the entire protein need of the population.

Anthropologist William Arens denies that the Aztecs were cannibals at all. He argues that the conquistadors' accounts of cannibalism are biased, written in part to justify their own acts of butchery. After all, he points out, Christians had a divine mission to wipe out paganism and the eating of human flesh. Arens also believes that Sahagun and the other friars highlighted cannibalism and other idolatries partly out of their own fear of the Inquisition. He goes as far as to argue that accusations of cannibalism were more political than scientific, and he suggests that no conquistador actually saw an Aztec eating the body of a human sacrifice, or even any evidence of cannibalism.

Few anthropologists or historians agree wholeheartedly with either Arens or Harner. Most place considerable reliance on the testimony of the early friar-historians. Diego Duran describes a sacrifice at the temple of Huitzilopochtli in which the thigh of the victim was cut off and handed over to his captors, where "it was carried away and eaten, each receiving his part, the number depending on the number of those who had captured him—never more than four" (1971, p. 95). Such careful division and consumption of sanctified flesh—it was nothing less—may have been commonplace among a people described by Duran as experts at eating at other peoples' expense. "Yet," he adds significantly, "there are no people who manage to

Warriors and prisoners. From the Codex Mendoza. Courtesy, Bodleian Library, Oxford. MS. Arch. Selden A.1. folio 65.

survive with less food, when it is at their own expense" (1971, p. 95).

Definitive proof of cannibalism can only come from the dispassionate testimony of the archaeological record. Archaeologist Eduardo Matos Moctezuma has been digging into Tenochtitlan's Templo Mayor, where he has found stacks of intact skulls, carvings, and caches of ritual objects from all over Mesoamerica. But he has never found any human bones broken up for food. According to Bernal Diaz and the friars, the Aztec ate human flesh at home. So far no one has excavated any houses in the ancient capital. When they do, the presence or absence of butchered bones may settle the cannibalism question once and for all. The weight of the historical evidence at present favors a belief in some ritual consumption of human flesh.

War, human sacrifice, and cannibalism held heavy symbolic meaning for Aztec existence. Battle, whether in heaven or on earth, was never a struggle between the forces of good and evil, as it has so often been in Christian history. The Aztecs saw war and sacrifice as an eternal order, as a means to an end—the end of perpetuating a doomed world. Through encouraging a deepening piety and the systematic use of terror, the Aztec rulers led their people into an existence where human sacrifice became a self-sustaining, integral part of their lives, perhaps even an instrument of political policy. As the population grew, so did the incidence of war and human sacrifice. It may be significant that the greatest incidences of human sacrifice, and the likelihood of cannibalism associated with it, occurred when the Aztec empire was expanding rapidly. The sacrifice of adult males from conquered provinces may have had the effect of reducing the number of able-bodied warriors capable of inciting, or taking part in, rebellion. Conceivably, human sacrifice was indeed a means of population control and pragmatic political strategy. But history shows there is a point at which a satiated population turns and rebels against an unbearable burden; where, perhaps, the burden of the dead weighs heavily on the minds not only of the priests and the ruler, but of the nation as a whole. There is some reason to believe that an increasing philosophical polarity between ferocity and mercy was causing acute tensions within Mexica society by the time of the Conquest.

The philosophical ambivalence of Aztec civilization shows acutely in the striking contrast between the ferocious cults of war and human sacrifice on the one hand and those of benevolence, humility, and mercy on the other. The rising cults of the war-god Huitzilopochtli and the peace-loving, philosophical Quetzalcoatl at different ends of the divine spectrum reflect this dualism. Undoubtedly the contradiction between war and humility was reflected in deep tensions between militant Tenochtitlan and more peace-loving cities like Texcoco. Nahuatl literature offers many examples of this strange conflict of ideals:

There is nothing like death in war,
nothing like flowery death
so precious to the Giver of Life:
Far off I see it: my heart yearns for it!
(Coe, 1962, p. 168.)

This poem, and many others, expresses in rich imagery the deep mystical, yet militaristic view of the world that sustained and balanced an ambivalent Aztec civilization. But this civilization of metaphysics and numbers was overthrown by weapons of steel and gunpowder. This beautiful world fled to the "place that is beyond us," when the temples were razed, the codices destroyed, and the idols thrown down. And when the gods were dead, the people perished as well.

esto, parece ser cosa muy buena, y
sabrosa, ya me sano, y quito la en
fermedad, ya estoy sano: y mas
otra uez le dixo el viejo. Señor.
beued la otra vez, porque es muy
buena la medicina, y estareys
mas sano. Y el dicho quetzalcoatl,
beujo la otra vez de que se embo
rracho, y començo a llorar triste
mente: y se le moujo, y ablan
do el coraçon, para yrse, y no se
le quito del pensamiento lo que
tenja, por el engaño, y burla,
que le hizo, el dicho nigromanti
co viejo. Y la medicina que be
ujo, el dicho quetzalcoatl, era
vino blanco de la tierra: hecho
de magueyes, que se llaman teu
metl.

tlapia ieveuetlacatl, âmonono
tzazque. auh iniquac ticalmo
cuepas, occeppa tipiltontli timu
chicas. njman icmoioleuh in
Quetzalcoatl: auh inrevento ie
no ceppa qujlhuj, tlaoque xoco
miti, inpatli, njman qujto in
Quetzalcoatl veventze caamo
piquiz, njman qujlhuj inveve
to, maca xoconmiti timotoli
niz, macannel noço mixquac
xocontlali motonal motolinis.
macanachito xoconmopalolti.
auh in Quetzalcoatl: njman
conpalo achiton: auh catepan
vel conjc, njman qujto inQue
tzalcoatl: tlenj cacenca, qualli,
in cocoliztli caocenpolo, campa
noia cocolli caocmo njnococoa,
njman qujlhuj inveuento, ca
occe xoconj caqualli inpatli ic
chicaoaz inmonacaic, auh ni
man ic ienoceppa ce conjc, njman
ic ivintic, njman ieic
choca veltellelquiça, ic vpcan
moioleuh in Quetzalcoatl, vncā
tlapan injiollo. aocmoconilca
caoaia, çaie inqujmattinenca
inqujmattinemja velqujolma

CHAPTER 10　　The Gods and the Ceremonies

You live in heaven;
you uphold the mountain,
Anahuac is in your hands.
Awaited, you are always everywhere;
you are invoked, you are prayed to.
Your glory, your fame is sought.
You live in heaven;
Anahuac is in your hands.

Cantares Mexicanos, 35, V. Leon-Portilla, 1963, p. 81.

A page from Volume 3 of Sahagun's General History *on the origins of the gods.*

"New words are these that you speak; because of them we are disturbed, because of them we are troubled." The Mexica were offered the solace of the Cross after the Conquest, a solace that they embraced with extreme reluctance. The wise men were soon called upon to defend their faith before the Catholic friars who arrived in Tenochtitlan in 1524. The friars denied that "the Lord of the Close Vicinity, to Whom the heavens and earth belong," was a god at all. The wise men listened carefully to the Christian message, thanked the friars, and then eloquently pointed out that they had learned their religion from their ancestors, who "taught us all their rules of worship, all their ways of honoring the gods. Thus before them, we do prostrate ourselves; in their names we bleed ourselves; our oaths we keep, incense we burn, and sacrifices we offer. It was the doctrine of the elders that there is life because of the gods; with their sacrifice, they gave us life . . ." (Leon-

Portilla, 1963, pp. 63–66). To reject the gods was to destroy the people themselves.

The close relationship between the Mexica and their gods was forged on the themes of fertility and creation, the great triumph and tragedy of the rising and setting Sun. They surrounded the intricate story of the challenges to the Sun's authority with a complex mythology and theology. They felt a constant need to reach out to their gods, the multifaceted deities that served as bridges between different parts of a complicated, numinous world. Many civilizations have been convinced that humans and gods shared at least some family likeness, a likeness that gave the people confidence that the world would continue. But the Mexica had no myth that joined human beings on earth with the remote gods. The only link between them occurred in elaborate rites during which people sought to feed the gods, to placate them and ensure that the world continued. Beyond the earth was an unknowable cosmos regulated by the unchanging verities of the ever-moving calendar. The gods also lived within this cosmos. Like humans, they had birth days and lived with all the luck and misfortune that such days and day signs brought. In that sense, they, too, were subject to the whims and caprices of fortune.

THE GODS

Bernardino de Sahagun and Diego Duran described the Aztec gods and the religious beliefs associated with them in hopes that an understanding of them would help them to stamp out idolatry. "The Indians worship idols in our presence, and we understand nothing of what goes on in their dances, in their marketplaces . . . in the songs they chant (when they lament their ancient gods and lords)," wrote Duran (1964, p. 55) as his justification for years of what his contemporaries regarded as near-heretical research.

"Just to list all known deity names and appellations would require many pages," writes Henry Nicholson

(1971, p. 408) of the Mexican pantheon. Most of the deities were thought of in anthropomorphic terms, as having certain forms and attributes, among others. Each had its own diagnostic combination of insignia which was shown in many codices and sculptures, symbolic depictions that enabled the faithful to identify the god and his or her roles. Individual signs and symbols might be shared by different deities, but the combinations were unique to a particular divinity.

The invisible gods were thought to live in the thirteen layers of the heaven, most of them in the highest stratum. The deities of the underworld dwelt in Mictlan, others at specific earthly locations where they were especially important. They were related to one another, but in no systematic way as, say, many of the Greek deities were. Nor was there a hierarchy of gods and goddesses. The Mexica thought of their deities in dual, quadruple, and even quintuple forms. The quadruple ones were associated with the four cardinal directions; the quintuple ones added a center to the four directions. Even more important were patron deities, gods and goddesses from the existing pantheon associated with particular social, political, or economic groups. These groups might range from entire tribes, like the Aztecs, to small calpulli or artisans' guilds. Even individual people might have their own special divine patrons, usually the deity associated with their day of birth.

The Mexica enjoyed the patronage of an exceptionally powerful divine patron: they considered themselves the chosen people of the Sun God Huitzilopochtli. In fact, the cult of this particular deity may have begun as a carefully contrived political strategy. The vizier Tlacaelel vigorously promoted the cult of Huitzilopochtli as a way to stiffen the imperial ambitions of the Mexica in the early fifteenth century. Huitzilopochtli had once been a minor tribal god, but Tlacaelel's orators and historians deliberately made him into a major deity. They painted a vivid picture of ancient priests carrying the divine image and sacred relic bundle of Huitzilopochtli wherever the Mexica went. The god urged the

people on to ever more heroic acts and inspired them to greatness. His priest-leaders acting as intermediaries between the people and the god, he became the *alte-peyollotl,* the "heart of the community." When the Mexica founded Tenochtitlan, their first act was to erect a shrine to Huitzilopochtli who now symbolized their power and independence. When they conquered another city, they burned its temple and carried off the sacred images of its patron gods. Huitzilopochtli would reign over the vassal state instead.

The Mexica believed that they lived only through the grace of the gods, the deities who gave them suste-nance, rain, and everything that flourished on earth. Almost every act, however trivial, was surrounded with a religious symbolism that is difficult for us to compre-hend. The theme of primeval creation, of divine crea-tivity, underlay all other religious themes in Mexica

Ehecatl-Quetzalcoatl and Tezcatlipoca. From the complete facsimile edition of the series CODICES SELECTI, published by the Akademische Druck- u. Verlagsanstalt, vol. XLIV: CODEX BORBON-ICUS.

society, and it embodied the most abstract of philosophical thought.

Ometeotl was the primordial creative power, the personification of the godhead, the all-pervasive divinity. This figure could be a bisexual unity or a male-female pair (male: Ometecuhtli, Tloque Nahuaque, and so on; female: Omecihuatl, Citlalicue, and so on), the primeval parents of gods and humans. Ometecuhtli and Omecihuatl were the constant creators of life, the gods who lived in the thirteenth, highest heaven and who sent the souls of infants from heaven to earth.

Ometeotl was, in many ways, the recipient of all the Mexicas' prayers and sacrifices, even if these were specifically directed toward more active gods who partook of his all-pervasive divinity. Ometeotl may have been the primordial creative force, but the main practical tasks of the Creation fell on the two great gods Tezcatlipoca and Quetzalcoatl.

Tezcatlipoca was the supreme god of the pantheon, a virile, youthful, and all-knowing deity who was associated with the four directions and colors. He was a quadruple supernatural personality, associated with the calendar, the sun and moon, even banqueting and revelry. He was the arch-sorcerer, the god of darkness, the night, and the jaguar, the animal associated with darkness, power, and wisdom. Henry Nicholson has argued that his origins may go back to the ancient obsidian mirror, the shining device used in primeval divination rituals. "Smoking Mirror," "he who never gets old," was often depicted wearing an obsidian mirror in his hair, another covering the place where one of his feet had been lost to the Earth Monster. Tezcatlipoca was caparisoned like a warrior armed with atlatl, spears, and shield. No god better personifies the fatalistic thinking that pervaded Aztec religion than this dread, powerful deity.

One of the most universal of all Aztec gods was the "Plumed Serpent," Quetzalcoatl. The feathered serpent was an age-old concept in Mexican religion, one that may have preceded Teotihuacan, a symbol of the fertility that comes from water and rain. Quetzalcoatl was a god with many tasks. As Creator, he played a key role in the creation of humans at the very beginning of the Fifth Sun. He had close ties with the fertility of the soil in another role, as Ehecatl, the wind, and, in yet another role as Venus, the Morning Star, he was associated with the dread, warlike Tlahuizcalpanteculi. Above all, Quetzalcoatl was a saintly, priestlike god, the patron of the calmecac, the nobles' school. He was the god of learning and culture, of ancient lore, the god of civilization itself. The divine Plumed Serpent had even assumed mortal form in the personages of the priest-rulers of Toltec Tula. It was the legendary Toltec high priest Topiltzin Quetzalcoatl who fled from Tula to the east to escape the wrath of Tezcatlipoca's followers. He set sail over the ocean, promising one day to return. This ancient and much revered god was the very symbol of holiness and gentility. His was a life of fasting and penitence, of priestly behavior. Quetzalcoatl was usually depicted wearing a red, bird-like mask. His face and body were black. He always wore a conical head-dress and a garment with a seashell-like front, and he usually carried the priestly incense bag.

Huitzilopochtli was *the* patron god of the Aztecs, the diety who had prophesied their greatness and led them to magnificent imperial deeds. A minor god elevated to greatness by imperial propagandists, Huitzilopochtli became the very personification of virile warriorhood, a young, brave god, who sought constant human sacrifices as his rightful due. He seems to have been a transfiguration of Tezcatlipoca, with blue-and-yellow-striped face and a warrior's helmet in the form of a hummingbird, its beak acting as a visor over the face. The peerless soldier, Huitzilopochtli carried a special shield and brandished darts like the indomitable *xiuhcoatl,* the Serpent of Fire, a snake-headed boomerang encrusted with turquoise that he could turn into a thunderbolt that incinerated all that stood in its way. He led the Mexica from Aztlan, inspired them to greatness, and helped them found Tenochtitlan. A much narrower diety than cosmic gods like Quetzalcoatl and

Tezcatlipoca, Huitzilopochtli was the special represen-
tative of the Mexica, the god who sanctioned their wars
and their rites of human sacrifice.

Xiuhtecutli was the fire god, the life-giving warmth
of the perpetual fire that sustained human life. The
eldest of the gods, he was associated with the coronation of rulers, who were usually confirmed in their offices on his most auspicious day, 4 Acatl. Fire was a
central concept in Mexican religion, the symbol of en-
during life, rekindled at the beginning of every fifty-
two-year cycle in the calendar.

The fertility of crops and life-giving rain were also
dominant themes in Mexican theology. These were associated with a small army of gods, among them Tlaloc,
the god believed to control the rains that fertilized all
crops, and especially goddesses. "To [Tlaloc] was attri-
buted the rain; for he made it, he caused it to come
down . . . . He caused to sprout, to blossom, to leaf out,
to ripe, the trees, the plants, our food" (Sahagun, 1, p.
2). He appears in many forms, sometimes in quadruple,
even quintuple manifestations. His *tlaloque,* a group of
dwarfish assistants, had different colors and cardinal
directions assigned to them. Tlaloc always wore a distinctive facial mask with goggle eyes. His body was
black, his mask and clothing blue. He wore a headdress
topped with white heron and green quetzal feathers.
Paper banners sprayed with rubber adorned his back.
His wife, sister, or mother (the roles vary) was Chalchiuhtlicue, a water goddess with close ties to the
maize-earth goddess. Ehecatl, the Wind God, had four
directions and personified the winds that preceded rain
storms.

A number of female deities were associated with
maize cultivation, among them Chicomecoatl. Under
the name Xilonen she was the goddess of the young
maize plant that produced the *xilotl,* the young, green
maize ear. Ometochtli was associated with maguey and
with pulque, the intoxicating beverage brewed from it.
The assistants of Ometochtli were known collectively as
Centzon Totochtin, "Four Hundred Rabbits," and
they enjoyed close spiritual links with Tlaloc's tlaloque.

They were patrons of revelry, alcohol, and drunkenness.

Teteoinnan, "Mother of the Gods," the earth mother, was worshipped by doctors and midwives and was identified with many major and minor deities, among them Coatlicue, the mother of Huitzilopochtli. These goddesses supervised sexual desire, sin, pregnancy, childbirth, and feasting.

Lastly, Xipe Totec, "Our Lord the Flayed One," was closely linked to the earth mother and was worshipped all over Mexico. Xipe was a fertility god whose gladiatorial rituals, the *tlahuahuanaliztli,* signalled the beginning of spring. The god himself was typically depicted wearing a flayed human skin.

The welfare of the Aztecs, indeed the very existence of the universe, depended on the proper nourishment of the gods and the sun with the sacred elixir of human hearts and blood. Tonatiuh, the Sun God whose attributes merged with the primeval Ometeotl, was the ultimate recipient of all human sacrifice. He was the patron of warriors, the people pledged to his service who supplied the prisoners for sacrifice and assuaged his insatiable appetite. When warriors died for him, they received as their due the privilege of eternal life and the pleasurable daily task of accompanying Tonatiuh to his zenith.

Wherever the Aztecs turned, they felt the presence of the gods. These colorful, sometimes grotesque, figures dominated the Mexica. Propitiated by complex public rituals and a constant supply of human hearts and blood, their power and charisma far overshadowed that of any ruler or conquering army. They were Mexico, the Fifth Sun, the divine host faithfully served by a hierarchy of devoted priests and hundreds of thousands of slavish believers.

THE PRIESTHOOD

Literally thousands of people served the temples and the gods. Like the secular bureaucracy, the *teopixque,* the priesthood, had a highly organized hierarchy. While every important temple had at least one fulltime

Mask of Xipe Totec in gray volcanic stone with traces of red paint. From the Valley of Mexico, exact location unknown. Height: 9 inches (22.8 cm). Courtesy, Trustees of the British Museum.

priest, the Templo Mayor and other major shrines boasted large staffs of religious functionaries. Priestesses and lay people served the gods as well. The whole priestly organization exercised an enormous influence over the daily life of the Aztecs and had a major say in the affairs of state.

Families dedicated their children to the priesthood before their teens. Young commoners or nobles entered a temple calmecac as *tlamacazton* ("little givers of things") to learn basic ritual activities and perform menial chores. Soon they became *tlamacazqui* ("givers of things"), young priests who entered the regular ecclesiastical ranks. Subsequently they advanced from rank to rank about every five years. Only the most qualified and devout aspired to the lofty status of *tlenamacac* ("fire giver"), the priests who wielded the obsidian-bladed sacrificial knife. Many clerics were engaged full-time in teaching activities, as well as in the organization and staging of major and minor religious functions. It was they who made incense offerings, blew the conch trumpets at intervals throughout the night, and kept the eternal fires burning in the temples. Two high officials of equal rank headed the priesthood and presided over the rituals at the Templo Mayor in Tenochtitlan. *Quetzalcoatl totec tlamacazqui* supervised the shrine of Huitzilopochtli, while *Quetzalcoatl tlaloc tlamacazqui* saw to Tlaloc's needs. Each was a very saintly person, "of righteous life; of pure heart, good, and humane; who was resigned; who was firm and tranquil; a peace-maker, constant, resolute, brave ... who had awe in his heart" (Sahagun, 3, p. 67).

The ruler and his chief vizier also exercised considerable influence in religious affairs. They were responsible for adherence to the religious calendar, and they carried out important ritual functions at major public ceremonies. They distributed food to the poor and even performed ritual dances upon occasion. Secular and religious affairs were closely entwined in what might almost be called a check-and-balance system. The priests crowned the ruler, but he selected the highest religious officials. Both secular and religious authorities possessed considerable political power, yet one could not function without the other. But above all, the prosperity of every Aztec, and of the state itself, depended on the continual placation of the gods. This was the task that engaged a priesthood of thousands of major and minor functionaries at the time of the Conquest.

The priesthood was deeply committed to the state religion and spent much of its time in the exercise of routine ecclesiastical duties—temple cleaning and maintaining the endless round of incense offerings and prayers, as well as tending the sacred fires. Every cleric performed routine religious duties, whether supervising a major ceremony or merely sweeping the temple steps. The priests lived together within temple precincts and practiced sexual abstinence. (Some may have married, but the evidence is uncertain.) They performed an unvarying round of offerings, prayer, and penance that included the drawing of blood. They usually dyed their bodies black with soot from the smoke of resinous wood, and they never cut their hair, which often reached to the knees, so that their braided locks "looked like a tightly curled horse's mane" (Duran, 1951, p. 114). The resinous soot so blackened and caked the hair that it could never be disentangled. They bound it, instead, with white cotton cords. Streaks of caked blood from constant autosacrifice flowed down the temples of every priest. Each was committed to a single deity, and each was expected to live the exemplary life. Even the conquistadors were impressed by their piety and gentleness.

Women too could be dedicated to the service of the gods. Parents would take an infant girl to the temple and make repeated offerings of an incense ladle and some copal. These constituted an agreement that the girl would enter the priesthood as a *cihuatlmacazqui* ("female giver of things"). Many priestesses later left the priesthood to marry, a move that had to be sanctioned by both parents and calpulli leaders. Some priestesses did spend their entire lives in religious service. They taught younger priestesses, impersonated goddesses, and spent a great deal of time weaving and embroidering the fine cloths used to decorate the idols and the temples.

Not all temple functionaries were fulltime clerics. Some people vowed their services to the temple for a limited time as a way of gaining divine favor: "All this time they were serving in the temple, the men by themselves, and the women by themselves, with much seclusion and chastity. The men served by sweeping and guarding the temple, and the women by cooking for the idol different foods which they placed and offered before their idol . . ." (Kubler and Gibson, 1951, p. 29). The laws of chastity and good behavior were strictly enforced. Those who deviated were summarily hung. Many calpulli members and specialized artisans participated in special ceremonies or feast days that honored their particular patron deity. Every member of society had a chance, indeed an obligation, to take part in the rituals and ceremonies that maintained the state's good relations with the divine pantheon.

The Aztec priesthood had duties well beyond their merely religious ones. The priests were the repositories of sacred and historical law, those who educated succeeding generations in the great accumulated body of philosophical knowledge. They foretold the future, read and interpreted the sacred books, and interpreted omens. Many priests accompanied the army into battle and took prisoners on their own account. Most important of all, they acted as the link between the pantheon and mere mortals, interpreting not only the will of the deities, but the role of humanity within the forbidding cosmos.

THE RITUALS

The rulers of the Aztec empire expended prodigious amounts of time, energy, and tribute on elaborate ceremonies to honor the gods. A measured cycle of public festivals signaled the passage of the seasons and key moments in the agricultural cycle. Every public ceremony varied in its details, but the overall pattern of celebration was much the same. The participants nor-

249

mally began with a period of fasting, *nezahualiztli,* which usually lasted about four days. The fasters would only take a single meal a day, a repast unseasoned by chilis or salt. They also abstained from sexual relations and washing. Sometimes the priests conducted an all-night vigil, *tozohualiztli,* on the day before a festival.

The major ceremonies were elaborate, carefully organized productions conducted in eye-catching settings intended to impress spectators and to promote loyalty to the gods that stood behind the community, the city, and the state. Most began with temple offerings of flowers, food stuffs, rubber-spattered papers, and clothing. "Thus were offerings made: with food and with capes were offerings made, and with all kinds of living things—perchance turkeys, perchance birds ... or whatever was newly formed—perchance maize ... or flowers" (Sahagun, 2, p. 181). Copal incense was burned at the shrines. "They dedicated the incense burner to the four directions, thus offering incense. And when they had offered [incense] to the four directions, then they threw [the incense and the coals] into the brazier" (Sahagun, 2, p. 181). Libations of pulque were poured at the hearths, too.

The most important offerings were symbolic or actual sacrifices. The priests offered hundreds of animal sacrifices every day, mainly by beheading quail *(tla-quechcotonaliztli)*. The ritual of autosacrifice, offering one's own blood, was a favorite public and private act of penance. The penitent drew blood by pricking the body with a maguey spine. The priests were the most ardent practitioners, sticking their ear lobes and other fleshy parts of the body with the spines. The bloody spines were then stuck into plaited grass balls or laid on a bed of green branches, or the blood was spattered on pieces of offering paper. They also "cut their ears with an obsidian blade, and then took out blood from about the ears" (Sahagun, 2, p. 185). Others pierced their flesh with a fine obsidian point "that there they might pass a straw [through it], upon the morrow the straws were swept up and gathered; and the straws were much bloodied" (Sahagun, 2, p. 184). The ultimate and most holy offering was that of human sacrifice.

Every ceremony involved singing and dances and sometimes processions where priests would impersonate the deity. The Mexica honored professional singers and dancers, who were carefully trained in the calmecac to create and recite songs commemorating the gods and extolling the deeds of the rulers. A special temple caretaker, the *tlapizcatzin,* trained the hymn singers. He was in charge of "the songs of the devils, of indeed all the sacred songs that none might do ill [with them]. Greatly was he concerned that they teach the sacred songs ..." (Sahagun, 2, p. 195). Orchestras of drums, rattles, flutes, whistles, and shell trumpets accompanied the songs and dances. Most major festivals ended with feasting and jollity on a large scale, activities sometimes sponsored by the ruler and the leading nobles as a community benefit.

THE MONTHLY CEREMONIES

Silence never fell over the temples of Tenochtitlan. The watchful priests orchestrated not only the vast public ceremonies but a host of minor rituals and regular offerings: "Each day, when the sun arose, quails were slain and incense was offered. And thus were quail slain: they wrung the necks of the quail and raised them, dedicated them to the sun." The priests invoked the sun: "The sun hath come forth—the shafts of heat, the torquoise child, the soaring eagle." They offered incense four times during the day and five times during the night, "the first time when it was dark; the second time, when it was time to sleep; the third time, when the shell trumpets were sounded; the fourth time at midnight; and the fifth time, near dawn" (Sahagun, 2, p. 202).

The sixteenth-century missionary historians identified at least eighteen annual festivals that fell at the end of the months *(veintena)* of the secular year. Most of them were linked to major events in the agricultural cycle, and it was no coincidence that no less than eleven of the monthly ceremonies were devoted to the rain god Tlaloc and to the fertility goddesses who presided over water, maize, and the land. The most elaborate fertility rituals fell during the major agricultural months between March and October. For example, the *Tlacaxiehualiztli* festival, the "Flaying of Men," took place in mid- to late-March and honored Xipe Totec. It featured mock skirmishes, human sacrifices, and the famous gladiatorial sacrifice ritual where an honored prisoner, with feather-decked, useless weapons and tied by the waist to a rock, battled against a series of warriors. The doomed and dying victim was then sacrificed to the gods with great reverence. The priests wore the flayed skins of the slain for twenty days. During this ceremony valiant warriors received prized insignia, and the tears of sacrificed children ensured a propitious rainfall.

Tozoztontli fell in late April or early May, the "Small Vigil," a planting festival when offerings were made in the fields and more children were sacrificed. *Ochpaniztli,* "Road Sweeping," the harvest festival, came round in the first three weeks of September. At this time the state organized a general clean-up of temples, roads, canals, and public buildings. Seeds and maize cobs were offered up, and human impersonators of the gods were sacrificed, sometimes by decapitation, sometimes by the bow. Once again, valiant soldiers were honored with capes and other fine insignia. *Teotleco,* in late September or early October, honored the "Arrival of the Gods," the appearance of maize-flour footprints in the temple signaling the return of the deities. *Panquetzaliztli,* the "Raising of Banners," fell just over two months later, a great celebration involving not only nightly dances by warriors and prostitutes, but a great procession that wound its way through the streets of the city from the Templo Mayor through Tlatelolco and the suburbs before returning for the inevitable human sacrifices at the starting point.

Other important rituals fell at longer intervals. Every four years, a version of the *Izcalli* festival, "the Planting

Above: Priest impersonating the maize goddess. From the complete facsimile edition of the series CODICES SELECTI, published by the Akademische Druck- u. Verlagsanstalt, vol. XLIV: CODEX BORBONICUS. Drawing, Sally Black.

Above, right: Gladiatorial sacrifice honoring Xipe Totec. From the complete facsimile edition of the series CODICES SELECTI, published by the Akademische Druck- u. Verlagsanstalt, vol. XXIII: CODEX MAGLIABECHIANO CL.XIII.3. Drawing, Sally Black.

of Flowers," honored the fire god Xiuhtecuhtli with sacrifices of victims disguised as the god, while the greatest nobles danced in their finest regalia. On this auspicious day children were assigned male and female godparents, dedicated over fire, and then their ears were pierced. Every eight years *Atamalcualiztli,* "the Eating of Water Tamales," gave new life to the maize. Everyone fasted strictly for seven days, eating only one bland meal of tamales soaked in water at midday. At this festival everyone danced; indeed, it was called "the Dance of the Gods." The dancers dressed as hummingbirds, butterflies, beetles, as "sleep," as vegetable sellers, even as "the poor." They danced before an image of Tlaloc facing a water pot filled with serpents and live frogs. One group, the Mazateca, actually grabbed the live snakes with their teeth and ate them as they danced. There were processions and feasting on fruit tamales. The elderly prayed that they might live another eight years. "Thus was given respite to the maize every eight years," writes Sahagun, (2, p. 164), "for it was said that we brought much torment to it . . . as we troubled [our food] to death, thus we revived it."

Once every fifty-two years, all the people of Central Mexico joined in perhaps the most solemn religious event of all, *Xiuhmolpilli,* the "Tying of Years," the name signifying the bundles of reeds that signalled the

passing of the years. On the prescribed day of the "New Fire" all domestic hearths were extinguished and household idols thrown out. Every family threw away its cooking utensils and cleaned house with meticulous care. At nightfall everyone climbed onto roofs or up to other good vantage points. Pregnant women and children covered their faces with maguey leaf masks. Mothers kept their young ones awake, for a dozing child would turn into a mouse if the great ritual failed.

Meanwhile the priests climbed to the summit of Uixachtlan, a sacred hill on the outskirts of present-day Mexico City. A high-ranking victim, often a prisoner of war, was spread-eagled on the sacrificial stone as the priests watched the heavens. Precisely at midnight, they would rip out the victim's heart and twirl a fire stick to kindle a new flame in the chest cavity of the dead warrior. A great shout went up as torches were lit from the flames and the universe was reborn for another fifty-two years. Teams of runners bore the new fire to temples, schools, and households while the people bled their ears in deep penance and life began again. Woe betide the nation if the fire-making ceremony failed. The world was them doomed, darkness would cover the earth, and the celestial monsters would devour every living thing as the Fifth Sun ended. This drama

The New Fire ceremony. From the complete facsimile edition of the series CODICES SELECTI, published by the Akademische Druck- u. Verlagsanstalt, vol. XLIV: CODEX BORBONICUS.

of anxiety and fear, the "New Fire" ceremony, expressed the very essence of Aztec belief.

THE MOVABLE FEASTS

The Mexica celebrated many more modest ceremonies whose dates were fixed by the divinatory calendar. Each feast honored the deity or deities associated with the particular day-sign upon which it fell. The idols of the god or goddess were elaborately decorated, and offerings of incense, quail, and sometimes human victims were laid before them. The inevitable fasting, processions, singing, and dancing commemorated the day. The most important of these was the 4 Movement ceremony when a messenger to the Sun God was sacrificed exactly at noon. Everyone fasted and shed blood in penance. Merchants displayed their wealth on 4 Wind. Another celebration took place on 7 Flower, the day-sign of the patron deities of the painters and seamstresses. Two Rabbit was the special festival for the maguey farmers and the gods of pulque. Major public ceremonies also commemorated special events—the dedication of a new temple or military victories. But many rituals were also celebrated at a personal level: stages in the life cycle, rites conducted by merchants returning from a long journey, planting ceremonies, and even the simple task of naming a child. Religion and ritual pervaded every aspect of Aztec life.

DIVINATION

The great public ceremonies and rituals influenced the fate of the Mexica as a nation. But the gods presided over the personal fates of the Aztecs as well. A sharp line divided the highly organized state cults and the supernatural beliefs that served private ends. The saintly Ehecatl-Quetzalcoatl was the patron not only of the priesthood as a whole, but of the diviners and magicians, the private practitioners, as it were, many of whom were also clerics.

255

The Mexica referred to diviners and magicians as *Nahualli,* and they consulted them frequently on a private basis. These people were not only diviners, but curers, illusionists, and oracles. *Cualli nahualli* were benevolent practitioners, the diviners, rain-makers, and curers. The *tlahueliloc nanahualtin* were black magicians, malevolent sorcerers who often took the disguise of owls. People employed them to harm others, to bewitch and destroy their victims by burning their effigies and bringing all sorts of misfortune.

The *ticitl,* or "doctor," was a "knower of herbs, of stones, of trees, of roots .... He provides health, restores people, provides them splints, sets bones for them, purges them ... he lances, makes incisions in them, revives them" (Sahagun, 10, p. 30). The Aztecs used all manner of herbs and plants to treat medical problems from gout to chronic sneezing. Their tictli used at least one hundred thirty-two herbs to cure diseases and heal wounds. They used the sweat bath, in childbirth, in fever cases, and to relax the patient, much as we use the hot tub today. Military tictli accompanied Aztec armies, setting broken bones and treating wounds with a mixture of maguey sap and other compounds.

Peyote and mushrooms were among the most important Aztec medicines. Both peyote and the sacred mushrooms *(teonanacatl)* were considered effective against fever, and the mushroom worked for gout as well. "The mushroom saddens, depresses, troubles one," wrote Sahagun (11, p. 130). "It makes one flee, frightens one, makes one hide. He who eats many of them sees many things which make him afraid or make him laugh. He flees, hangs himself, hurls himself from a cliff, cries out, takes flight. One eats it in honey . . . ." Perhaps sacrificial victims were dosed with mushrooms before their death.

Yet other specialists were known as *tlapouhque,* "counters." Most expert and honored among them were the *tonalpouhque,* the diviners who could interpret the significance of the two-hundred-sixty day-signs of the sacred calendar. They determined the auspicious

days for infants' naming ceremonies and foretold peoples' fates through their birthdates. Every day-name in the 260-day cycle, the twenty day-signs and thirteen day-numbers, were either lucky, unlucky, or indifferent, so much so that one's birthdate served as a form of one's soul *(tetonal)*. The diviners would take into account a multitude of factors in assigning names and establishing the correct days for such auspicious events as the coronation of rulers, the start of wars, the planting of crops, or the beginning of a journey. They also interpreted dreams, for which purpose they consulted special "books of dreams."

The *tlaolchayauhqui* ("one who scatters maize kernels") were important diviners who read the scatter patterns of maize grains on a white cotton mantle to diagnose diseases. Many such practitioners were women. Divination may also have been accomplished by observing the subject in the surface of a water-filled pot or in a polished obsidian mirror. The astrologers, the *tlaciuhqui*, did their work by watching celestial signs and the procession of the heavenly bodies. Some diviners used self-induced hallucination—fasting, auto-sacrifice, or consuming hallucinogenic plants—as part of their practice. In their trances, they gave oracular answers to questions posed.

The Spanish quickly destroyed the public cults of the Aztecs, but the magicians and diviners continued to flourish individually long after the Conquest right under the noses of the missionaries. Indeed, they can be found practicing in Indian Mexico to this day.

A woman diviner using maize kernels and beans to diagnose her patient's illness. From the complete facsimile edition of the series CODICES SELECTI, published by the Akademische Druck- u. Verlagsanstalt, vol. XXIII: CODEX MAGLIABE-CHINAO CL.XIII.3.

V

THE COLLAPSE OF THE FIFTH SUN

The only persons to profit by the whole business are the lawyers, prosecuting attorneys, notaries, solicitors, and the persons sent to verify the damage done by the cattle. In short, all is show and pretence, with much giving of false, defective, and lying testimony. Nothing that I might say would suffice to expose the enormity of the things that are done.

Alonso de Zorita, *Life and Labor in Ancient Mexico,* 1963, p. 271, on the seizure of Indian lands for cattle grazing.

porque el que mas podia correr,
que otros, tomaua la tea de pino:
y ansi muy presto, casi en un mo
mento llegauan, asus pueblos: y
della luego venjan, a tomar to
dos los vesinos della. Y era cosa
de ver, la mucha dumbre de
los fuegos, en todos los pueblos,
que parecia ser de dia: y pri
mero se hazian lumbres, en
las casas, donde morauan,
los dichos mjnjstros, delos ido
los.

¶ Capitulo doze. de co
mo la gente. despues de
auer tomado. fuego nu
euo, renouauan todos
sus vestidos, y alhajas:
donde se pone la figura
de la cuenta de los años.

De la dicha manera, hecha
la lumbre nueua, luego los ve
zines, de cada pueblo, e cada
casa, renouauan sus alhajas:
y los hombres y mugeres, se ves
tian de vestidos nueuos, y po
njan enel suelo, nueuos peta
tes, e quebrauan todas sus cosas

ca quitototzaia, quimotlaloch
tiaia: inic iciuhca caxitzque in
chan, quimomamacatiquiça, qui
mocuicuilitiquiça, ic mopapa tla
tiui. Amo uecauh, amo machiztli.
can isquichcauitl, y, in conaxitia
ia, in quicueponaltiaia: çan achi
tonca in nouiiampa, cuecuepoca
timoteca tletl, cuecuepocatiqui
ca: no umpa achto quitquitiqui
ca, quitlamelaoaltiuetzi inin
teupan, inincalmecac, inincacal
pulco: çatepan ic moiaoa, tepan
cemani in nouiian tlaltlaxilacal
pan, yoan in calpan.

¶ Inic matlactlomume.
capitulo, uncan mitoa: in que
nin inisquich tlacatl, inicoac
omocuic in iancuic tletl: auh
inicoac, y, muchi tlacatl, quia
cuiliaia initlaquen, yoan in
isquich calitlatquitl.

¶ Niman icoac, isquich ian
cuiia, in calitlatquitl: inoquich
tlatquitl, in cioatlatquitl, in
petlatl, in tolcuextli, inicpalli:
muchi iancuic in moteca, ioa
in tenamaztli, in texolotl. No
iquac iancuic nequentilo, net

CHAPTER 11

The Spanish Conquest

Thus he [Moctezuma] thought—thus it was thought—that this was Topiltzin Quetzalcoatl who had come to land. For it was in their hearts that he would come, that he would come to land, just to find his mat, his seat.

Fray Bernardino de Sahagun, *General History,* 12, p. 3.

Page 258: Chalchiuhtlicue. From original drawing by Alonso Caso. Courtesy, Fondo de Cultura Economica, Mexico City.

Left: A page from Volume 7, Chapter 12, of Sahagun's General History, *"in which is told [the manner of conduct of] all the people when the new fire was taken. . . ."*

"These natives are of brownish color. Both sexes pierce the ears and wear golden pendants in them, and the men pierce the extremity of the underlip, down to the roots of the lower teeth. Just as we wear precious stones mounted in gold upon our fingers, so do they insert pieces of gold the size of a ring into their lips . . ." (McNutt, 1912). The firsthand accounts of people who had witnessed the momentous encounters between the Aztecs and the Spanish adventurers between 1519 and 1521 or who had seen the Indians brought back to the Spanish Court shaped Western perceptions of Aztec civilization for generations.

Christopher Columbus had landed in the Indies just as the Aztec empire was reaching its zenith. Within a generation Spain controlled the West Indies, and by 1515 the opportunistic crowd of adventurers and colonists who had raped the islands of Cuba and Hispaniola began to look westward for the fabled El Dorado of boundless gold and untold wealth. There was no lack of volunteers to man the ships that sailed in quest of a short-cut to the fabulous riches of the Orient.

For their part, the Mexica had no idea what lay beyond the horizons of the eastern sea. All they knew was that the god Quetzalcoatl had vanished over the ocean, vowing to return one day to reclaim his kingdom. Now their wise men grew certain that the near future held terrible dangers. Their world was suddenly beset with unexplained, evil portents. For ten years before the Spaniards landed in New Spain, the Aztecs were plagued by omens that foretold their coming. The inhabitants of Tenochtitlan panicked. "An omen of evil first appeared in the heavens. It was like a tongue of fire, like a flame, like the light of dawn." The pointed, wide-based flame caused consternation in the city. "There was shouting; there was the striking of the palm of the hand against the mouth." Ululating war cries rang through the streets, striking fear into noble and commoner alike. Then the shrine of Huitzilopochtli at Tlatelolco inexplicably burst into flames. The priests urged on the firefighters, but all was destroyed. Next lightning suddenly struck the roof of a temple of the fire god Xiuhtecutli. More evil omens appeared. A flaming comet raced through the afternoon sky scattering sparks and leaving a long trail in the heavens. The waters of Lake Texcoco suddenly surged and boiled on a flat calm day, destroying houses on its islands. Worse, people reported hearing a woman walking around in the dark of night weeping and wailing. "My dear children, we have to go! Where can I take you?" she lamented.

One day some fishermen snaring birds caught a brown crane with such a strange crest that they took it to the calmecac where Moctezuma happened to be meditating. The ruler stared in amazement at its mirror-shaped crest, "round, circular, as if pierced in the middle. There appeared the heavens, the stars—the Fire Drill [constellation]. And Moctezuma took it as an omen of great evil when he saw the stars and the Fire Drill. And when he looked . . . a second time, he saw, a little beyond, what was like people coming massed, as conquerors, coming girt in war array. Deer bore them upon their backs" (Sahagun, 12, pp. 1–3). The court soothsayers only scratched their heads. Soon Moctezuma started imagining that two-headed people were approaching him, only to vanish when he spoke. The inexplicable portents preyed on the minds of the ruler and his devout advisers.

Moctezuma's uneasiness was confirmed in 1517. Messengers brought confidential reports of white-bearded visitors to Maya country in distant Yucatan, strangers from over the ocean who fought with the local people. A year later a tax collector named Pinotl hurried from the Gulf Coast to report seeing winged towers loaded with white-faced, long-bearded men. Pinotl had communicated with the visitors in sign language and traded gold for green glass beads. These "winged towers" were the ships of the Spanish captain Juan de Grijalva, sent from Cuba to follow up on the discovery of the Yucatan in the previous year. Grijalva coasted as far east as Veracruz and the northern limits of Aztec domains before sailing away to the east. But he told Pinotl he would soon return.

The tax collector's tidings filled Moctezuma with dismay. Then he remembered the legend of Quetzalcoatl and his vow to return to reclaim his homeland. Soon he was convinced that "this was Topiltzin Quetzalcoatl who had come to land. For it was in their hearts that he would come to land, just to find his mat, his seat" (Sahagun, 12, p. 9). This belief more-or-less determined the course of events for the next two years.

The story of the conquest of Mexico by Hernando Cortes and a tiny army of conquistadors, made famous by the writings of William Prescott and others, ranks among the classic epics of Western history. The best impression of the Conquest comes not only from the pens of the Spaniards who were there, but from the Mexica themselves. Cortes wrote five letters to King Charles V that provide much gripping detail on the campaigns and on Tenochtitlan itself. Bernal Diaz wrote his reminiscences of the Conquest fully fifty years after the event, but it is as if we are fighting alongside him, so vivid are the scenes he remembers. The Indian chronicles, faithfully recorded by Bernardino de Sahagun in the twelfth volume of his *General History,* provide a startling contrast. The oral histories tell of the

dread omens that preceded the arrival of the Spaniards, of Moctezuma's belief that Quetzalcoatl had returned to claim his birthright, a conviction shattered only when Cortes finally arrived in Tenochtitlan. Looking at the Conquest from both sides is like looking into a two-sided mirror. The Aztecs could see their strange visitors with their "bodies . . . everywhere covered; only their faces appeared. They were very white; they had chalky faces; they had yellow hair . . ." as nothing but gods, people with iron weapons, armor, borne on the backs of "deer . . . as tall as roof terraces" (Sahagun, 12, pp. 19–20). The Mexica reacted then as one would now to a confrontation with visitors from outer space. For their part, the Spaniards were amazed, fascinated, and horrified by a society that had a wonderful sense of

Hernando Cortes. A portrait by the German medal-maker Christoph Weiditz in 1529. UCSB Library. Courtesy, Regents of the University of California.

beauty, glittered with gold, yet practiced human sacrifice on a grand scale.

CORTES REACHES TENOCHTITLAN

The Spaniards had originally sailed west from Cuba in 1517 in search of gold and "any other kind of wealth." When some of Grijalva's ships returned from the encounter with Pinotl with tidings of a great, gold-rich kingdom in the far interior of the new lands to the west, the Spanish Viceroy Diego Velasquez immediately planned a more ambitious expedition. He passed over his kinsman Grijalva in favor of a thirty-four-year-old soldier-adventurer, Hernando Cortes. History has painted this remarkable man in many guises, as a great, almost legendary general, or as little more than a gold-hungry robber. That he was a man of great cunning and shrewdness and a charismatic leader is beyond question, for his dealings with the Aztecs show how well he understood their weaknesses and preoccupations. He also commanded extraordinary loyalty from the motley collection of six hundred soldiers, freebooters, friars, and minor artisans, who flocked to his eleven ships. Their only common allegiance was to Cortes himself, an allegiance so intense that the Viceroy soon realized that his new commander might become a powerful and uncomfortable rival. He tried to prevent him from setting off. Cortes simply ignored his messages and sailed away to the west, armed with an official mandate that gave him a remarkable degree of latitude. He was to learn all he could about the new country and to take possession of it in the name of the Crown. He had no authority to conquer or colonize the new lands, for Charles V had not given permission for a new colony. Unconcerned by such bureaucratic niceties, Cortes used the flexibility of his instructions to the full, and changed history in the process.

The expedition first landed on the island of Cozumel off the east coast of the Yucatan. There Cortes found a marooned Spaniard, Jeronimo de Aguilar, who had traveled for eight years among the Maya and learned

their language. He was pressed into service and became a valued interpreter. So did a woman called Marina, who was given to Cortes after a violent battle with a large force of Indians along the coast in Tabasco. Over three hundred locals died in the conflict, and seventy conquistadors were wounded. Cortes licked his wounds, made an uneasy peace with the people, and coasted westward to Veracruz, where he anchored on Holy Thursday, 1519. There he met envoys from Moctezuma.

Moctezuma Xocoyotzin had prepared for the encounter with great care. He sent five high-ranking priests and warriors to Veracruz. They carried rich gifts which included four complete sets of divine regalia, two for Quetzalcoatl, and one each for Tezcatlipoca and Tlaloc. The ambassadors approached the ships in canoes. The Spaniards greeted them cautiously, then allowed them aboard. Each emissary "touched the earth" before Cortes. They greeted him as they would a god and arrayed him in the regalia of Quetzalcoatl:

The Spaniards landing in New Spain. From the Florentine Codex. Courtesy, University of Utah Press, Salt Lake City.

266

"They put him into the torquoise serpent mask with which went the quetzal feather head fan . . . . And they put him into the sleeveless jacket . . . . And they put the necklace on him" (Sahagun, 12, p. 15). The bedecked Cortes asked them if this was all they brought, had them bound in irons, and fired off a large cannon. The emissaries fainted with fright, then they were revived and given refreshment. Cortes offered them swords and other European steel weapons and challenged them to a fight. The ambassadors refused, frantically rowed ashore, and fled back to Tenochtitlan as fast as their legs would carry them. When Moctezuma heard that Cortes had accepted Quetzalcoatl's regalia, "he was terrified, he was astounded . . . his heart saddened; his heart failed him" (Sahagun, 12, pp. 19–20) He caused two prisoners to be sacrificed in the presence of the emissaries and sprinkled them with the blood of the victims, for "they had gone to very perilous places . . . they had gone to see, to look into the faces, the heads

Right: Moctezuma's envoys present gifts to Cortes, then are terrified by the sound of gunfire (page 268). From the Florentine Codex. Courtesy, University of Utah Press, Salt Lake City. Drawing, Sally Black.

of the gods—had verily spoken to them" (Sahagun, 12, p. 18).

The tlatoani now instructed his officials to treat Cortes generously in the hope that liberality would discourage the strangers from visiting Tenochtitlan. In truth, the Aztecs did not know what to do. Their unwelcome visitors behaved in strange ways. Unlike Quetzalcoatl or any other gods, the visitors detested human blood and hearts, and preferred sweet foods that seemed indigestible to Indian palates. Moctezuma sent more messengers to the coast, this time with "captives so they might be prepared: perchance [the Spaniards] would drink their blood" (Sahagun, 12, p. 21). He ordered the local people to ply the visitors with all the food they wanted, their sorcerers to cast spells on the white men. The spells had no effect whatsoever. The conquistadors again made it clear they were nauseated by blood and human sacrifice. But the lavish gifts including a "disk in the shape of the sun, and as big as a cartwheel and made of very fine gold" (Sahagun, 12, p.

22), went down well. Cortes became even more determined to call on Moctezuma.

Cortes soon discovered that although the Aztecs might be rich, they were very unpopular with the local people who groaned under their tribute demands. So he began to play a double game, encouraging dissatisfied chiefs to join him against their oppressors. At the same time he ignored recall instructions from Viceroy Velasquez and founded a garrisoned town at Veracruz. Next he calmly bypassed the Cuban authorities and sent a ship direct to Spain with dispatches to Charles V that described his wonderful discoveries. He also sweetened the news and the highly irregular communication by promising the King not only the official "Royal Fifth" of the gold found, but all of Moctezuma's treasure as well. As soon as the vessel had sailed, Cortes burned his remaining ships to maroon the Velasquez supporters among his men. On August 16, 1519, he set out for Tenochtitlan at the head of a tiny army of three hundred to three hundred fifty men armed with crude muskets, ten cannons, four light guns, and sixteen horses.

Hernando Cortes's route from the Gulf of Mexico to Tenochtitlan and the retreat from the capital to Tlaxcala. Data from Nigel Davies, The Aztecs, *p. 248.*

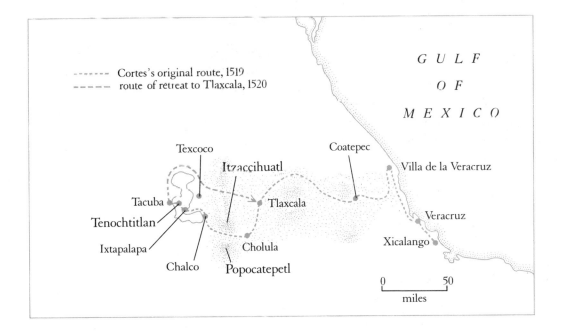

Moctezuma watched quietly and indecisively as the conquistadors marched towards the highlands. He could not decide whether he was dealing with temporal or immortal foes. Cortes was unopposed until he reached Tlaxcala, 7,000 feet (2100 m) above sea level. Tlaxcala was an independent state surrounded by Aztec fiefdoms, an obvious ally in any campaign against its long-time enemy, Tenochtitlan. The Spaniards had learned much about the Mexica on their way to the highlands, of their vast armies, their impregnable capital, and their huge supplies of gold. The stories of fabulous wealth merely strengthened Cortes' resolve. The Tlaxcalans opposed his tiny force in several small engagements and two major battles. The Spaniards found themselves confronted by thousands of brightly dressed Indian warriors. By keeping their ranks tightly knit and making effective use of their horses and ordinance, the conquistadors weathered the mob attacks. Frightened by the cavalry, unused to the smoke and noise of cannon and the terrible wounds they inflicted, in the end the Indians were routed and the Spaniards carried the day. Nevertheless, Cortes lost two hard weeks and two horses in subduing the Tlaxcalans. Large-scale defections among his enemies, however, had made his task easier.

Cortes was generous in victory, accepting but modest tribute and gifts, including wives for his captains. But the Tlaxcalans politely refused to abandon their religious beliefs or their practice of human sacrifice. The Spaniards did not press the point, for their position was at best exposed and precarious. Moctezuma was rightly concerned about an alliance between his long-time enemy and the newcomers, and Aztec diplomats soon arrived at Tlaxcala. They tried to dissuade Cortes from his new ties, and offered to guide him to Tenochtitlan in the hope that they could prevent any further entanglement with their foes. Cortes found himself in the enviable position of being courted by both sides.

Tlaxcala lay close to Aztec-ruled Cholula, the ancient center of Quetzalcoatl worship. Ignoring the pleadings of the Tlaxcalans, who feared treachery, Cortes boldly entered the town without resistance. Warned of ambushes, he massacred the assembled nobles in the temple precinct, killing some four to five thousand Indians, looting the city, and rewarding the Tlaxcalans with cotton garments and salt. The Spaniards kept the gold. No one knows quite why Cortes ordered the massacre. Perhaps it was to demoralize the Cholulans—and the Aztecs. "They received a blow they will remember for ever," wrote Diaz (1963, p. 199). Realizing that Moctezuma had spies everywhere, Cortes made a point of ordering the Tlaxcalans to release their prisoners instead of sacrificing them. Then he ordered the Cholulans to give up human sacrifice and their "customary bestialities," reminding them that their gods had deceived them.

His strategies succeeded in thoroughly confusing the Mexica. Everything he did seemed most un-Quetzalcoatl-like. Moctezuma was still convinced that the god was returning in vengeance. His soothsayers saw a vision of Tezcatlipoca leading the Spaniards, crying "Nevermore will there be a Mexico; it is already gone for ever . . . ." The dejected tlatoani bowed his head and awaited for the inevitable.

The conquistadors marched ever closer in triumph. "They arrayed themselves for war. They girt themselves; they bound on well their battle dress. Then their horses: thereupon they were, each one, disposed, arranged in rows, placed in order, put in line" (Sahagun, 12, p. 39). Iron swords flashed, horses neighed, dogs panted and sniffed. Periodically the arquebusiers (soldiers carrying light firearms) fired their pieces. "They each exploded, they each crackled, were discharged, thundered, disgorged. Smoke was spread, smoke was spread diffusely, smoke massed all over the ground . . . . By its fetid smell it stupefied one, it robbed one of one's senses" (Sahagun, 12, p. 40). Thoroughly puzzled, the Indians watched the Spaniards approach. " 'So be it,' said the people of Tenochtitlan. 'Let us be accursed. What more can be done? We are bound to die, we are already bound to perish. Yes, we can only await death' " (Anderson and Dibble, 1978, p. 27).

Hernando Cortes and Moctezuma Xocoyotzin met on a causeway on the outskirts of Tenochtitlan on November 8, 1519. Tens of thousands of Indians watched from rooftops and canoes as the conquistadors marched into the city. The two men bowed deeply to one another. Moctezuma gazed on the countenance of Cortes and addressed him with ceremony: "Thou hast come to arrive on earth. Thou hast come to govern thy city of Mexico; thou hast come to descend on my mat ... which I have guarded for thee .... And now it hath been fulfilled; thou hast come" (Sahagun, 12, p. 44). There can be little doubt that Moctezuma was certain he was in the presence of the divine Quetzalcoatl. At least he was playing it safe.

The meeting between Cortes and Moctezuma. The interpreter, Marina, is in the center. From the Florentine Codex. Courtesy, University of Utah Press, Salt Lake City. Drawing, Sally Black.

While the astounded conquistadors explored the wonders of Tenochtitlan, Moctezuma and his advisers played for time. They soon realized their visitors were interested in gold to the virtual exclusion of everything else, and they agreed to send regular tribute to Cortes' sovereign, presumably on the assumption that tribute was only payable when payment was enforced. Far worse were the strangers' theological demands. Cortes and his friars demanded that Huitzilopochtli's idols be thrown down and a cross erected in their place. Furthermore, all human sacrifice was to cease. "I had the temples which they occupy cleansed for they were full of the blood of human victims who had been sacrificed, and placed in them the image of Our Lady and other saints all of which made no small impression on Moctezuma and the inhabitants" (Cortes, 1928, pp. 90–91). Mystified by Quetzalcoatl's strange behavior, Moctezuma began to plot Cortes' destruction.

Meanwhile, Cortes had problems of his own. Rumors of treachery on the coast made it imperative for him to return to Veracruz. So he took Moctezuma as a hostage to ensure the loyalty of his people. This was a grave mistake, but an understandable one—Cortes believed Moctezuma to be an absolute monarch like Charles V, when in fact his power was subject to many subtle restraints. Magnanimously, and in desperate hope that all of his captors would depart, the ruler gave the conquistadors the entire contents of the palace treasure room. Virtually all that survives today of Moctezuma's treasure is a feather shield in the Museum für Volkekunde in Vienna. Most of the gold was melted down, and what remained in Mexico ended up as gambling stakes. Again, Moctezuma's strategy backfired: his generosity just whetted the Spaniards' appetite for more.

By this time the uneasy Aztec leadership had lost confidence in Moctezuma. Matters came to a head while Cortes was away in Veracruz. He had left Pedro de Alvarado in charge of his Tenochtitlan garrison, a tough, direct soldier with none of Cortes' diplomatic skills. Feeling increasingly isolated and threatened by the overwhelming superiority of the Aztecs around him, Alvarado ordered the massacre of hundreds of nobles at a festival. The furious Indians attacked the conquistadors and besieged them in the palace where they were quartered. When Cortes returned with reinforcements, he found the city ominously calm. Most canoes had vanished, some bridges had been knocked down as if in preparation for a siege. Next day thousands of warriors blockaded the Spaniards in the palace of Axayacatl for a week. The vacillating Moctezuma was killed during the stand-off, either by his own people, or perhaps by the Spaniards. Cortes lost so many soldiers that his only hope was to withdraw from Tenochtitlan. Only a quarter of his force managed to reach the mainland alive, there to fight its way back to friendly Tlaxcala. The Spaniards survived only because Cortes was shrewd enough to realize that he could make up for inferiority in numbers by killing Aztec nobles rather than common soldiers who were easily demoralized by the death of their leaders.

Both sides now realized that a fight to the death was inevitable. The Mexica chose a brave warrior named Cuauhtemoc as tlatoani in Moctezuma's place. He tried to unify his allies in the face of the Spanish threat, but with little effect. His predecessors' policies of ruthless exploitation and terror backfired. Meanwhile Cortes exploited the divided loyalties of the Aztecs' neighbors, preventing his enemies from gathering an army large enough to overwhelm his superior weapons by sheer numbers. He secured the countryside, moving against cities that rebelled and drawing up decrees based on Spanish law that sentenced any rebellious allies to slavery. This gave him an official, and legal, mandate to enslave as many Indians as he wished. His military tactics were carefully designed to confuse his adversaries and to deny them the kind of decisive mass battle they sought. Then some leaders of Texcoco saw in Cortes a chance to dominate the Basin, and they joined the conquistadors, giving them access to the lake. This was his big break. Cortes built a fleet of

Conquistadors besieged by an Indian army. From the Florentine Codex. Courtesy, University of Utah Press, Salt Lake City.

armed galleys to protect his army's flanks as it advanced along Tenochtitlan's seemingly impregnable causeways.

The siege of Tenochtitlan lasted ninety-three brutal days. Cortes separated his army into three divisions that fought their way along the city causeways. The Mexica put up a desperate defense and slowed the Spaniards, who were unable to deploy their cannon in close quarters. But they made the mistake of pausing to sacrifice their prisoners to Huitzilopochtli instead of pressing their advantage. The horror-stricken soldiers saw their companions taken prisoner and sacrificed: "Then they kicked the bodies down the steps, and the Indian butchers who were waiting below cut off their arms and legs and flayed their faces, which they afterwards prepared like leather gloves, with their beards on" (Diaz, 1963, p. 387). Cuauhtemoc displayed his grisly trophies in front of the temple of Tlatelolco and sent them round to neighboring centers in an attempt to raise support.

Cortes now changed his tactics. He blockaded the city. "There was hunger. Many died of hunger. There was no more good, pure water to drink—only nitrous water. Many people died of it— contracted dysentry which killed them. The people ate anything—lizards, barn swallows, corn leaves, saltgrass . . ." (Anderson and Dibble, 178, p. 79). Cortes renewed his attack in mid-July. He sent his Indian allies ahead to tear down the city house by house and to fill in the canals. Then the horsemen charged and cleared the way for the artillery. The city fell after a last desperate stand on the steps of the temple of Tlalelolco. The streets literally were paved with the dead and wounded. "The city looked as if it had been ploughed up," wrote Diaz (1963, pp. 406–407). "The roots of any edible greenery had been dug out, boiled, and eaten, and they had even cooked the bark of some of the trees. There was no fresh water to be found; all of it was brackish." For three days and three nights, the emaciated survivors streamed out of the ruins. Cuauhtemoc was tortured to reveal where he had hidden his gold until the conquistadors realized they had taken most of it before the siege. The rest had vanished in the waters of the lake. Entire quarters of the city were demolished and looted. Only some sixty thousand of the original three hundred thousand defenders survived.

Tenochtitlan fell less than two years after Cortes first arrived in the capital. The Spaniards succeeded partly because of their vastly superior war technology and long-term military tactics. The Europeans' steel swords were devastating in the sort of hand-to-hand fighting the Aztecs preferred. The razor-sharp blades could slice through wooden shields and past obsidian-bladed clubs, inflicting terrible wounds. Their noisy muskets and cannons had some shock effect, but they were inaccurate and slow to reload. Horses provided battlefield mobility; savage dogs struck fear even into very brave warriors. The Spaniards used their superior weapons not to capture prisoners, but to achieve long-term victory against an enemy trained to fight for short-term advantage, to win short, single campaigns. The Aztecs had no concept of a military campaign that lasted for months. They specialized in hand-to-hand combat aimed at capturing prisoners for sacrifice. But even these tactics were faulty, for they lost their numerical advantage by advancing in mass and engaging in battle only on a small front. As time went on, the advantage of numbers was lost as more and more Indian allies joined Cortes' army.

The Conquest pitted an isolated, battle-hardened expeditionary force against a brave, driven people who were convinced that every act of war was imbued with deep symbolism. The Mexica had long used war to feed the relentless maw of the gods and to keep an ill-matched patchwork of vassal states in order. With a skilled enemy exploiting their uneasy allies, they found themselves on their own. All they could do was to defend themselves desperately against a puzzling foe quite unlike any adversary they had ever encountered. This small and determined band of gold-hungry adventurers were accustomed to long and arduous military campaigns, and it was inevitable that they would pre-vail. They brought not the divine benevolence of Quet-zalcoatl but suffering, death, exotic diseases, and slavery.

dias en otro. y dende aotros cinco dias enotro de manera que el q̃
to quintanario, era la fiesta del dios que se celebraua enel mes q̃
se seguia: los cinco dias que son mas delos trezientos y sesenta de
do el año. tenjan los por valdios, y haziagos: y ansi no hazian cue͠
dellos para njnguna cosa. Pero cuenta tenjan contodos los dias de
y con todos los meses del año, y con todas las quintanas del año, que
quatro en cada mes.

¶ Otra cuenta tenjan estos naturales que nj sigue la cuenta del a
nj delos meses, nj delas quintanas, que impropriamente se puede de
zir semanas. Esta cuenta, tiene veinte caracteres, como esta pinta
en la tabla, que esta detras desta hoja: a cada vno destos caracte͠
atribuyan treze dias: en las quales reinaua vno destos caracteres
manera que cada vno reinaua treze dias, y el circulo que estos ca͠
res consus dias hazian, son dozientos y sesenta dias: el qual cir͠
lo, tiene ciento y cinco dias menos, que vn año. Esta cuenta se vs
ua para adiuinar las condiciones, y successos dela vida, que tendr͠
los que naciessen. Es cuenta delicada, y muy mentirosa, y sin njn
fundamento de astrologia natural. Porque el arte dela astrologi͠
judiciaria, que entre nosotros se vsa, tiene fundamento en la astr͠
gia natural, que es en los signos, y planetas del cielo, y en los curs͠
y aspectos dellos. Pero esta arte adiuinatoria siguese, o funda s͠
en vnos caracteres, y numeros, en que njngun fundamento natur͠
ay, sino solamente artificio fabricado, por el mesmo diablo, nj
posible que njngun hombre fabricasse, njn ventasse esta art͠; p͠
que no tiene fundamento, en njnguna sciencia, nj en njnguna ra͠
natural: mas parece cosa de embuste y embaimjento, que no co͠
razonal, nj artificiosa. Digo que fue embuste y embaimjento, p͠
enramdar, y desatinar agente de poca capazidad, y de poco e͠
tendimjento. No obstante esto, era tenjda en mucho, esta arte a͠
nadeia o mas propriamente hablando embuste ß embaimjent͠
diabolico: y tambien los que la sabian, y vsauan era muy honra͠
y tenjdos: porque dezian las cosas por venjr, y del vulgo eran ten͠
dos por verdaderos, aunque njnguna verdad dezian sino a͠
y por cierto. Esta arte, nj sigue años, nj meses, nj semanas, nj
[...], nj olimpiadas, como algunos soñando dixeron, y afir͠
con falsamente. [firma]

CHAPTER 12 The Aftermath of the Conquest

And ... it is ... admitted by all ... that the Indians throughout the Indies never did any harm to the Christians: they even esteemed them as coming from heaven, until they and their neighbors had suffered the same many evils, thefts, deaths, violence, and visitations at their hands.

Bartolomé de las Casas, *Very Brief Account of the Destruction of the Indies,* 1953, p. 1.

Part of the apology from Volume 5, Appendix of Sahagun's General History, bearing his signature.

"Under the old system of government, then, the whole land was at peace. Spaniards and Indians alike were content, and more tribute was paid, and with less hardship, because government was in the hands of the natural lords." Alonso de Zorita wrote his *Brief Relation of the Lords of New Spain* in the 1560s, nearly a half-century after the Conquest. In it he compared the state of affairs before the fall of the Aztec state with the result of several generations of bribery, corruption, and thievery at the hands of "Spaniards, mestizos, and mulattoes who know the native language" (Zorita, 1963, pp. 116–117). "Lords and commoners alike have been impoverished," he reported. "All have suffered great spiritual and temporal decline." It was as if the Aztec civilization had vanished without trace.

It was not until a decade after the Conquest that the whole of Mexico, or New Spain, was under secure Spanish control. Some Indian groups were easily subdued, others resisted to the death. Tens of thousands of people died in dozens of bloody encounters, adding

to an already accelerating population decline. A rapid breakup of indigenous society was inevitable in the face of a civilization armed with overwhelming technological superiority. Both sides confronted each other in terms of their own cultural values, often making decisions in their best short-term interests with little thought for long-term consequences. Inevitably, those at a technological disadvantage lost, simply because their leaders could not call on the huge reservoirs of labor that had fought their wars, built their temples, and fed their city populations in the past.

The new masters of Mexico came from a culture that had only just emerged from a form of feudalism which bound individuals to families and powerful lords. The Spaniards represented a newly united nation of individ-

Sketches by Christoph Weiditz of two Indians at the Spanish Court in 1528. They wear feather mantles and aprons and have jewels set into their faces.

ual people linked by loyalties to a remote, symbolic monarch and to the Faith, the ultimate cohesive belief that overrode all others. As a whole they were devout people, with an official passion for legalism and an unshakable belief in the rightness of their Divine Mission to settle and convert New Spain. But as individual people, the horde of adventurers, government officials, and clerics who descended on New Spain were not so typical. Their characters tended to great extremes. Many were rapacious plunderers who came for the gold and a life of ease. "As if they were monkeys they seized on the gold," remembered a Sahagun informant. "It was as if their hearts were satisfied, brightened, calmed. For in truth they thirsted mightily for gold; they stuffed themselves with it; they starved for it; they lusted for it like pigs" (Sahagun, 12, p. 31). Such people cared nothing for the Indians, thinking of them as convenient slaves, as little more than beasts.

At the other extreme were the vociferous and powerful officials and priests who believed that the Spanish Crown's divine mission was to carry Christianity to all corners of the globe. Powerful advocates of this viewpoint, the Dominicans and Franciscans argued that the government's primary responsibility was the conversion and welfare of the Indians. "The means to effect this end are not to rob, to scandalize, to capture or destroy them, or lay waste their lands, for this will cause the infidels to abominate our faith," wrote the celebrated Dominican Bartolomé de las Casas (Hanke, 1949, p. 21), a ferocious champion of Indian rights.

Both factions realized that their views would prevail only through political influence at court. They engulfed the Spanish government in what can best be called a war of books, theoretical controversies that raged for decades. Nearly everyone who came in contact with the Indians felt they were inferior. They lacked Christianity, after all, and written legal codes, among many other "civilized" accomplishments. How were they to be treated? Aristotle had written that all inferior people were fated to be slaves. Were the Indians in this category? Or were they free people, perhaps lapsed Chris-

tians from long-forgotten missionary endeavors centuries earlier? So strongly did the Dominicans feel
about the issue that they carried it to the Pope himself.
On June 9, 1537, Pope Paul III issued two famous
decrees—*Sublimis Deus* and *Veritas ipsa*—that spelled
out the issue in no uncertain terms: "Man is of such
condition and nature that he can receive the faith of
Christ and whoever has the nature of man is fitted to
receive the same faith" (Hanke, 1949, p. 25). The Pope
forbade any Christian to deprive Indians, or anyone
else for that matter, "of their freedom . . . of the do-
minion of their possessions, and [they] must not be
reduced to slavery."

All these maneuvres in far-away Spain were to little
avail. The debates waged fast and furious, royal decrees
were issued, and legal points won that had little to do
with the realities of life in New Spain. The Spanish
Crown's agonies of conscience did it credit, but its
officials lacked the swift communication and the local
authority to enforce any laws passed to protect the
Indians from the colonists. Only the loosest legal

Bartolomé de las Casas. UCSB
Library. Courtesy, Regents of
the University of California.

framework governed the settlers' treatment of the Indians. The Mexica suffered desperately at the hands of an unscrupulous people far enough away from home to get away with almost any behavior.

While these debates were at their height, Diego Duran wrote that "this most fertile and rich land, together with its capital Mexico, has suffered many calamities and has declined with the loss of its grandeur and excellence and the great men who once inhabited it" (1964, p. 213). Even high-minded missionaries and officials like Diego Duran felt themselves betrayed by the tragic course of events. They believed that Spain was giving valuable new benefits to the Indians—not only Christianity, but regal and legal authority, writing, literature, town life, the Spanish language, and European notions of labor. There were immediate and obvious benefits: new crops, domestic animals, iron tools, as well as European dress (including trousers). Everyone expected that the Indians would receive these gifts gratefully and accept radical changes in their lives without question. Few Spaniards had even a vague understanding of Indian society, with its communal land ownership and complicated kinship rules. Puzzled and angered when the Indians resisted, they turned to force, missionary instruction, and government decree, none of which worked either.

The Mexica soon adopted valuable, practical innovations like the breeding of cattle and sheep, plows that were superior to digging sticks, wheeled carts, and iron tools. But when it came to land ownership, political institutions, or spiritual beliefs, they stalled. Land ownership was a duty, a gift given by a higher supernatural power, not a right, they believed. The Spanish system that vested land-ownership in an individual person was totally alien to them. They wondered, for example, whether acreage owned by "the Crown" was in the hands of a supernatural god or a land-owning king. The colonial system of governance was even more incomprehensible. The Indians discovered that priests, not secular rulers, provided moral leadership, while an army of anonymous lay officials did little to protect them.

Promises were routinely broken, and the bureaucratic pyramid of the Spanish officialdom appeared totally useless. The only way to resist was to withdraw as much as possible from the Europeans. People turned inward, relying on their familiar, close-knit family and community patterns, and lay low. These underground institutions perpetuated many traditional values, even if outward signs—religious observances, architecture, and dress—appeared Spanish to the casual observer. "These people are reluctant to abandon things familiar to them," wrote Diego Duran (1964, p. 4) with prophetic accuracy. Many Indian values and social institutions have survived more than four centuries of alien rule.

ENCOMIENDAS

The victory at Tenochtitlan left Cortes and about a thousand Spaniards with the entire Aztec heartland at their feet. A year later the Crown confirmed Cortes as Captain General and Governor of New Spain. Reaping the fruits of his stupendous victory, he became master of a huge estate, entitled to the services of thousands of Indians to cultivate his lands. Tribute that had once flowed to the tlatoani now came to the Captain-General instead. Cortes found himself caught between the official policies of the Crown which stipulated justice and order and the informal practices of his own followers who were out for a quick profit. He also inherited the problems of the notorious *encomienda* system.

The Spanish word *encomendar* means "to give in trust." The encomienda, originally invented in Spain as a temporary grant of rights in order to gather tribute, had been transported to the Indies as a convenient way of entrusting the Christian welfare of the local people to Spanish colonists. The Crown granted a group of Indians to a settler, who had the right to extract tribute or forced labor from them in exchange for their religious conversion and protection. In practice, the colonists forced their Indians to farm their lands *and* to pay tribute in pesos, chickens, capes, and domestic labor. Long before the Conquest the encomienda had given rise to terrible abuses and cruelty in the Indies. Charles V expressly forbade using this system in New Spain, but Cortes found himself in an impossible situation. The encomienda was the only way he knew to govern both his unruly settlers and the vanquished Aztecs. So he ignored the royal order. By the mid-1550s, four years after Cortes' death, 130 *encomenderos* in the Basin of Mexico controlled the fate of more than 180,000 Indians. These privileged families abused their charges far more severely than had any earlier Aztec ruler on the flimsy pretext that they had to guard against threats of rebellion. It took most of the sixteenth century for the Crown to reassert its control over Aztec labor, tribute, and governance.

Based on forced labor, the encomienda did perpetuate many features of the trade and tribute systems of earlier times. The colonial masters of New Spain respected the craftsmanship of their workers. But the artisans who had once created fine gold ornaments and feather shields no longer had a market for these status symbols. Now the need was for carpenters and masons, tailors and potters. The traditional craft centers did continue to flourish, and the pre-Conquest markets remained open, frequented by Indian and Spaniard alike. While drastic changes took place in the indigenous economy, the supply of staples such as cacao continued along centuries-old trade routes. A few Spaniards and mestizos (those of half Indian-half Spanish blood) traded with European markets on a very large scale, but most local needs were met through market structures that were a direct legacy from pre-Hispanic times.

THE BLACK LEGEND ?

The Conquest brought not only new systems of governance and material innovations, but hidden perils as well. The steady stream of settlers that arrived in New Spain brought new infectious diseases with them. A black conquistador in the siege of Tenochtitlan introduced smallpox to Mexico. The beseiged city suffered its first epidemic in 1520. Indians died like flies. Other unfamiliar diseases—smallpox, measles, and typhus—ravaged the Indian population during the next century. Catastrophic smallpox epidemics decimated the Indians between 1545 and 1548 and again from 1576 to 1581. Demographers Sherburne Cook and Lesley Byrd Simpson used colonial archives and censuses to calculate that the population of central Mexico was 6,427,466 in 1540, sharply down from an estimated 11 million in 1519. By 1607 the Indian population was less than a fifth of that of a century earlier. The Basin population declined from 1.5 million to 325,000 between 1519 and 1570. Indian members began to rise again only in the late seventeenth century.

Earlier historians were unable to explain this sudden population decline. Fairly naturally, they turned to the vociferous writings of Bartolomé de las Casas, who had thundered in indignation about the terrible crimes of the conquistadors. "The reason why the Christians have killed and destroyed such infinite numbers of souls is solely because they have made gold their ultimate aim, seeking to load themselves with riches in the shortest possible time" (Sanderlin, 1971, p. 44). So the historians blamed the conquistadors, accusing them of mass genocide and ruthless exploitation. Stories of a "Black Legend," of gruesome and bloody massacres of Indians by conquistadors and friars, gained wide currency in the seventeenth and eighteenth centuries, especially when unsavory stories of Catholic repression in the Yucatan circulated through European courts. Spanish intellectuals were furious at such imputations. They countered indignantly, citing example after example of government humanity to counter charges of genocide. Most authorities now agree that the major cause of the population decline—it fell 3 to 6 percent annually during the first half-century of colonial rule—was the devastating epidemics of new diseases like measles and influenza. Colonial policies of forced resettlement that led to starvation may also have contributed to the decline, as did famine and overwork in Spanish mines and plantations.

A depiction of Spanish cruelty to Indians that appeared in Las Casas' treatise on the subject, published in 1598. UCSB Library. Courtesy, Regents of the University of California.

A tiny minority that never exceeded 1 to 2 percent of the total population dominated the Indians. Spanish archives tell us that these Spaniards were mainly semi-literate, unskilled, poverty-stricken males in their mid- to late-twenties, escaping virtual starvation at home. They came seeking wives and intermarried with the Indian population, creating a new class of Mexicans, the *mestizos,* who tended to acquire European culture. They became landowners and small businessmen, developing a distinctive culture mainly derived from Spain but incorporating many traits from Mexican Indian societies. The mestizo lifeway eventually became dominant in the colony, and later in the Republic of Mexico itself. The number of "full-blooded" Spaniards in New

287

Spain probably never exceeded 5 percent of the population.

LAND AND ENVIRONMENTAL CHANGE

The Spaniards also irrevocably altered the heavily exploited pre-Hispanic environment. They cut down extensive stands of timber for lumber to build Mexico City—and for firewood. Their plows penetrating far deeper into the Basin soils than digging sticks, stripped nutrients from the earth. The European farmers grew new crops—wheat, sugar cane, olives, and vines—while the Indians still preferred their traditional staples of maize and beans. Enormous herds of cattle and sheep rapidly denuded the natural vegetation and changed the landscape forever. Stockraising remained a European activity, for the Indians showed little interest in ranching. They did, however, constantly complain that Spanish herds encroached on their lands. The new farmers dug their own drainage systems while filling in the Mexicas' ingenious canal system. Thousands of chinampas fell into disuse. Within a few generations the combined effects of soil erosion and altered drainage had rendered much of the Basin useless for agriculture.

Nevertheless, the Indians managed to eke out a living from the land, largely because they had many fewer to feed from the surviving chinampas. Large acreages of the drier, more infertile soils once sown with maize were now planted with maguey cactus. The Mexica had confined the drinking of pulque to ceremonial occasions. Unfettered by traditional constraints, their successors turned to pulque to escape from the harsh realities they daily faced. All efforts to control drinking by government decree, whether by the friars or secular authorities, failed abysmally. A population undergoing mass, catastrophic stress rarely responds to legislation.

Where the Indians abandoned land, the settlers purchased it. More often, they simply usurped hundreds of acres, or took over land by bribery or through spurious grants. Under Spanish law, cattle breeders had rights of common pasturage, and the Indians found their fields overrun with settlers' herds. Realizing that this was often the preliminary step to a land grant, they responded by fencing their acres, even building new villages in the way of the cattle. These efforts were usually in vain. Something like half the agricultural land in the Valley of Mexico passed from Indian to Spanish ownership in the first century after the Conquest. So chaotic were farming conditions that Indians sometimes starved while Europeans grew special crops to feed their cattle and sheep.

SOCIAL CHANGE AFTER THE CONQUEST

The highly stratified Aztec society of earlier times became more and more homogeneous under the impact of Spanish colonial rule. At first the nobles fared somewhat better than the common people—some of Moctezuma's descendents were even granted encomiendas. A tlatoani ruled, at least nominally, in Tenochtitlan until the death of Don Luis de Santa Maria Nacatzipatzin in 1563. Some tlatoque retained nominal titles and privileges and were permitted to carry arms, to wear Spanish clothing, and to ride horses or mules as signs of their status within Indian society. A few nobles achieved considerable prosperity, especially those who lived close to Spanish towns and the few who could adjust readily to the European way of life. Most of these had also received at least a rudimentary education at the hands of the friars.

In some ways the Conquest enhanced opportunities for upward mobility among commoners. Some Indians in domestic service and a few enterprising small businessmen learned how to exploit the new system. They acquired land, engaged in profitable trading ventures, and became nobles in everything except birth. As time went on, birthright became less important than imagination and entrepreneurial drive. The status of the nobility was undercut still further when the colonial government insisted on wage payments rather than tribute for services rendered. These regulations under-mined the authority of the tlatoque and made achieve-ment rather than birthright the criterion for prestige and authority.

Most of the earliest Spanish settlers in New Spain were illiterate and unrefined, even by sixteenth-century standards. Yet they became the upper class of the new society, together with the educated clerics, lawyers, and high-ranking officials who came out to establish mis-sions and to administer the new colony. At the pinna-cle of colonial society were the "Peninsulares," people of Spanish birth who emigrated to New Spain. They held the highest religious and secular offices, much to the frustration of the "Criollos," the Spaniards born in the New World. The Criollos hated the arrogant and superior Peninsulares, who, in turn, looked down on them as languid, unproductive citizens debilitated by the Mexican climate to which they were born. The locally born colonists could hold posts in the govern-ment, but they were rarely able to achieve the highest offices in the colony. Many of them were prosperous ranchers and businessmen.

Relatively few Spanish women emigrated to New Spain, so the colonists married local wives. Spaniards married Indians, mestizos married one another, Indians married mestizos. By the early 1800s, about a third of the population was mestizo. In time, mestizos occupied all of the social strata in New Spain. Some were virtual grandees, others were culturally indistinguishable from Indians. The status of both mestizos and mulattoes, those born of Spanish men and black slave women, was as vague and ill-defined as that of the Indians was well-set. The Mexica and their tribal neighbors were at the base of the social pyramid. Indian educational institu-tions like the calmecac and telpochcalli gave way to totally inadequate substitutes such as the friars' mission schools. Institutionalized warfare was soon a vague memory, and the elaborate rewards and social status it conferred vanished with the Conquest. The old Indian class structure melted away in the face of wage-earning and personal achievement. Polygamy was outlawed by

Featherwork shield that was probably sent to Europe by Hernando Cortes. The coyote depicted on the shield is a version of the Aztec fire god. The fire god is outlined in flame, and the tufted border also signifies flames. Courtesy, Museum für Volkerkunde, Vienna.

both Church and state soon after the fall of Tenochtitlan. Only the calpulli remained almost intact, for it provided a convenient equivalent to the Spanish barrio, a unit from which tribute could be collected and laborers drafted. But the calpulli was no longer a military entity, and its patron gods were those of Christianity rather than those of the Aztec pantheon.

Within a few generations of the Conquest, Aztec society was a homogeneous, poverty-stricken shadow of its former hierarchical self. Only a small number of well connected or exceptionally able people managed to prosper on their own or succeeded in adjusting successfully to the new order.

CABICERAS AND CONGREGACIONES

The rapid alienation of Indian lands and the disintegration of the Aztec social order coincided with a new

291

system of governance based on the Spaniards' urban experience in the Old World. The colonists created a network of major cities surrounded by "head towns," *cabeceras,* ruled by former Indian rulers, and lesser settlements, *sujetos,* organized into villages and parishes. Many once-important centers vied to become cabeceras, for this designation gave their rulers access to lucrative tribute privileges that could compensate for revenues lost at the Conquest. As time went on, the cabeceras came under the rule of a governor, or *cacique,* and council. At first the office coincided with that of a tlatoani, but the authorities were afraid of powerful indigenous rulers and tended to encourage dual appointments. The cabecera became a way of channeling labor, tribute, and agricultural surplusses to the government. The Indians were left alone, provided they paid their taxes on time. The government appointed *corregidores* in each cabecera, elected officials, paid from local taxes, who served as magistrates and tax collectors. But this was only the beginning, for the corregidores milked their charges for whatever they could get. Many of them traded illegally with the Indians, forcing them to buy back produce at exorbitant prices. As Spanish control of Mexico tightened, the Indians became alienated and lost all their social mobility. As time went on, the Indians increasingly disengaged themselves from Spanish political and social life. Their symbolic defense was nonparticipation.

Under Aztec rule, communal land ownership had been controlled by the calpulli. Now the Indians were reduced to selling their land to stave off economic catastrophe—to buy food and pay taxes. They were sometimes regrouped in smaller, more compact communities known as *congregaciones,* a resettlement device originally intended to make people more accessible to forcible conversion. The Indians complained with justification that they were better off on their traditional lands, where cherished tribal loyalties could be fostered and continued. Unfortunately they lacked the political organization and unity to speak with anything like one voice or to maintain a united front in the face of European encroachment. Rather than be herded into congregaciones, many Indians moved into the cities or onto the great *haciendas,* ranches that now supplied the produce that Indian farmers had once provided. Both the cities and the haciendas needed large numbers of Indian laborers to function effectively, and the people who filled these needs severed their ties with their traditional homes, adding to political and social alienation. So much Indian land was lost by the policy of congregacion that many communities starved. The trouble was that most Spanish immigrants were nonfarmers, so the land simply lay fallow and people went hungry.

MISSIONARIES AND CHRISTIANITY

"Any other human belief opposed to the Faith loses the quality of the Faith itself . . . since idolatry has not been totally erased from their minds, they mix the Christian Faith with heathen beliefs. Thus the Faith among them is superficial . . ." (1971, p. 2). Diego Duran deeply believed that the Mexica should be converted to Catholicism, but he had no illusions about the difficulties that faced the friars who followed in Cortes' footsteps. The Crown regarded the conversion of the Indians as an urgent and necessary priority, a preliminary to cultural and social reform. The earliest efforts, at best superficial, involved mass conversions by traveling missionaries without any permanent base of operations. The Christian mission began with a vengeance in 1524 with the arrival of twelve Franciscans. They caused a sensation among the Indians by walking barefoot all the way from Veracruz, poor, humble men quite unlike the arrogant conquistadors. They began by confronting the Aztec wise men with their Christian teachings. It was then that the Mexica priests laid out their own basic beliefs and pointed out that the people would die without the solace of their gods. Huitzilopochtli and Tezcatlipoca had failed to avert the fall of

Tenochtitlan. "It is the doctrine of the elders that there is life because of the gods; with their sacrifice, they gave us life . . . . And now are we to destroy the ancient order of life?" they asked (Leon-Portilla, 1963, p. 66). The friars swept all such pleas aside in a torrent of mass conversions.

Once the missionaries had mastered Nahuatl, they planned a long-term educational program to give Christian training to young nobles, the potential leaders of Indian society. At first the missionaries succeeded. The Indians as a whole abandoned their loyalty to the old gods, pagan temples, and human sacrifice. The most zealous advocates of the new spiritual order were younger people who had been through the Church schools. A timely miracle helped. On December 9, 1531, an Aztec with the Spanish name of Juan Diego

Detail from Diego Rivera's "The Legend of Quetzalcoatl," from the National Palace, Mexico City. The white-faced, blond-haired Quetzalcoatl is seen seated with the outlines of the pyramids of the sun and moon behind him. He is surrounded by young men who offer him pulque in a drinking gourd. The four Indians at his left depict the four cardinal directions. Photo, Lesley Newhart.

294

saw a beautiful Indian woman dressed in shining robes on the Hill of Tepeyacac, once a shrine of the mother of Huitzilopochtli. The radiant woman spoke to him in Nahuatl and said she was the mother of God. The vision took hold, despite fierce resistance from the friars, and the Indian Virgin of Guadalupe is venerated throughout Mexico to this day.

Superficially, the Indians were attracted to the elaborate rituals and colorful ceremonies of the Catholic church. Some of their own traditional practices surrounding marriage, penance, and fasting bore some resemblance to Christian ritual. But a simple transfer of allegiance was simply impossible. The friars were unable to get across the deeper meaning of Christian doctrine, the significance of such abstract concepts as virtue and sin. Many Indians simply added God to their pantheon of deities and counted the saints as members of an anthropomorphic pantheon of lesser gods. The hardest belief to shake was the notion that the gods had to be sustained by humans with food and drink.

The Indians liked the early friars, partly because they functioned within the traditional social framework, and partly because they lived close to their parishioners, suffering the same hardships as they did. The Indians had always respected their priests, whatever gods they venerated. But this respect often turned to hate when zealous prelates bore down on transgressors and backsliders. Some idolators were executed, others sentenced to exile and service in the monasteries. Whippings were commonplace, imprisonment routine. In 1525, the Church embarked on a systematic campaign to remove all signs of idolatry. In 1531, Bishop Zumarraga of Mexico boasted that he had destroyed five hundred pagan shrines and twenty thousand idols. Unfortunately he burned hundreds of priceless codices as well. The Indians' "volunteer" work that built the first churches and monasteries was replaced by forced labor in the 1530s. The friars responded to criticism by arguing that they were educating people with the mental abilities of ten- or twelve-year-old children.

Eventually the church became a wealthy and complex bureaucracy, and its influence on Indian society declined sharply as the people withdrew into themselves. The governance of thousands of small communities lay in local organizations: the barrio, the local chapel, and the *cofradia,* the parishioners' association. These Indian-supported organizations provided their members with small, intimate associations of their own that provided havens against social stress and racism. The cofradia became a symbol of community welfare, each with its patron saint, whose Christian name disguised cherished beliefs that went back to earlier times. This fusion of beliefs was—and is—best expressed in community *fiestas,* regular celebrations of patron saints and holy days. The services, processions, and public feasting that accompanied them combined both Christian observance with costumes, masks, displays, and dancing that gave the Indians a sense of community and common identity. The Aztec preoccupation with rain and water, for example, can be discerned even today in public festivals like the annual jaguar fights for rain that take place every May in the towns of Acatlan and Zitlala in Guerrero, Mexico. The masked fighters crack whips at one another in contests that look very much like sacrifices for rain. Until fairly recently, people were sometimes killed in these fights.

The Spaniards ruled Mexico for over three hundred years. They succeeded in reorganizing millions of Indians into a large political unit that kept most of the population out of the mainstream of colonial society. Confronted with the terrible reality of Quetzalcoatl's second coming and alienated from their new, exploitative masters, the people retreated into their own communities, taking the tatters of their beliefs and values with them. Only scattered remnants of traditional Aztec society survive today, and the relentless onslaught of twentieth-century industrial civilization endangers even these. Perhaps it is as well that their ancestors placed limited value upon life on earth and lived close to *miccatzintli,* the state of death:

It is not true, it is not true
that we came to live here.
We came only to sleep, only to dream.
(Leon-Portilla, 1963, p. 123.)

References

The following works are quoted from in the text. The most commonly quoted work is Bernardino de Sahagun's *General History*. In the interests of brevity, these references appear as "Sahagun, 3, p. 2," and so on.

Anderson, Arthur O., and Charles E. Dibble.
1978   *The War of Conquest: How It Was Waged Here in Mexico*. Salt Lake City: University of Utah Press.

Chimalpain, Domingo Cuahtlihuanitzin.
1889   *Differentes historias originales de los reynos de Culhuacan y Mexico, y de otras provincias*. Ed. R. Simon. Paris: Bibliotheque Linguistique Americaine.

Coe, Michael.
1962   *Mexico*. New York: Frederick A. Praeger.

Conway, William Martin, ed.
1889   *Literary Remains of Albrecht Durer*. Cambridge: Cambridge University Press.

Cortes, Hernando.
1928   *Five Letters of Cortes to the Emperor* (originally written 1519–1526). Trans. J. Bayard Morris. New York: W.W. Norton Company.

Diaz del Castillo, Bernal.
1963   *The Conquest of New Spain*. Trans. J.M. Cohen. Baltimore: Pelican Books, Penguin Books.

Duran, Diego.
1964   *The Aztecs: The History of the Indies of New Spain*. Trans. Doris Heyden and Fernando Horcasitas. Norman: University of Oklahoma Press.

1971   *Book of the Gods and Rites* and *The Ancient Calendar*. Trans. Doris Heyden and Fernando Horcasitas. Norman: University of Oklahoma Press.

Hanke, Lewis.
1949   *The Spanish Struggle for Justice in the Conquest of America*. New York: American Historical Association.

Kubler, George, and Charles Gibson.
1951   "The Tovar Calendar," *Memoirs of the Connecticut Academy of Arts and Sciences,* vol. 11.

las Casas, Bartolomé de.
1953   *Very Brief Account of the Destruction of the Indies* (written in 1542). Ed. Lewis Hanke. New York: Columbia University Press.

Leon-Portilla, Miguel.
1963   *Aztec Thought and Culture: A Study of the Ancient Nahautl Mind.* Trans. Jack Emory Davis. Norman: University of Oklahoma Press. Copyright 1963 by the University of Oklahoma Press.

Motolinia, Toribio.
1951   *History of the Indians of New Spain* (written between 1536 and 1543). Trans. Francis Borgia Steck. Washington D.C.: Academy of American Franciscan History.
1951   *History of the Indians of New Spain* (written between 1536 and 1543). Included in *Documents and Narratives Concerning the Discovery and Conquest of Latin America.* Ed. Elizabeth A. Foster. Berkeley, Calif.: The Cortes Society.

Nicholson, H.L.
1971   "Religion in Pre-Hispanic Central Mexico." In *Handbook of Middle American Indians,* vol. 10, pp. 395–446. Austin: University of Texas Press.

Ricard, Robert.
1966   *The Spiritual Conquest of Mexico.* Berkeley: University of California Press.

Sahagun, Fray Bernardino de.
1950–1969 *Florentine Codex: General History of the Things of New Spain* (originally written in 1369). Trans. Arthur O. Anderson and Charles E. Dibble. Salt Lake City, Utah, and Santa Fe, New Mexico: University of Utah Press and School of American Research.

Sanderlin, G., ed.
1971 *Bartolomé de Las Casas: A Selection of His Writings.* New York: Alfred A. Knopf.

Sanders, William T., Jeffrey R. Parsons, and Robert S. Santley.
1979 *The Basin of Mexico: Ecological Processes in the Evolution of a Civilization.* New York: Academic Press.

Tezozomoc, Fernando Alvarado.
1975 *Cronica Mexicayotl.* Mexico: Universidad Nacional Autonoma de Mexico.

Zorita, Alonso de.
1963 *Life and Labor in Ancient Mexico* (written in the 1570s or 1580s). Trans. Benjamin Keen. New Brunswick, N.J.: Rutgers University Press.

Guide to Sources

A rich and diverse literature surrounds the Aztec civilization, a literature remarkable for its high quality and challenging debate. The general reader is best advised to start with one of the widely available general summaries before venturing into the more technical publications. On the assumption that most readers of this book will be English-speaking, I have concentrated on English language sources in this Guide. These are also the sources which provided most of the material for this volume.

General Works

Gene S. Stuart, *The Mighty Aztecs* (Washington, D.C.: National Geographic Society, 1981) provides an exciting narrative for the wider audience. Even more useful is Frances Berdan, *The Aztecs of Central Mexico: An Imperial Society* (New York: Holt, Rinehart and Winston, Inc., 1982). This is a college text, but crammed with useful insights and information. I found it invaluable in preparing this book. Nigel Davies, *The Aztecs: A History* (Norman: University of Oklahoma Press, 1973) covers the rise and fall of the Aztecs with great clarity, a sometimes admittedly conjectural historical account injected with vivid descriptions of Mexica society. The same author has written two further books that describe the centuries before the Aztec empire: *The Toltecs Until the Fall of Tula* (Norman: University of Oklahoma Press, 1977) and *The Toltec Heritage From the Fall of Tula to the Rise of Tenochtitlan* (Norman: University of Oklahoma Press, 1980). Both are based on fragmentary and diverse sources, so much so that legend and historical fact are sometimes almost impossible to unscramble. Two classics round out the general descriptions: Jacques Soustelle, *Daily Life of the*

Aztecs On The Eve of the Spanish Conquest (Palo Alto, Calif.: Stanford University Press, 1961) and C.G. Valliant, *Aztecs of Mexico* (Baltimore: Penguin Books, Inc., 1944). Both give vivid accounts of Aztec daily life and institutions. The archaeology of the Basin of Mexico is brilliantly covered by William T. Sanders, Jeffrey R. Parsons, and Robert S. Santley, *The Basin of Mexico: Ecological Processes in the Evolution of a Civilization* (New York: Academic Press, Inc., 1979). This highly technical monograph is state-of-the-art as far as settlement archaeology is concerned, and I have drawn on it extensively here. Muriel Porter Weaver, *The Aztecs, Maya, and Their Predecessors: Archaeology of Mesoamerica* (New York: Academic Press, Inc., 2nd. ed., 1981) is one of several widely available syntheses of Mesoamerican culture history and was a major source for this work.

Prologue

Two works trace the early history of research into Aztec civilization. Ignatio Bernal's *A History of Mexican Archaeology* (London: Thames and Hudson, 1981) covers the subject from an archaeological perspective. Benjamin Keen, *The Aztec Image in Western Thought* (New Brunswick, N.J.: Rutgers University Press, 1971) is the definitive work, surveying major and minor researchers and literary and artistic attitudes from the Conquest up to modern times.

Bernardino de Sahagun's works are best approached through Charles E. Dibble and Arthur J.O. Anderson's *Florentine Codex: General History of the Things of New Spain* (Salt Lake City: University of Utah Press, and Santa Fe: The School of American Research, 12 vols., 1950–1975), a definitive translation and critical analysis of the Franciscan's great work. Nothing gives a better impression of the complexities of Aztec ethnohistory than this magnificent work. Munro Edmonson (ed.), *Sixteenth Century Mexico: The Work of Sahagun* (Albuquerque: University of New Mexico Press, 1974) contains a fascinating set of essays on the man and his research methods. Diego Duran, *The History of the Indies of New Spain* (New York: Orion Press, 1964, translated by Doris Heyden and Fernando Horcasitas) and *Book of the Gods and Rites* and *The Ancient Calendar* (Norman: University of Oklahoma Press, 1971, same translators) provide another perspective on the sixteenth-century Aztecs. These works have been pivotal sources for this book.

William Prescott, *History of the Conquest of Mexico* (New York: Harpers, 1843) is a "must" for any serious student of the Conquest. For all its romanticism and false imagery, it remains a compelling narrative.

The Handbook of Middle American Indians (Austin: University of Texas Press, general editor, Robert Wauchope) provides useful essays on Aztec archaeology and historiography, especially the provocative essays on ethnohistorical sources in Volumes 13 to 15. It was invaluable in compiling this chapter.

Chapter 1: Tolteca and Chichimeca

This chapter navigates through a plethora of speculative historical accounts. Sahagun's informants are one basic source, as are other sixteenth- and seventeenth-century chronicles well described by Nigel Davies in his two volumes on the Tolteca and the Toltec legacy, already mentioned. Teotihuacan is well described by René Millon (ed.), *Urbanization at Teotihuacan,* vol. 1 (Austin: University of Texas Press, 1973), a volume that includes comprehensive maps. Tula is published in a variety of monographs and other works, and is well summarized for beginners in Muriel Porter Weaver's *The Aztecs, Maya, and Their Predecessors,* chapter 7 (see General Works). The legend of the Fifth Sun is fully described in Chapter 12, and references are given there. Charles Dibble's translation and critical analysis of the sixteenth century *Codice Xolotl* (Mexico City: Publicaciones del Instituto de Historia, no. 22, 1951) is invaluable for Chichimeca history, as are the classic passages in the tenth volume of Sahagun's *General History* (see Prologue).

Chapter 2: The Rise of the Mexica

Diego Duran's *Historia* (see Prologue) is a basic source for this chapter, as are various other chronicles including Fernando Alvarado's *Cronica Mexicayotl,* originally written in 1609 (Mexico City: Universidad Nacional Autonoma de Mexico, 1949). Nigel Davies' *The Aztecs* (see General Works) is a comprehensive, critical source in English, while Toribio Motolinia's *History of the Indians of New Spain,* written between 1536 and 1543 (Berkeley, Calif: Cortes Society, 1950), is also useful. The archaeological evidence is discussed in great detail by Sanders, Parsons, and Santley in the Basin Survey monograph already referred to (see General Works).

Chapter 3: The Subsistence Base

Bernardino de Sahagun (see Prologue) is our best guide to Aztec subsistence activities. Volumes 2, 8, and 11 are especially informative. Sanders, Parsons, and Santley (see General Works) provide the definitive synthesis in the Basin Survey volume. Warwick Bray, *Everyday Life of the Aztecs* (New York: G. P. Putnam's Sons, 1968) is a readable summary and can be combined with Soustelle's *Daily Life* (see General Works). Much of the literature on subsistence is scattered in specialist works, but these summaries will guide you to more detailed references.

Chapter 4: Tenochtitlan

Bernal Diaz, *The Conquest of New Spain* (Baltimore: Pelican Books, Inc., 1963, translated by J.H. Cohen) gives a superb eye-witness account of Tenochtitlan, and can be combined with Cortes' *Five Letters to the King of Spain* (New York: W.W. Norton, Inc., 1928, translated by J. Bayard Morris). The recent excavations at the Templo Mayor are described by Gene Stuart in her *The Mighty Aztecs* (see General Works). Edward Calnek has written a series of important papers on the city based on archival sources. See his "The Internal Structure of Tenochtitlan," in Eric R. Wolf (ed.), *The Valley of Mexico* (Albuquerque: University of New Mexico Press, 1976, pp. 287–302).

Chapter 5: Government and Empire

The classic account of the growth of the Aztec empire is in Diego Duran's *General History* (see Prologue), which also describes the extraordinary range of tribute that flowed to the capital. Sahagun's volume 6 (see Prologue) is informative on the processes of governance and the Aztec bureaucracy. He also devotes an entire volume to the merchants. Nigel Davies' *The Aztecs* (see General Works) analyzes the Aztec state critically, using all available sources. Warfare is vividly described by Bernal Diaz and by Duran (see Prologue), while James Cooper Clark (ed.), *Codex Mendoza* (London: Waterlow and Sons, 1938) provides vivid illustrations of costumes, tribute, and trade objects.

Chapter 6: The Exemplary Life and Chapter 7: Nobles and Commoners

These chapters are written almost entirely from Bernardino de Sahagun's *General History* (see Prologue). His sixth volume is an authoritative guide to the basic tenets of Aztec life and conduct. No one has improved on his summary. The same book also surveys the life passages of an Aztec family in elegant detail, while Diego Duran's *Historia* (see Prologue) gives many details of different social classes. Aztec kinship and social organization are an academic minefield, summarized by Duran and Sahagun, but most importantly by Alonso de Zorita in his *Life and Labor in Ancient Mexico,* originally written in the 1570s or 1580s (New Brunswick, N.J.: Rutgers University Press, 1963, translated by Benjamin Keen). He describes the calpulli in some detail, compares conditions under Indian and Spanish rule and gives much information on class structure. Patricia Anawalt's *Indian Clothing Before Cortes* (Norman: University of Oklahoma Press, 1981) is an exquisite, scholarly summary of Indian sumptuary laws and clothing before the Conquest. The illustrations are superb.

Chapter 8: Artisans and Merchants

The tenth volume of Sahagun's *General History* (see Prologue) deals specifically with the pochteca and their rituals. Soustelle and Valliant describe Aztec craftsmanship in some detail. Berdan's *Aztecs of Central Mexico* is especially informative on economic matters, as this is her specialty within the field. (See General Works for publication data on all three volumes.)

Chapter 9: Cosmos and Creation

A rich and satisfying literature surrounds Aztec philosophy and literature. Miguel Leon-Portilla's *Aztec Thought and Culture: A Study of the Ancient Nahuatl Mind* (Norman: University of Oklahoma Press, copyright 1963, translated by Jack Emory Davis), is crammed with useful ideas and information. So are Burr Cartwright Brundage, *The Fifth Sun: Aztec Gods, Aztec World* (Austin: University of Texas Press, 1979) and Alfonso Caso's *The Aztecs: People of the Sun* (Norman: University of Oklahoma Press, 1971). Sahagun and Duran (see Prologue) are, of course, seminal. Angel Maria Garibay K.'s *Historia de la Literatura Nahuatl* (Mexico City: Editorial Porrua, 1953–1954) is a fundamental source, as is Miguel Leon-Portilla's *Pre-Columbian Literatures of Mexico* (Norman: University of Oklahoma Press, 1969). For astronomy and calendrics, try Anthony F. Aveni, *Skywatchers of Ancient Mexico* (Austin: University of Texas Press, 1980) and Alfonso Caso, "Calendrical Systems of Central Mexico," in Gordon F. Ekholm and Ignatio Bernal (eds.), *Handbook of Middle American Indians* (Austin: University of Texas Press, vol. 10, 1971, pp. 333–348). Cannibalism and human sacrifice have generated much controversy. William Arens, *The Man-eating Myth* (Oxford: Clarendon Press, 1969) is a provocative essay that basically denies the Mexica were cannibals at all! Michael Harner, "The Ecological Basis for Aztec Sacrifice," (*American Ethnologist,* 1977, 4, 1, pp. 117–135), summarizes the protein arguments. Bernard R. Ortiz de Montellano, "Aztec Cannibalism: An Ecological Necessity?" (*Science,* 1978, 200, pp. 611–617), demolishes them.

Chapter 10: The Gods and the Ceremonies

Anyone seriously interested in Aztec religion should consult what is widely agreed to be the fundamental source: H.B. Nicholson, "Religion in Pre-Hispanic Central Mexico," in Gordon F. Ekholm and Ignatio Bernal (eds.), *Handbook of Middle American Indians* (vol. 10, 1971, pp. 395–446). Chapter 12 is written almost entirely from this brilliant paper. Diego Duran's *Book of the Gods and Rites* and *The Ancient Calendar* (Norman: University of Oklahoma Press, 1951, translated by Doris Heyden and Fernando Horcasitas) are basic sources, as is Sahagun's second volume (see Prologue).

Chapter 11: The Spanish Conquest

The Conquest is best followed through eye witness accounts: Hernando Cortes, *Five Letters of Cortes to the Emperor, 1519–1526* (New York: W.W. Norton, Inc., 1962, translated and edited by J. Bayard Morris) and Bernal Diaz, *The Conquest of New Spain* (Baltimore: Pelican Books, Inc., 1963, translated by J.M. Cohen). Read these in conjunction with Arthur J.O. Anderson and Charles E. Dibble *The War of Conquest: How It Was Waged Here In Mexico* (Salt Lake City: University of Utah Press, 1978) to obtain a two-sided view of the events of 1519–1521. William H. Prescott, *History of the Conquest of Mexico* (New York: Harpers, 1843) is one of the classics of American literature and should be on any serious reader's bookshelf. Sahagun's twelfth volume (see Prologue) is seminal.

Chapter 13: The Aftermath of the Conquest

Robert F. Berkhofer, *The White Man's Indian: Images of the American Indian from Columbus to the Present* (New York: Alfred A. Knopf, Inc., 1978) summarizes attitudes of Europeans towards American Indians and touches on Spanish Colonial policies. Charles Gibson's *The Aztecs Under Spanish Rule* (Palo Alto, Calif.: Stanford University Press, 1964) is a masterly description and analysis of Aztec society after the Conquest based on colonial archives, anthropological data, and other sources. Arthur J.O. Anderson, Frances Berdan, and James Lockhart, *Beyond the Codices: The Nahua View of Colonial Mexico* (Berkeley: University of California Press, 1976) is a useful source book.

The great debates about colonial policy are well summarized by Lewis Hanke, *The Spanish Struggle for Justice in the Conquest of America* (New York: American Historical Association, 1949). See also: J.H. Elliot, *Imperial Spain* (New York: St. Martin's Press, Inc., 1964) and Roger Bigelow Merriman, *The Rise of the Spanish Empire in the Old World and in the New. Volume II: The Catholic Kings* (New York: Cooper Square Publishers, 1962). For colonial history, see: François Chevalier, *Land and Society in Colonial Mexico: The Great Hacienda* (Berkeley: University of California Press, 1963); George Foster, *Culture and Conquest: America's Spanish Heritage* (Chicago: Quadrangle Books, Inc., 1960); Oscar Lewis, *Life in a Mexican Village* (Urbana: University of Illinois Press, 1951); and Michael Meyer and William L. Sherman, *The Course of Mexican History* (New York: Oxford University Press, 1970). Robert Ricard's *The Spiritual Conquest of Mexico* (Berkeley: University of California Press, 1966) covers missionary endeavors.

Lastly, a novel that gives a vivid, if often overpainted, view of Aztec life through the eyes of a *pochtecatl* turned Eagle Knight! Gary Jennings' *Aztec* (New York: Atheneum Publishers, 1980) is based on uncritical research but brings much dry data to fictional life. But take it with a pinch of salt!

Index